CONSTITUTIVE VISIONS

WITHDRAWN
UTSA LIBRARIES

RHETORICAND**DEMOCRATIC**DELIBERATION

EDITED BY CHERYL GLENN AND J. MICHAEL HOGAN
THE PENNSYLVANIA STATE UNIVERSITY

Rhetoric and Democratic Deliberation is a series of groundbreaking
monographs and edited volumes focusing on the character and quality of
public discourse in politics and culture. It is sponsored by the Center for
Democratic Deliberation, an interdisciplinary center for research, teaching, and
outreach on issues of rhetoric, civic engagement, and public deliberation.

A complete list of books in this series is located at the back of this volume.

CONSTITUTIVE VISIONS

INDIGENEITY AND COMMONPLACES OF NATIONAL
IDENTITY IN REPUBLICAN ECUADOR

CHRISTA J. OLSON

The Pennsylvania State University Press | University Park, Pennsylvania

Cataloging-in-Publication data is on file at the Library
of Congress.
ISBN 978-0-271-06198-6 (cloth : alk. paper)
ISBN 978-0-271-06199-3 (pbk. : alk. paper)

Printed in the United States of America
Published by The Pennsylvania State University Press,
University Park, PA 16802-1003

The Pennsylvania State University Press is a member
of the Association of American University Presses.

It is the policy of The Pennsylvania State University
Press to use acid-free paper. Publications on uncoated
stock satisfy the minimum requirements of American
National Standard for Information Sciences—
Permanence of Paper for Printed Library Material,
ANSI Z39.48–1992.

For ANNA, *and our next adventure*

TABLE OF CONTENTS

ILLUSTRATIONS

PREFACE: THE PRECARIOUS POLITICS OF GOING THERE

"How Ecuadorean journalists are teaching the Indians to read and write and like it." So begins "Alphabet in the Andes," a brief, English-language article written by an Ecuadorian author and published in the United States in 1945 and in Ecuador in 1949.[1] The article—about Indians, literacy, and national life—not only gives a glimpse of ethnopolitics in its own moment but also offers an instructive opening anecdote for this early twenty-first-century book about rhetoric, visual culture, and indigeneity.

"Alphabet" tells the story of a literacy project run in the Quito area by the Ecuadorian Unión Nacional de Periodistas (UNP, National Journalists' Union). The first page of the article introduces us to its main characters: pitiable, malleable Indians and initially skeptical but quickly trained teachers. It gives as well a brief profile of one indigenous student, Rafael Llumiquinga, whom the strength of literacy moved from "unwashed" and unpleasantly aromatic into cleanliness and confidence. Utterly changed, the article notes, Llumiquinga "wrote to the local paper, saying that at last he felt like a man" (27).

After praising the work done by the UNP, "Alphabet" next describes a visit by literacy researchers from the United States sent to the project by the U.S. Office of the Coordinator of Inter-American Affairs (CIAA) and the Walt Disney Company. According to "Alphabet," the motion pictures those visitors brought to encourage literacy and improve hygiene "were almost too successful." They drew new students to the project in droves, overflowing rooms and lending a powerful new efficiency to the labor of teaching and learning (28).

As much as it celebrates the outcomes of the literacy projects discussed—both the pen-and-paper strategies of the UNP and the motion-picture efforts of the CIAA–Walt Disney expedition—"Alphabet" is also a celebration of influential visuality. The author, Miguel Albornoz, both praises the visual learning techniques employed in the program and emphasizes visual elements in his effort to draw in readers. He shows, in both areas, a significant faith in the power of seeing, and seeing anew. For Albornoz, the quality of literacy acquisition in the program is visible and tightly linked to an image-based taxonomy. In his descriptions, indigeneity and modernity are visually marked poles existing in generative tension, both diametrically opposed and inextricably connected. He pictures illiterate Indians as dirty and poncho-clad, clumsily premodern in the shape of their hands and the set of their bodies. Yet they are eager for access to development and its bright lights, colors, and straight lines. In response, literate (nonindigenous) teachers provide printed flashcards and cartoon filmstrips that teach hygiene and modern skills. Accessing text and image transforms those miserable, mud-caked Indians into clean, bright-eyed, and trembling protocitizens. From ponchos, dirty fingernails, and crowded rooms to filmstrips, electric lights, and shining faces, acquiring literacy (and modernity) proves a thoroughly visual affair in Albornoz's hands.

Published first in the U.S. government periodical the *Inter-American* and then four years later in an Ecuadorian travel magazine, *Ecuador*, "Alphabet" had two different audiences. The *Inter-American*, the official organ of the CIAA, was distributed to U.S. State Department affiliates throughout the Americas. In Ecuador it would have been read by U.S. expatriates, members of the U.S. diplomatic corps, and Ecuadorians affiliated with those groups. The short-lived tourism magazine *Ecuador*, for its part, carried an appealing image of Ecuador to potential tourists both within the country and throughout the Americas. Its articles in Spanish and English situated Ecuador as a picturesque, culture-rich, and accessible nation. Both versions of the article, then, reached outward. They offered their story of literacy learning and national progress to an audience indirectly involved in the UNP's project yet, in many cases, intimately connected to it by their shared goals of modern development.

That sharp anxiety over modernity (and its lack) consumed both Ecuadorian political elites and the larger inter-American politics of development in the mid-twentieth century. In response, they launched a full-spectrum assault on the secondary signs of lingering rusticity, a status embodied particularly by indigenous peoples. "Alphabet," in other words, resonates topically with other Ecuadorian documents of its era. It resonates as well in its form: oriented primarily in textual terms—literacy rates and economic statistics, political projects and historical analyses—it relies heavily on the shaping force of *seeing* to spark identification and generate movement. The visual link that Albornoz makes between indigeneity and national development in his article was not, in other words, unusual. Yet his article's faith in the power of vision—to change Indians and inspire readers—offers a concise representative anecdote for the ways that seeing indigeneity and seeing national identity have long run parallel in Ecuadorian civic life.

Using artifacts such as "Alphabet in the Andes," this book traces textual and visual arguments about the nation threaded through more than a hundred years of Ecuadorian history. It takes up the specific example of Ecuador because that country has a long, rich, and well-documented history of explicit nation making and has consistently relied on the force of vision to carry that nation making forward. Like "Alphabet," in other words, Ecuador offers an evocative representative anecdote for the rhetorical intersections of visuality and nationalism. Giving close attention to the constitutive force of vision as demonstrated so powerfully by the Ecuadorian example, this study unravels the multivalent nature of nationalism and the ways its shaping, matter-making influence extends across representative forms.

These opening pages preface that analysis by calling attention to a set of parallel concerns visible in the image-saturated matrix of "Alphabet in the Andes." They suggest that the article's troubling confidence in the benefits of literacy, the reliability of interpretation, and the ability of U.S. American experts to "go there"—in this case, to Highland Ecuador—ought to unsettle and oblige scholars today. Though it might be easy to dismiss "Alphabet" as a historical example of misguided developmentalist propaganda, we would do better to engage "Alphabet" and artifacts like it as barometers for the power relations that infuse every interpretive project and haunt every effort to present a history.

* * *

"Alphabet" narrates literacy acquisition as provided through increasing levels of outside intervention. The nonindigenous Ecuadorian professionals of the UNP provide literacy training to indigenous communities pictured as uncivilized, unhygienic, and uncertain of their own potential. As Albornoz puts it, the members of the UNP began their project knowing "they had taken over a big job when they set out to teach the illiterates of the region to read and write." They discovered, however, "that the hardest part was to convince the misery-ridden highland Indians that it was possible for them to learn at all" (27). Indigenous Ecuadorians, according to Albornoz, desperately need outsiders to transform them into lettered people. They are passive, neglected subjects awaiting the benevolent intervention of others.

But indigenous communities are not the only ones in need of outside enhancement. U.S.-based literacy experts, funded by government agencies and corporate investment, further propel literacy learning forward through the latest in pedagogical technology, teaching Indians to "like it" at an ever more efficient pace. Albornoz describes their arrival using language that blends the CIAA's origins in the Second World War with its commitment to social hygiene, describing the arrival of "five new allies" in the "anti-illiteracy campaign": "Mickey Mouse, Donald Duck, . . . Jose Carioca, and two new cartoon characters called José and Ramón" (28). These Disney "reinforcements" make possible new progress in the battle against a social disease—illiteracy—that "afflicts" nearly two-thirds of Ecuador's population. The full and modern might of United States arrives, once again, to carry the day.

The article's tale of intervention contains a sort of twentieth-century paternalism easily read, today, as problematic: imperialist, developmentalist, and neocolonial. It ought also, however, serve as a cautionary tale of the dangers of intervention and analysis. As U.S.-based rhetoric and visual-culture scholars increasingly imagine a wider and more complex field of inquiry for our work, we would do well to look closely at our uncomfortable kinship with predecessors such as "Alphabet" and the CIAA-Disney expedition.

In light of the tradition so baldly represented in "Alphabet," I am not confident that it is ever possible for U.S.-based or U.S.-trained scholars to completely transcend the history and perspectives of Euro-U.S. hegemony. Whether we restrict our inquiries to U.S. and European contexts or travel beyond them, we are inevitably informed by assumptions born of those contexts.[2] The historical invasions and interventions of the Euro-U.S. world—political colonialism, economic globalization, cultural imperialism—now touch most points of the globe. They color not only our analyses but also the scenes we encounter. We would be as foolish to deny how thoroughly they infuse our analytical means as we would be irresponsible to simply accept them as given. Whatever our subjects and their relative proximity to ourselves, scholarship is a messy, partial pursuit. Power relationships always infuse our historiography; our analytical lenses always skew as much as they reveal. Any rhetorical history, then, must incorporate tactics that trouble the scope and certainty of its own claims. We must, as the rhetorical historian LuMing Mao urges, produce scholarship that examines "the power dynamics within representation" across cultural and political borders. We must also call attention to how those power dynamics inevitably work within our own representations of rhetorical practice.[3]

Rhetorical historians moving beyond their field's long-standing focus on the United States and Europe have some good resources for considering the ethical quandaries of analysis.[4] Yet the specific challenges of taking rhetorical historiography beyond its familiar Euro-U.S. sphere have only recently been the subject of direct discussion.[5] Much remains to be considered. The existing scholarship generally encourages what Mao calls a "dialogic process": "troubling our own modes of thinking and being . . . deftly moving between self and other, the local and the global, and the contingencies of the present and the historical imperatives of the past."[6] Mao suggests that for both ethical and intellectual reasons, traveling rhetoricians need to critique, expand, or even set aside our learned habits of analysis—including our basic definitions of rhetoric's key concepts (e.g., persuasion, argument). Such analytical flexibility will allow more robust accounts of the diverse ways in which humans influence one another.

Yet even in the case of such careful research and writing, the "power dynamics within representation" remain active in our scholarship. For scholars researching and writing about Latin America, that means that we work constantly in light of the history encapsulated in "Alphabet." That history of influence and intrusion demands explicit strategies of recognition that—without descending into ethical paralysis—acknowledge how U.S. hegemony infuses scholarship. The next several pages offer my version of that strategy: a guide for reading *Constitutive Visions* as itself implicated in power dynamics and shaped by the limits of its analytical means and methods. Inspired by the troubling images at work in "Alphabet," it outlines three critical recognitions that ought to condition the reader's encounter with the text ahead. Those recognitions—invitations to rethink—map out the ways this text negotiates the precarious politics of traveling scholarship.

Recognition #1: Dominant rhetorics are always haunted by practices that call the dispersion and coherence of that dominance into question.

The first lesson worth taking from "Alphabet" is a lesson of absence, of the part of the story that wasn't told but could have been. "Alphabet" narrates literacy acquisition as brought into indigenous communities from outside: concerned, well-meaning Ecuadorian journalists and foreign visitors provide programs backed by the full support of national governments and familiar corporations. That hopeful narrative, however, hides a more complicated story of literacy training denied and interrupted.

In "Alphabet," indigenous people are imagined as naturally and passively illiterate. Descriptions of rough hands, accustomed to wielding pick axes, not pencils, make clear just how foreign the delicate work of writing is to the beginning indigenous student. Yet the article also imagines indigenous people as protoliberal subjects, as hungry for a modern, Western life as soon as it is made available to them. When indigenous students realize that they can read and write, those awkward hands tremble with excitement; they write letters to the editor and appear in class the next day cleaned and manicured, where once they were dirty and unkempt. The article positions indigenous illiteracy as "the biggest enemy of Ecuadorean progress" and envisions the nonindigenous college students, journalists, and literacy experts who teach classes as saviors of both the individual Indians before them and the nation as a whole (28).

That tale—that literacy first became available to Ecuador's indigenous communities thanks to the good will of the nonindigenous state and private interest—covers over a longer and more complicated history. The truth is that at least a decade before the UNP, CIAA, and Walt Disney arrived, indigenous people—having been actively excluded from state-funded schooling—began building their own literacy programs and, for their trouble, faced violent retribution from landowners and bureaucratic repression from the government.[7] Not telling (or not knowing) the history of that earlier struggle for literacy serves a specific purpose in "Alphabet," given the article's propagandist goals and elite, international audiences. It locates agency outside of indigenous communities to aggrandize and moralize the intervention of others. Taking at face value the story of literacy learning and national progress told in "Alphabet" and similar artifacts, then, would mean acquiescing to the same "power dynamics within representation" at work in the original piece. For a rhetorician today, the interaction and overlap of these conflicting projects—indigenous organizing, state-sponsored literacy projects, and U.S. foreign aid—ought themselves to provide the substance of analysis. Such an approach takes better account of the constitutive efforts of both hegemonic and subaltern groups; it tracks both dominant trends and counterforces, both successful and failed persuasion.

Giving attention to multiple levels of intervention is especially important in the Ecuadorian context, where so much of state formation occurred in the efforts of a light-skinned, European-identified, white-mestizo minority to solidify and maintain its political and social control.[8] As the historical anthropologist A. Kim Clark argues, in the case of Ecuadorian nation-state formation, "neither dominant nor subordinate groups can be fully understood except in relation to each other." Indeed, Clark continues, even dividing Ecuadorian society into monolithic categories of "dominant" and "subordinate" risks erasing the internecine conflicts within and among subgroups that were also essential to evolving constitutions of

Ecuadorian national identity. White-mestizo landowners in different regions sometimes saw their interests in conflict; urban elites viewed rural leaders as inferior rustics; indigenous caciques and "governors" used their privilege to participate in the networks of administration that exploited lower-class indigenous labor. Understanding the processes of Ecuadorian nation formation thus requires sorting through the messy accumulation of persuasive artifacts that negotiate, challenge, and attempt to secure often contradictory ideas of the national public. It also, as Clark implies, benefits from a rhetorical orientation. Those multiple relations among "dominant and subordinate groups should be thought of as characterized by contention, struggle and argument."[9] Such focus on argument and dispute includes tracking persuasion in a number of registers and from across a variety of social positions, including those positions sometimes visible only between the lines of dominant discourse.

In what follows, then, analyses of elite efforts to imagine the nation-state are repeatedly interrupted by histories of resistance and discussions of rhetorical failure. Those turns toward the claims of subalterns and the infelicities of national narratives serve the scholarly interest of providing a robust history of a complex rhetorical ecology. They also, however, should remind readers that there are layers upon layers at work beneath the analyses offered here, that these tales are contested and contestable, and that they elide almost as much as they illuminate. Every switch of register or social position, in addition to signaling a shift in argument, should remind readers of interpretation's moral ambiguities and the stories yet to be explored.

Recognition #2: U.S.-based interpretations of Ecuadorian contexts are in debt to Ecuadorian interpretations.

In "Alphabet" there is some sense of conversation between the Ecuador-based literacy projects run by the UNP and the U.S.-based expedition supported by Disney and the CIAA. Miguel Albornoz, the article's author, was an Ecuadorian—a liberal diplomat who later worked in the prodevelopment government of Galo Plaza Lasso (1948–52) and served as the Ecuadorian ambassador to the United Nations. The article, though written in English and published first in the United States, offers an Ecuadorian's perspective on literacy programs and spends its first half describing and praising the efforts of the UNP. At the same time, though Albornoz depicts the UNP's low-tech efforts as essential in a country with limited rural electrification, there is no question that such local projects pale in comparison to the motion picture–stoked modernity of the CIAA-Disney expedition. The UNP provides the quotidian labor; the CIAA and Disney push the cutting edge.

Certainly Albornoz had reason to present his article as a tale of glitzy U.S. intervention. His original audience (readers of the *Inter-American*) was primed for a pro-U.S. tone and a celebration of modernity in its most narrow definition. If Albornoz's article is a savvy response to a particular rhetorical situation, however, it also accedes to the expectations of its readers in ways that reinforce assumptions about unequal economies of knowledge. Albornoz writes as an insider—an Ecuadorian speaking of the Ecuadorian situation—yet he privileges an exterior method and the perspectives of outside intervention. He leaves out not only the history of indigenous-led organizing but also a rich Ecuadorian analytical milieu in which social scientists, labor organizers, local communities, and national politicians all actively debated the future implications of the so-called Indian problem. According to "Alphabet," the possibilities for progress in indigenous communities and in Ecuador as a whole are altered primarily by theories brought into the country from abroad (both the Laubach method used by the UNP and the films from the CIAA–Walt Disney); Ecuadorian theories and practices fade into the background. Choosing not to acknowledge the active debate within and emphasizing instead imported methods shapes the stories available about Ecuador and shifts the fulcrum of analysis outside the Ecuadorian context. Recognizing that shift and the reduced possibilities for productive synthesis that it entails ought, once again, to prompt recognition among present-day scholars from the United States: we will always carry the history of our analytical tools along with us but need not leave those tools unchanged.

Constitutive Visions emerges at the confluence of two powerful streams of scholarship. On the one hand, it draws deeply from a long history of rhetorical theorizing that includes consistent concern for the making and maintenance of the *polis*. On the other, it enters an Ecuadorian context flush with critical scholarship about the trials and mechanisms of national identity. Its challenge, then, is to allow the two to come together without letting one overwhelm the other. This is a slightly different challenge than the one posed by recent scholars who have questioned the applicability of the term "rhetoric" in non-Western contexts. Laying aside the rather thorny question of whether post-Columbian Latin America is or is not "Western," this dispute over the appropriate scope of rhetoric still risks leading rhetoricians' attentions astray because it assumes that rhetoric is a static concept—usually a somewhat thin version of the Greek *Rhetorike*. In that assessment, rhetoric is, indeed, incapable of approaching non-Western contexts. It would also, however, be unable to provide insight into the twenty-first-century United States or eighteenth-century Britain.

Thankfully, rhetoric need not be chained by its Greco-Roman roots. Instead, rhetoric can be approached as the English word applied to a large set of human practices: those forms of communication that have designs on the values, beliefs, and actions of others.[10] The pages ahead regularly use rhetorical terms of art: *topos, synecdoche, ethos.* The meaning and purpose of those terms, however, is not primarily tethered to definitions articulated in the fourth century B.C.E. Instead, they are live analytical terms, charged with the energy of contemporary rhetorical theory and contemporary Ecuadorianist scholarship. At its best, the analysis here holds those two strands in close, generative proximity.

Taken in this sense, rhetoric is highly portable and its tools quite flexible. The important question is how sensitive the rhetorical method is—how well it captures fine-grained differences of context and moment. And the challenge for rhetorical analysis situated in long-ignored contexts is to calibrate its claims in relation to the existing body of scholarship, some of it quite rhetorical in nature, already in place.

Most anywhere rhetoricians might travel today, they will encounter prior and ongoing analytical work done by other scholars, local experts, and community members. Much of that work may pursue rhetorical questions or contain rhetorical implications. Mao's call for rhetoricians to find ways to "[trouble] our own modes of thinking and being" and "deftly [move] between self and other, the local and the global, and the contingencies of the present and the historical imperatives of the past" takes on new meaning in that context.[11] While Mao may appear to emphasize an *internal* process of increased critical awareness on the part of the researcher, the fact of foregoing scholarship ought to remind us that such expansion does not occur in isolation. Interaction with others and others' analyses calls into question our existing ways of thinking and brings to light other understandings and methods. In the final product, those interlocutors appear not only in the form of citational support for the new argument but also as having profoundly influenced both the argument itself and the tools used to achieve it.

Ecuadorian and Ecuadorianist scholars have frequently treated the larger areas of concern addressed in this text. That long-term interest in the processes of nation making is, in fact, part of what makes Ecuador such a rich site for analyzing the rhetorical contours of national identity. Those scholars have also, often, asked and answered questions reasonably described as rhetorical in nature.[12] *Constitutive Visions*, then, is far from the first study of rhetorical practice in Ecuador, and its understandings of what rhetoric is, how it circulates, and how it influences are shaped by those foregoing studies.

In the pages ahead, readers will encounter that potentially generative interaction in the frequent citation of both rhetorical theorists and Ecuadorianists and in the ways my analyses bring those two streams into conversation. Seeing those moments of confluence ought to remind readers that theories are live objects and that rhetorical theory needs to be alive to the influence of those histories and ideas already at work in new contexts. In this case, they draw attention to the ways that Ecuadorian scholars' assessments of national discourse drive and reshape the rhetorical terms and histories engaged here.

Recognition #3: Processes of representation and identification take place over the long term; resistance and social change invisible at any given moment may become clear under a wider lens.

The hopeful assertions about the magic of literacy in "Alphabet" ring false today. Its depiction of drastic change occurring in a single day or through a single film focuses attention entirely on the moment of literacy acquisition and the programs that fostered that moment, eliding longer histories of oppression, intervention, and resistance. In the article, having learned to read and write, María Hermelinda Cuichán becomes a citizen, and an "old peon" announces that "his employers could not fool him on the payroll any more" (27, 28). "Alphabet" asks readers to accept a version of the "literacy myth" (the assumption that citizenship and economic opportunity flow naturally and inevitably from acquisition of literacy), reaching beyond the immediate gains made by individual students to imagine a nation transformed.[13] The article gestures toward a larger history, one in which illiteracy disenfranchises and landowners exploit laborers. The racist strategies, colonial interventions, and structural inequalities that sustained that long history, however, are quickly (and implausibly) erased by the bright light of motion-picture literacy.

In "Pan-Historiography: The Challenges of Writing History Across Time and Space," Debra Hawhee and I argue for the value of pursuing histories that stretch across long periods.[14] We suggest that, contrary to the common assumption that long-span histories must skim over details and textures, careful pan-historiography can in fact reveal textures and complexities that develop over time and might be hidden from a deep but narrowly focused analysis. Aware of the pitfalls illustrated by "Alphabet's" limited scope,

Constitutive Visions attends to the long-term processes of national identity, tracing how changing tactics and shifting power relations both contest and serve an overall appearance of national coherence.

Bringing a long history into play sends rhetorical historians looking for other routes to literacy and obliges them to consider the processes that made illiteracy and indigeneity synonymous yet still tied indigeneity to national identity. It forces discussion of how Cuichán's claim that literacy makes her a citizen or the old peon's assertion that his employer will no longer be able to cheat him articulate with the long struggles over citizenship and conscripted labor surrounding those claims. Such pan-historiographic attention makes possible a more robust narrative. It positions Albornoz's empowered indigenous learners not only in light of the populist indigenous movements of the 1930s and 1940s but also in relation to the political shift in 1861 that made the franchise theoretically possible for literate Indians, in conversation with paintings of "miserable" Indians from the 1880s that helped establish the visual taxonomies in "Alphabet," and in tension with debates from the 1920s over indigenous workers' capacity to make contracts.

This book, then, engages a pan-historiographic method to come as close as possible to the multivocality and rich texture of the history of nationalism it outlines. Each chapter draws together at least two periods of Ecuadorian history, usually a stretch in the mid-to-late nineteenth century and another in the mid-twentieth. The total span of the book runs from 1857 to 1947, with the conclusion moving the analysis into the twenty-first century. Rather than offer a step-by-step history of those ninety-plus years, however, each chapter juxtaposes events and artifacts from different periods, using such oblique illumination to draw attention to both continuity and change. In addition to serving an analytical purpose, that pan-historiographic juxtaposition should remind readers of the far longer history into which the study intervenes. As Hawhee and I note, even the broadest pan-historiography represents a choice: "historiography always involves making selections."[15] In this study, the visibility of such selections should call the reader's attention to the lived complexities that exceed, sprawl beyond, and distend the circumferences drawn.

Going There

The narrative of literacy, modernity, and indigeneity in "Alphabet" is populated by Indians with red ponchos and shining black eyes, by upsetting aromas and rough hands, by cartoon characters, journalists, and the CIAA. The analyses presented in *Constitutive Visions* are not so different. Work-scarred hands and bright ponchos fill the canvases of artists and the speeches of political candidates and, in turn, the pages of this book. Neither is the text's origin in the U.S. academy so entirely different from that of the literacy experts described in "Alphabet." This study may not precisely carry the backing of the U.S. federal government or a major transnational corporation, as did the CIAA–Walt Disney expedition, but it has, indirectly, received funding from the U.S. Department of Education and the Andrew W. Mellon Foundation.[16] A blue U.S. passport grants visaless passage through the immigration checkpoint at Mariscal Sucre Airport in Quito, a privilege not reciprocated for Ecuadorian-passport holders standing in line on arrival in Miami or Houston. In both Quito and Madison, ATMs dispense crisp twenty-dollar bills on demand, but U.S. dollars buy much more in Ecuador than they do in the United States—a fact that might aid the Ecuadorian relatives of migrants living in the United States but not those who travel to the North. An academic title and affiliation with a U.S. university grant access to museums and archives in Ecuador, while many Ecuadorian scholars travel to the United States or Europe to earn degrees with sufficient *caché* to secure academic positions in their home country. *Constitutive Visions* is, in other words, not exactly *unsponsored* by the political and economic might of the United States.

The influence of the United States may not be what it once was, and Ecuadorians have long been roundly critical of their northern neighbors' assumptions of access (at least in private). Still, there is no question that travel from the United States to Ecuador, whether as a twentieth-century corporate-funded literacy expert or a twenty-first-century university-employed rhetorician, necessarily invokes troubling questions of power, access, and representation. If this study has absorbed some of the lessons made available through the jarring assumptions in "Alphabet" and sought to mitigate them by paying attention to resistance, by reading rhetorical theory in light of Ecuadorian scholarship, and by keeping in mind the long span of history, it certainly leaves other lessons as yet unlearned. Those missed lessons haunt these pages. Taken properly, however, that haunting can be productive. It pushes the reader to learn, again and again, the generative contradictions of rhetorical historiography.

ACKNOWLEDGMENTS

Books do not write themselves. That unfortunate fact, however, is accompanied by a far more pleasant one: no one writes a book by herself. This book bears out that reality. It owes its shape, its depth, and its material to the many individuals and institutions in the United States and Ecuador who supported its creation over the past seven years. This text, I hope, does credit to the energy they expended in its favor.

Many organizations, programs, and people made the international task of researching and writing *Constitutive Visions* possible. The Center for Latin American and Caribbean Studies at the University of Illinois provided funding for early research trips to Ecuador through a summer Foreign Language and Areas Studies fellowship and a Tinker Field Research Grant. The Department of English at the University of Illinois supported my major research trip, and the women's organization P.E.O. (Professional Educational Organization) funded a year of writing following that research. The Rhetoric Society of America generously recognized my work with its annual Dissertation Award in 2011. The graduate school at the University of Wisconsin–Madison funded a return trip to Ecuador. And the Ethel and William Gofen Faculty Development Fund, given to the UW-Madison Department of English, provided a semester of leave essential to the completion of this manuscript.

In Ecuador I conducted the bulk of my research at the Economic and Cultural Libraries of the Banco Central del Ecuador (later the Ministerio de Cultura), at the Casa de la Cultura Ecuatoriana "Benjamín Carrión" and at the Archivo Metropolitano de História de Quito. Yesenia Villacrés at the Banco Central and Ministerio de Cultura and Diego Chiriboga at the Archivo Histórico were especially instrumental in making those efforts successful. The staff at the Archivo de la Función Legislativo, the Archivo Nacional, the Museo Jacinto Jijón y Caamaño, the Museo Metropolitano Alberto Mena Caamaño, and the Biblioteca Aurelio Espinosa Pólit also provided important support. Soledad Kingman, Alba Galecio, and Yolanda Wuth provided access to the collections of their respective fathers, sharing stories and generously encouraging my inquiries. The Casa de la Cultura "Benjamín Carrión," the

Centro Cultural Metropolitano, the Fundación Posada de las Artes Kingman, Alba Galecio, the Ecuadorian Ministerio de Cultura, and Yolanda Wuth all generously gave permission for me to reprint images.

Ecuadorianist scholars—especially María Arboleda, Marc Becker, Ernesto Capello, A. Kim Clark, Rosario Coronel, Valeria Coronel, Alexandra Kennedy Troya, Eduardo Kingman Garcés, Erin O'Connor, Amalia Pallares, and Trinidad Pérez—have offered years' worth of advice, support, and feedback essential to this study and my intellectual growth. Martha Moscoso, for her generosity and encouragement stretching back more than a decade, deserves particular recognition—I would never have begun thinking about national identity, visual culture, and Ecuador without her.

The field of rhetoric deserves greater attention than it generally receives, not least for its tradition of phenomenal mentoring for junior scholars. I thank Michael Bernard-Donals, Ralph Cintrón, Jessica Enoch, Cara Finnegan, Debra Hawhee, Gail Hawisher, Brad Hughes, Jordynn Jack, Peter Mortensen, Roxanne Mountford, John Murphy, Catherine Prendergast, Paul Prior, Jenny Rice, Susan Romano, Spencer Schaffner, and Morris Young for the ways large and small that they have invested in my intellectual and professional growth. Ralph Cintrón, Cara Finnegan, and Peter Mortensen have also continued to serve as mentors and models. Above all, I owe a debt of gratitude and friendship to Debra Hawhee, whose intellectual and professional guidance is without parallel.

My peers within and beyond rhetorical studies have made my academic career thus far amazingly pleasant and rich. Sarah Alexander, Sarah Alderfer, Elizabeth Baldridge, Jim Brown, Caroline Gottschalk-Drushke, Sarah Hallenbeck, Cory Holding, Sam Looker, Lauren Kroiz, Alli Meyer, Kim Hensley Owens, Janine Solberg, Jon Stone, Kate Viera, Amy Wan, and Jordan Zweck have been especially central to that experience. Janine, Kim, and Amy have received and responded to reams of e-mails in ways that kept me going through the crazy patches. Lauren, Janine, Kate, and Amy have, among them, read nearly every word of this book at least twice. Its evocative turns of phrase, its solid arguments, and its well-organized moments owe much to those untiring readers, and its clunky shortcomings are certainly signs of their advice left unheeded.

Sufficiently thanking my family for the years of encouragement, laughter, and love they have provided would itself be a book-length project. My parents gave me many of the skills an academic needs to survive and keep sanity intact, and they have loved me even in the moments I didn't apply those skills. My sister models hard work, balance, and love of living; I still hope to be more like her when I grow up. Anna Henning has been there throughout, and I am better for it. She reads when pressed into service, listens to ideas as they develop, and, just as often, pulls me from the world of rhetorical history into the world of food and walks and new adventures.

In all fairness, the coffee shops where every last word of this study came into being deserve closing thanks: Café Kopi in Champaign; Este Café in Quito; Peregrine, Tryst, and Modern Times Café in Washington, DC; and EVP Coffee in Madison. Neither they nor the people acknowledged here can be held responsible for the following pages. I, however, am grateful to them for enabling this book to develop as successfully, as pleasantly, and as quickly as it did.

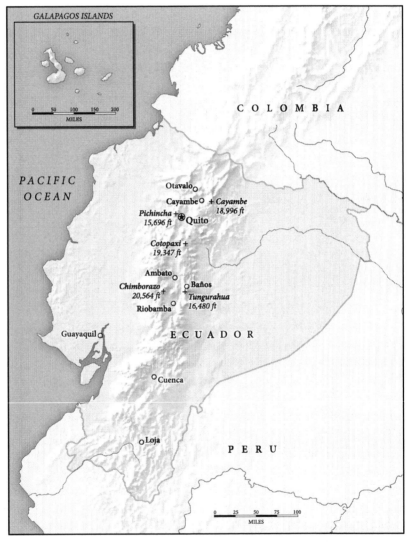

GALAPAGOS ISLANDS

0   50   100   150   200
MILES

COLOMBIA

PACIFIC
OCEAN

Otavalo○
Cayambe○ +Cayambe
                18,996 ft
Pichincha +⊕
15,696 ft Quito

Cotopaxi +
19,347 ft

Ambato○
Chimborazo   ○Baños
20,564 ft+ +Tungurahua
Riobamba○   16,480 ft

Guayaquil○

ECUADOR

○Cuenca

0   25   50   75   100
MILES

○Loja

PERU

Map 1.   Ecuador, selected cities and mountains. Map by Erin Greb Cartography.

A *rondador*. A man with dark eyes, wearing a poncho, holding a panpipe to his lips. With those words I could begin a description of any of the three images sitting on the desk in front of me (figs. 1–3). And I could go further: an image made in the Ecuadorian Andes, an indigenous man, a figure that circulated and has been copied and reproduced, an object intended to envision the nation.[1]

The similarities among these images—an early twentieth-century watercolor painting, a midcentury photograph, and a twenty-first-century cloth doll—are far from coincidental. Even a cursory review of Ecuadorian art books and Internet databases turns up dozens of rondador images produced over a 150-year span and crafted by a diverse array of makers: indigenous merchants, foreign visitors, and white-mestizo artists, among others. Despite their historical spread and varied creators, all these images share common features. The overall look and use of the rondador have remained remarkably stable from the first *rondín* paintings of the nineteenth century to the present-day photographs available on Flickr. That repetition and resilience draw attention to three themes: the rondador appears in many forms but circulates especially prominently in artifacts of visual culture; his image has been taken up over time by a spectrum of rhetors concerned with Ecuadorian national identity; and his indigeneity is an essential part of his ability to stand in for the nation.

As such, that ubiquitous rondador is one figure among many whose circulation and use in the Ecuadorian context illuminate the urgent questions underlying this study: how do strong identifications, such as national identities, come into being and sustain themselves? How do those identifications make claims on future change? To answer those questions, this book tracks the ways that the rondador and his image kin—peasants at market, public works conscripts, festival participants, and more—have served as strange synecdoches for Ecuador. Reviled and excluded in much of daily life, those indigenous subjects reappear in images as representative members of the national

Fig. 1. Joaquín Pinto, *Rondín*, 1900. Watercolor on paper. "Album de personajes populares." Private collection.

Fig. 2.   Bodo Wuth, untitled photograph, ca. 1945. The original caption in *Letras del Ecuador* reads, "En el Continente Americano vive una raza triste" (In the American continent there lives a melancholy race). Reprinted with permission from the family of Bodo Wuth and the Casa de la Cultura Ecuatoriana "Benjamín Carrión," Quito, Ecuador. Photograph by Jessie Reeder.

body and are used to convene national identification. Their shifting and purposeful use highlights a basic reality that extends well beyond Ecuador: all national identity, all nationalism, is rhetorical.[2] But such rhetoricity does not exist only in the grand documents of national constitution or in the circulation

Fig. 3.   Cloth doll (rondador), purchased in Quito in 2011. Photograph by the author.

of individual, explicitly nationalist artifacts. Instead, it fills the interstices of daily life and infuses experience through a wide spectrum of modes and actions. Contradictory yet constitutive, the diffuse objects and ideas of national life accumulate into a thick common sense that is far more resonant than any individual artifact could be. Growing out of and inviting identification, that common sense creates publics, sustains them, and summons them to action.

Whether because of their country's small size and strong neighbors, its ethnic and geographic diversity, or its frequent political change, Ecuadorians have spent much of their history imagining national identity. Throughout that history of contestation, image makers—artists and authors, but also politicians, intellectuals, and journalists—have invested figures like the rondador with a long memory of what Ecuador looks like. The image history offered here tracks the interwoven claims about identity and sovereignty at work within that national vision. It takes the particular case of Ecuador—replete with images, political arguments, and intellectual analyses all aimed toward national identity—as instructive for the larger nature of identification. Tracking how national arguments gain force through ubiquity, repetition, and evolution, the study suggests a revision to the idea of the *topos*, or commonplace. In light of the work done by figures such as the rondador, it reimagines *topoi*—those resources for arguing from generally accepted opinion whose nature has been debated by rhetoricians since Aristotle—as *places of return in changing circumstances* that allow rhetors to make claims both on and from within the nation.

The resilient role played in national identity by figures like the rondador illuminates the ways that theories of rhetoric rely on the commonplace. Definitions of rhetoric often highlight argument or identification, language or artifact, situation or *civitas*. If we look closely, the commonplace lies beneath all those definitions and provides them force. Persuasion and identification rely on shared meaning. Texts, images, and objects must be mutually intelligible to gain influence. Situations and publics gain their shape from common experience and common appeals. As the pages ahead articulate, the commonplace is the basic terrain of rhetoric. Structuring rhetorical analysis around topoi puts useful emphasis on the contexts, practices, registers, and modes of purposeful communication. Working in that vein, *Constitutive Visions* repositions rhetorical theory in light of the Ecuadorian example and reimagines nationalism in light of a visually infused theory of rhetoric.

The analytical reconsideration offered here was inspired by the striking contradiction mentioned earlier: the idea of the Ecuadorian nation has often relied on images of indigenous people, but indigenous people themselves have equally often been excluded from active participation in the nation. Over time, the creation and repetition of commonplaces that connect indigeneity to the idea of the nation have aided in the maintenance of that contradiction, giving it conceptual force, naturalizing its paradoxes, and negotiating its complex rhetorical circumstances. With those commonplaces, socially dominant white-mestizo Ecuadorians reconciled concerns over their own modernity and imagined a coherent nation-state even in the midst of social upheaval and territorial contraction. Popular movements, middle-class artists, and indigenous people also engaged topoi of indigeneity and national identity, contesting the visions circulated by their elite compatriots and making space for themselves within the public body. In their interactions across places, times, and social positions, those multiple claims to the nation have woven a pervasive fabric of national identification able to absorb even resistance and contestation.

This study, written at a moment when scholars question the continued relevance of the nation-state as a primary category of identification, draws attention to an earlier moment of nation trouble.[3] Investigating the idea of the nation as a rhetorical process and product, *Constitutive Visions* suggests that nations have always been porous affairs. The problems of sovereignty and standing that trouble scholars of contemporary transnationalism are nothing new when seen from the perspective of the global South. *Constitutive Visions* traces the contradictory and piecemeal, yet enduring, visions of the nation that developed in Ecuador from the beginning of the popular republic. In the process it illustrates how nationalism—understood in rhetorical terms as a sustained, compounded process of identification—depends on elastic topoi to provide conceptual places of return in the midst of contestation and interrupted sovereignty.

The remaining pages of this introduction map the book's rhetorical terrain. They use those ubiquitous, repeated rondador images as a guide to three key aspects of my revised notion of the commonplace: circulation across modes, elasticity over time, and resonance within context. Discussion of those three elements, along with a brief history of the Ecuadorian scene, sets the stage for tracking national identity in Ecuador and for a renewed understanding of nationalism's rhetorical foundations.

The Terrain of the Commonplace

This study approaches topoi as nodes of social value and common sense that provide places of return for convening arguments across changing circumstances. That definition emerged from a need to understand the persistent patterns of national vision so prevalent in Ecuador as something other than a sign of stagnation. Research in archives and secondary material made clear that Ecuadorian rhetors—from criollo elites to subaltern indigenous people—returned repeatedly to shared themes of national identity and used those returns to make new social meaning and effect change. The anthropologist Emma Cervone shows indigenous communities engaging pre-Columbian social orders to invert white-mestizo control of social space; historian Eduardo Kingman Garcés's *La ciudad y los otros* follows the feudal patterns that underwrote the emergence of modernity in Quito; anthropologist Blanca Muratorio tracks the images of indigenous people that nineteenth-century Ecuadorian elites used to picture their nation in world's fairs and international expositions.[4] For all these Ecuadorianist scholars, what is old does not merely exert the power of tradition. Instead, it drives re-creation.

That sense that the familiar can serve a generative purpose resonates productively within the long history of rhetorical theorizing around the commonplace. It works particularly well with recent definitions put forward by the rhetorical theorists Carolyn Miller and Ralph Cintrón, who figure topoi, respectively, as "aid[s] to pattern recognition" and "storehouses of social energy."[5] Blending Cintrón's emphasis on social context with Miller's focus on familiarity and novelty and then reading both in light of the insights offered by Ecuadorian scholars, my definition of topos directs attention to issues of temporal and spatial circulation, stressing the moments and movements of the commonplace. Topos, thus defined, allows new insights into the rhetorical processes that foster, valorize, and give force to the common. It also makes clear the term's particular applicability to the rhetorical tactics of nationalism.

By virtue of its encounter with Ecuadorianist theories and with the work of contemporary rhetorical scholars, the notion of topoi invoked here is several steps removed from Aristotle's concern with finding ways to "reason from opinions that are generally accepted."[6] Like other more recent rhetorical scholars, I engage topoi to examine how the "generally accepted ideas" that Aristotle largely takes for granted emerge and gain their persuasive power in context.[7] That approach to topoi as intricately situated heuristics highlights, above all, their resilience. Topoi are elastic symbolic tools built from common sense that provide a stable tether point, allowing rhetors and publics to negotiate shifting terrain.

This move to alter topical theories in light of new contexts is itself nothing new. The rhetorical theorist Richard McKeon reminds us that the current proliferation of commonplace theories has its roots in ancient ambiguity. Their key terms, "places, topics, loci, commonplaces and proper places . . . were as

ambiguous in ordinary Greek as they are in ordinary English." Rhetorician
Michael Leff similarly notes that elaborating a systematic theory of topoi has
been at the center of rhetorical study from ancient times to the present. Such
effort has resulted in "a bewildering diversity of meanings," largely because
ancient sources simply do not agree.[8] Each era and context, it seems, recuper-
ates the commonplace for its own uses. It should not be surprising, then, that
our scholarly moment is less concerned with topoi as means of arrangement
and more concerned with topoi as ideological carriers and sources of invention.[9] The most driving commonplaces of late modernity are, after all, the
simultaneously meaning-filled and contentless terms of democracy and capital, economic liberalism and religious conviction, that pervade contemporary
common sense and underline our most pressing arguments.

It is in this sense, then, that commonplaces are what Cintrón terms
"storehouses of social energy." Those content-filled storehouses allow actors
from a wide range of subject positions to bring a shared sense of the world
"before the eyes" of the publics they convene. That common vision, conditioned by the social energy on which it is based, "organize[s] our sentiments,
beliefs, and actions in the lifeworld" and, in the process, nurtures public
common sense. Cintrón thus moves the emphasis of topical invention from
the action of individual rhetors to the social life of common sense and positions topoi as both products and means of public creation. Though Cintrón
does not develop the point, this understanding of the commonplace makes it
particularly applicable to the material and symbolic constitutions of national
life. The very idea of the nation relies on expansive, layered commonplaces
that appear to preexist any given rhetorical moment but are also generated
from each use in context. Understanding the commonplaces of nationalism,
then, requires seeking out those topics and topoi that, as Cintrón suggests,
"have sufficient *umpf* to actualize the body politic."[10]

Such forceful topoi, I propose, share three features that bear more
thorough discussion. The following sections perform that extrapolation,
unwinding the ways that commonplaces circulate across modes, maintain
elasticity over time, and gain resonance in context. Putting rhetorical theories, Ecuadorianist theories, and Ecuadorian history into conversation, that
exegesis expands the interpretive terrain of the commonplace.

Circulation Across Modes: Doing Rich Rhetorical Historiography

While most theories of the commonplace omit direct treatment of the visual, the ocularity of the term is hard to miss.[11] Whether defined in terms

of "pattern recognition," "invention, discovery, and insight," or "bringing-before-the-eyes," explanations of the commonplace generated by rhetoricians are shot through with the sensory and the visual.[12] Such implicit dependence is not incidental. As Ecuadorian art historian Alexandra Kennedy Troya asserts with regard to national identity and visual culture, "images are instruments of historical invention, . . . and along with texts written, read, or sung, they become national discourses that will be reinterpreted or re-elaborated in the hands of various social agents once their original purposes [commitments] have lost relevance."[13] Visual images are, in other words, frequent and natural carriers of the commonplace. Though commonplaces work across multiple expressive modes, leaving elements of visual culture out of the analysis prevents full understanding of the strong identifications of nationalism. Any robust treatment of topoi must attend to their accumulation and circulation across an array of symbolic forms (Kennedy Troya's "images . . . along with texts written, read, or sung"), as it is that very modal flexibility that allows them to become common.

As the case of Ecuador demonstrates, the need for a broad sensory awareness is especially profound in the study of national topoi. Commonplaces, in whatever form they circulate, function primarily to help publics see themselves and envision their interconnections with the imagined community. They are carriers of visuality in the sense invoked by Nicholas Mirzoeff, as "the visualization history . . . [a] practice [that] must be imaginary, rather than perceptual, because what is being visualized is too substantial for any one person to see and is created from information, images, and ideas."[14] Commonplaces allow access to the larger scene, speaking both to it and from within it. As Miller suggests, commonplaces illuminate the wider patterns that drive and organize social life.[15]

Rhetorical scholars, then, need to pursue what Cara Finnegan has called "rich rhetorical histories": studies that include "careful, situated investigation of the social, cultural, and political work that visual communication is made to do."[16] Doing otherwise in our analyses risks omitting important aspects of how publics come together, sustain themselves, and promote visions for the future. The circulation and repetition of images in the process of Ecuadorian nation formation are, in other words, essential to understanding the common sense–informing claims about national identity and republican sovereignty. Such an approach treats visual rhetoric not as "a unique genre of rhetorical artifact ('rhetoric' that is 'visual')" but as "a project of inquiry that considers the implications for rhetorical theory of sustained attention to visuality."[17]

In that spirit, it becomes both useful and necessary to track figures like the rondador that contribute to a commonsense national pattern and bring a vision of the nation before Ecuadorian and foreign eyes. The rondador, interpolated into the story of the nation, has circulated within and across moments, appearing in nineteenth-century traveler's books, in twentieth-century periodicals, and in twenty-first-century tourists' trinkets. In each moment, he makes the features of national life visible. Like the rondador, most of the artifacts of Ecuadorian visual culture examined in the coming pages come from genres suitable for mass reproduction or public dissemination (illustrations, murals, prints, etc.). Though it would be disingenuous to suggest that all of the images discussed here had truly popular circulation in their own time and place (economies of art and access always limit circulation, even in forms intended for wide consumption), their ability to move and their frequent reproduction helped make them common to the national milieu and available to those actively engaged in shaping national identity. In visual form, they helped sustain and circulate commonplaces that moved across modes. They thus are implicated even in the versions of those topoi that Ecuadorians encountered in political speech, in quotidian discussions, and in cultural ephemera. These images are rich sources of topoi. They popularize and make visible shared places of return. In their uptake and re-creation over time and space, they provide stable locales from which invention can occur and aid responses to new moments and new circumstances. They allow the nation to see itself again and again in new light.

Elasticity over Time: On Novelty and Tradition

The ubiquity of that repetition points to the second feature of topoi made particularly visible by the Ecuadorian context: their elasticity. The three rondadors introduced earlier speak eloquently for an understanding of the commonplace that highlights resilience. The figures are social types—ordered, condensed images of local character that inoculate the public body against the flux of daily life. That these resources for argument provide stability, then, is largely apparent. The rondadors from the early twentieth, mid-twentieth, and early twenty-first century are romantic, nonthreatening, and consumable. Given that each of those periods was marked by sustained resistance from indigenous communities and by significant elite anxiety over the threats that indigenous Ecuadorians posed to their authority, such passive availability is clearly both purposefully and persuasively deployed. It holds the public in place and manages the national body.

At the same time, we ought also to see that commonplace constancy as active and inventive. Ecuadorians have repeatedly used figures like the rondador to make new claims about national identity. The images provide a sense of stability that pervades even the shaky experiences of national change. In this sense, they point us toward a means of resolving the classic tension in rhetorical discussion of topoi, what Miller terms their simultaneously managerial and generative capacity.[18]

Over the course of their theoretical history, topoi have been celebrated as tools for building arguments and dismissed as sets of technical rules. As McKeon puts it, "The commonplaces of invention changed periodically from meaning devices for discovering something previously unknown to meaning familiar quotations in which something well known and widely esteemed is stated." Though the more tradition-based form of topoi has often been promulgated through guides and handbooks for orators, McKeon notes that rhetorical theorists since ancient times have argued for the inventive sense of topoi.[19] In light of that ongoing disconnect, there has been a relatively consistent contemporary interest in what might be called the central paradox of the topics: the fact that they house inventive possibility in the recitation of the familiar. Rhetoricians, again and again, seek to address those tensions between tradition and structure on the one hand and creativity and innovation on the other.

Informed by the Ecuadorian example, my treatment of topoi as places of return emphasizes invention but suggests that tradition and stability play a crucial role in that invention. The rondador and similar images are compelling in rhetorical terms not because they hold the national body still but because that apparent stillness constantly creates new possibilities. As a topos, the rondador allows for invention and development by grounding visions for the future on images of the past. Such a view of commonplaces gives further emphasis to what Miller terms the "generative potential of the familiar." For Miller, tradition and innovation interrelate within the topos: "A revived theory of topical invention should make novelty and decorum complementary and interactive, opposing impulses that can be implemented only in tension with each other." In this sense, a topos functions as "a point in semantic space that is particularly rich in connectivity to other significant or highly connected points." The commonness of "commonplace," in that sense, is derived from intersections and the ability to interlock with other locations and ideas. Miller emphasizes that connectivity is key to creating novelty out of the habitual. As techniques of pattern recognition, topoi push rhetors and audiences to recognize the "familiar [in] the unfamiliar, the known [in] the unknown" and then make new connections in light of that recognition.[20]

Seen in this light, topoi provide resources for innovative arguments because they allow audiences to recognize the contexts and structures from which novelty arises.

Within Miller's study, while topoi are generative and open-ended in a spatial sense, providing "a region of productive uncertainty" and "a space, or a located perspective, *from* which one searches," the temporal dimensions of their function are ambiguous.[21] Miller draws on McKeon, so it is reasonable to imagine that she, like McKeon, sees topoi as cyclical. McKeon describes the commonplace as the outcome of novelty grown old: "Invention, discovery, and insight are creative modes of departure from accustomed circumstances of the commonplace to transform the customary or the unnoticed into novelties. Widely known and authoritatively established novelties in turn become commonplaces and provide circumstances and subjects for new innovations."[22] Defining topoi as elastic or resilient, as "places of return in changing circumstances," presses against the idea that they gain their inventive potential primarily through a cyclical relationship with the new or a tendency to be replaced by novelty. A reliance on *return* directs attention instead to the lives and life spans of topoi: how they retain connectivity over time, are remodeled for new purposes along the way, and are constantly stretching and altering supposedly familiar terrain.

That insistence on seeing topoi as *live* over the long term again emerges from the parallel insights provided by Ecuadorianist scholarship about national identity. Scholars of Ecuadorian history broadly agree that national identity first began developing there more than twenty years after the 1830 creation of the political territory known as Ecuador. It was only in the 1850s and 1860s that economic and social pressures gave exigency to a sense of common identity that crossed regional boundaries. Not coincidentally, that moment coincided with the de jure integration of indigenous peoples into the republic in 1857, when indigenous people were no longer required to pay the separate "personal tax" or "tribute." The projects of nation building begun in the 1850s lasted well into the twentieth century. Such a drawn out and explicit process demands attention to the enduring textures and mechanisms of nation making and, in turn, to the importance of temporal resilience within theories of the commonplace.

To make sense of that simultaneously temporal and spatial resilience, and of the topos's ability to make novelty from the familiar, this study engages a diverse collection of archival documents drawn from a variety of moments and contexts. Taken together, those artifacts trace an intricate history of everyday and exceptional communication that has given commonplace force to visions of what it means to invoke the nation. Working from that wide concatenation of archival material (works of art, illustrations, petitions, proclamations, articles, essays, etc.) allows access to the long-term, commonplace machinations of identification and nation making in Ecuador.[23] It demonstrates as well how both everyday and exceptional artifacts participate in the creation and dispersal of commonplaces, serving both as part of the familiar substrate that allows novelty to emerge and as examples of that novelty itself.

By describing the opposite of the "everyday" in terms of the "exceptional," I suggest that both official and private realms produce everyday discourse and that the mundane and the extraordinary together merit rhetorical analysis. This study, then, challenges the frequent implication in scholarship that the opposite of "everyday" is "elite," as if elites did not have an everyday and subalterns never stepped outside of the ordinary. Defining "everyday" in terms of the quotidian and opposing it to the exceptional emphasizes the different levels at which commonplaces circulate in their role as sustainers of publics. It suggests that stability and change similarly occur at multiple levels.

The constant petitions of indigenous laborers and the revolutionary speeches of political elites both prompt change by drawing on the national familiar. They simply do their work at different levels and in different scopes. To understand images like the rondador as tapping the generative potential of the familiar, then, requires a theory of the topos that pays attention to quotidian availability, such as their ubiquitous presence in market stalls, postcard displays, periodical illustrations, and watercolor sketches; and extraordinary appearances, like their presence in oil paintings or invocation in national political campaigns. It also requires awareness of the political and documentary contexts in which those images have circulated. For that reason, the coming chapters move between artifacts such as political Constitutions, geography treatises, and oil paintings ("exceptional" rhetorical objects meant to be unitary and immense in their definitive scope) and popular petitions, congressional debates, and widely reproduced pictures ("everyday" rhetorical objects that constitute publics through their mundane repetition). They examine, in other words, how complexes of everyday and exceptional artifacts convene and sustain the elastic topoi of Ecuadorian national identity.

Resonance Within Context: Placing Rhetorical Ecologies

For most of their history, rondadors have served as powerful indicators of place. While themselves often sceneless, they grew from artistic movements and commercial purposes intricately tied to a sense of location. Rondadors have participated in tourist economies, providing evidence of a visit to Ecuador and standing in for the national experience. In the nineteenth and twentieth centuries, rondadors also aided internal arguments about Ecuadorianness: Ecuadorian image makers made them for Ecuadorian audiences who wanted a sense of national particularity. Whether made for local audiences or foreign ones, though, rondadors sought and projected a common place: Ecuador.

The spatial specificity of the rondador points us back toward the territorial implications of the commonplace. It illuminates as well how the constitutive, permeable interplay between identifications and territories informs the experience of national identity. When it comes to national common sense and national topoi, the question of how, where, and through what scenes topoi move is essential to understanding the social energy they channel. That focus on how topoi move and influence within contexts invites us into an ecological view of rhetorical practice.

The first definition of ecology, voiced by Ernest Haeckel in 1869, is frequently glossed as "the study of the interrelations of plants and animals with their environments."[24] Since 1985, Charles Krebs's definition of ecology as "the scientific study of the interactions that determine the distribution and abundance of organisms" has become more or less dominant.[25] It is not much of a stretch to understand rhetoric in ecological terms as the study of the symbolic interactions that determine the distribution and abundance of civic life. Commonplaces, in this sense, form the shifting terrain of rhetorical ecology. They ground identifications and allow us to recognize dynamic relationships among audiences, places, rhetors, and events.

In her generative rethinking of the rhetorical situation, Jenny Edbauer introduces the term "rhetorical ecology" to emphasize the interrelations of rhetorical elements "in a wider sphere of active, historical, and lived processes." Edbauer's ecological project is to develop "a framework of *affective ecologies* that recontextualizes rhetorics in their temporal, historical, and lived fluxes." That aim leads her to contest the "placed" aspects of rhetorical theories, noting that the social resides not in "fixed sites, but rather in a networked space of flows and connections." "In this way," Edbauer continues, "place becomes decoupled from the notion of *situs*, or fixed (series of) locations, and linked instead to the in-between en/action of events and encounters."[26] For Edbauer, place is always characterized by fluxes and processes, not sites. Location is displaced; place is dislocated.

While Edbauer's emphasis on flux treats an essential piece of ecology, its departure from situs risks losing what precisely is ecological about rhetoric. Rhetorical ecologies do highlight fluid populations and mobile interactions, but they are also, fundamentally, about placed confluences: communities, ecosystems, publics. My return to Edbauer's term in light of the Ecuadorian case finds me digging in my heels in support of location and situs. That recalcitrant interest in sites does not dispute Edbauer's insistence on circulation as one of rhetoric's key terms. Movement makes rhetorical practice. As Edbauer argues, no ecology is hermetically bounded; they are always permeable, though not necessarily in predictable ways. At the same time, no ecology is placeless. Even in light of Edbauer's insight that "rhetoric emerges already infected by the viral intensities that are circulating in the social field," no rhetorical act entirely transcends its location. It is that balance of flux and site that drives the rhetorical force of the commonplace (linking questions of place to the generative capacities of the topos).

The fact that ecology cannot be detached from place comes into focus as we consider its etymological root in the idea of *oikos*: ecology is the study of the "'home life' of living organisms." The root of "ecology," whether approached as biological or rhetorical, encourages attention to the relationships "between organisms [biological, discursive, symbolic, material] and their environments." Rhetorical ecologists, like scientific ecologists, "focus on the pathways followed by energy and matter as these move among living and nonliving elements of . . . [their] ecosystem."[27] Ecology is about populations and interactions, then, but it is also about paths and places. This is not so much a departure from Edbauer's claims as a reemphasizing of a less central point. Edbauer notes, after all, that a shift toward rhetorical ecologies allows us to "see that public rhetorics do not only exist in the elements of their situations, but also in the radii of their neighboring events."[28] Neighborhoods matter. Rhetorics circulate within and across places. Situs, if newly porous and crisscrossed with resource flows, remains powerful.

My fidelity to the territorial implications of the commonplace has two related motives, both shaped by contemporary concerns in rhetorical scholarship and by the placed histories at hand. First, rejuvenating a connection made by rhetorical theorist Scott Consigny in 1974, I suggest that rhetorical scholars ought to read our various spatialized theories in concert. We should view commonplaces, rhetorical situations, and rhetorical ecologies alongside one another to better understand the workings and possibilities of another concept whose placedness is often contested: the public.[29] The analyses ahead, particularly in chapter 2, enact that combinatory project. Second, seeing commonplaces in terms of situated publicity and rhetorical ecologies may help rhetorical scholars grapple with the complexities of expanding our own vision. As the field engages troubling questions about the relevance of rhetorical theory to contexts minimally touched by Greco-Roman traditions, it is useful to remember that persuasive practice emerges both from places

and from the forces that move across them. A new study of the topos, because it takes so seriously the question of place, pushes rhetorical scholars
to review the territories of our own identifications. The majority of rhetorical
scholars locate our work in places where classical rhetorical traditions overlap with, appropriate, or are washed away by other traditions of persuasion
and identification. In that context, careful attention to terrain—to common
and uncommon places—is essential. We need robust, flexible, and wide-
ranging theories of the topos: theories that have traveled and that travel well.

The particular location of Ecuador, the landscapes and common places
of a small Andean republic, also demand rhetorical scholarship that takes
terrain into account. While transnational topics of modernity, science, capital, and political ideology have crossed nation-state borders and permeated
Ecuadorian national argument, they have always also been moving across
specifically Ecuadorian topography. Making sense of the rhetorical work of
Ecuadorian national identity, then, requires careful attention to the particular
ecology of its common places and common visions. The purpose and use of
rhetorical theories must, similarly, shift to accommodate the forms and patterns at work in those places.

Each of the three elements of topoi discussed here—movement across
modes, innovation from tradition, and ecological placement—emphasizes
the interconnection among rhetorical objects, contexts, and effects as well as
their circulation among audiences and moments. They direct rhetorical analysis toward the lines of force and dependence that make identifications common. Shaped by the insights made available in the Ecuadorian context, this
reworked approach of topoi allows new understandings of how they authorize and sustain strong public identifications. It positions rhetorical artifacts
(images, texts, performances, etc.) not as isolated instances of persuasion but
as force-filled elements that move within persuasive fields and are engaged
by varied publics and counterpublics in the pursuit of a coherent, legitimate,
sustainable sense of a national "we."

Setting the Scene: The Argument from Ecuadorian History (a Brief History
of Ecuador)

Understanding the stakes and shape of that national "we" in the case of
Ecuador requires one more round of scene setting. This final section takes
heed of the reminder to place commonplaces. *Constitutive Visions*'s rhetorical
terrain is shaped by an Ecuadorian one, replete with boundaries, histories,

politics, and cultural contexts. To follow the study's rhetorical paths, then, readers need an overview of their Andean topography and of the ways that the pages to come traverse that terrain.

Such cartographic sketching could easily start in the pre-Columbian period: tracking the Inca Huayna Capac's invasion of what is now Ecuadorian territory or his son Atahuallpa's rise to power only to face the Spanish invaders.[30] Likewise, this history could begin in the colonial period with the Republic of Spaniards and Republic of Indians, whose different governing structures set the stage for future Ecuadorian policies, or with the influence of indigenous aesthetics in the so-called Quito School of sacred art.[31] Moving toward independence, it could trace the tribute system under which indigenous people provided significant income for colonial and early republican governments.[32] Or it might begin with Quito's status as the site of the first "Shout" for independence—in 1809, with the Quito department's subsequent slowness to achieve independence (on May 24, 1822), or with its separation from Simón Bolívar's Gran Colombia in 1830.[33]

This brief history of Ecuador actually begins, however, in the 1850s, when Ecuador formally abolished indigenous tribute (1857) and saw the founding of its first local postcolonial arts organization, the Escuela Democrática de Miguel de Santiago (1852). The year 1857 thus marks the moment when Ecuador, by law, recognized itself as incorporating rather than coexisting with its indigenous population—even if the end of tribute is best explained by its decreasing utility and not by an egalitarian urge toward inclusion.[34] For its part, 1852 introduces a rising concern with national vision, one that positioned history, territory, and population as integral elements of Ecuadorian image making. Those two early and thoroughly intertwined events on the path of nation making set constitutive scenes that were revisited and reimagined again and again over the next hundred years. The mapping here begins from those two events, using their impetus to aid readers' orientation to the two eras central to this study and to highlight the ways that political, artistic, and intellectual trends flowed together during those eras.

The Romantic Picturesque from Catholic Modernity to Secular Liberalism (1852–1906)

The 1850s saw some of Ecuador's first moves toward national integration. Prior to that, elites and subalterns alike tended to privilege local affiliation over national. Ecuadorian governments from the 1850s through the turn of the century invested in political centralization and cultural cohesion. They pursued cultural, political, and economic strategies designed to advance the nation and a sense of national identity. Civil society both drove and responded to that governmental orientation, and Ecuadorian criollos and white-mestizos launched periodicals, literary and philosophical societies, and artistic movements all aimed toward the idea of the nation.[35] Though elite economic and administrative interests were a primary impetus for the move toward national vision, the means for achieving such vision strayed well beyond those realms. The notion that Ecuador ought to have a claim on the affiliations and identifications of its population required full-spectrum engagement to bring into reality. Such "all available means" attention to nation formation appears in the founding documents of the Escuela Democrática de Miguel de Santiago, in the policies and institutions advanced by successive presidents, and in the cultural production of authors, artists, and intellectuals throughout the era. Those nation-making efforts took more than fifty years to reach their first, short-lived point of stasis. The first period of this study coincides with that early era of nation formation.

The second half of the nineteenth century was a period of intense political dispute. Catholic Conservatives and secular Liberals repeatedly clashed—with words, with images, and with bullets—over the fundamentally sacred or secular nature of the nation-state. That battle slowed the process of national-identity creation and set the scene for the more chaotic contests of the next century. The era under consideration here saw a gradual shift in political dominance of the presidency from the staunchly Catholic Conservative Party (1859–75) to the bourgeois banking- and export-dominated Progressives (1883–95) to the secular Liberal Party (1895–1916).[36] Though there were significant political and ideological differences among those groups, as the Ecuadorian historian Eduardo Kingman Garcés suggests, "they coincided, in large part, within the same process of constituting a State and a National Society" and, further, in their use of indigenous images within that process.[37] The ideological polarities dividing Liberals and Conservatives also existed within a shared aesthetic-conceptual milieu: a positivist romanticism whose sources lay primarily outside the borders of Ecuador but whose orientation was profoundly local.[38] Liberals and Conservatives, authors and artists, local officials and visiting experts all spoke the language of science and nature. They observed, recorded, and attempted to improve their country.

Politics, academics, and the arts were far from separate spheres in this era. The central characters of this study exemplify that fact: the artist Juan Agustín Guerrero and the author Juan León Mera both held elected positions and participated in party politics during their careers (Guerrero with the Liberals, Mera with the Conservatives). Conservative President Gabriel García Moreno joined visiting scientists as they scaled Quito's famous volcano, Guagua Pichincha, and was responsible for creating the country's first school of fine arts. The painter Joaquín Pinto alternately satirized and romanticized local culture in his art and also provided scientific illustrations for books of natural history. The archbishop of Quito, Federico González Suárez, mediated between Liberals and Conservatives at the turn of the twentieth century, hired Pinto to illustrate his study of pre-Columbian archaeological remains, and published a history of the Spanish Americas that exposed the vices of colonial authorities and helped justify independence. The country as a whole, and Quito in particular, had a small cadre of active nation makers, and they did their constitutive work in conversation and conflict with one another.

García Moreno, who dominated Ecuadorian politics between 1859 and his assassination in 1875, is usually credited with the first successful period of Ecuadorian state and national-identity formation. His authoritarian approach, fierce commitment to Catholic doctrine, and pursuit of scientific and educational advances sparked both great change and great resistance. He pushed through an official alliance with Rome in 1866, sponsored scientific expeditions, founded educational institutions, and promoted infrastructure projects. During his presidency, the arts began to flourish again in Ecuador after a period of decay during the early republic.[39] Though artists in this era worked in the shadows of Europe—their status often depended on their ability to train there—they also began to promote a new sense of Ecuadorian particularity. They painted local landscapes, extolled the heroes of the wars of independence, and sketched scenes of "local color" through a genre known as *costumbrismo*. Guerrero, Pinto, and Mera all came of age in this era and produced work that envisioned Ecuador's popular spirit, critiqued its foibles, and promoted its particularity. Those projects—artistic and administrative—advanced a vision of Ecuador as an integrated national whole, and they left clear marks on the political, architectural, scientific, and economic state of the nation.

After García Moreno's assassination in 1875, Ecuador entered a period of upheaval that eventually led to an alliance between Coastal agro-export interests and conservative Highland landowners. Pairing the social values of the Conservatives with bourgeois economic interests, these Progressive governments approached national development in terms of the booming market in cacao production and exportation on the coast. That outward turn also precipitated Ecuador's participation in the world's fairs and international expositions of the era. The Ecuadorian pavilions in Paris, Madrid, and Chicago featured Highland textiles and Coastal cacao; they vaunted a spirit of republican progress through paintings of heroes and martyrs; and they displayed landscapes and local customs in the romantic picturesque of the day.[40]

In general, the emphasis on national images continued to grow in aesthetic circles during that era. Mera began to publish prolifically and became a central figure in Highlands intellectual and political circles. His best known novel, *Cumandá*—a romantic tale set in the Amazon—appeared alongside hundreds of poems and essays, as well as a guide to the Constitution, a textbook on geography, a compilation of popular songs, and the text of the national anthem.[41] Pinto, becoming better known in Quito, produced large numbers of both costumbrista watercolors and traditional religious oil paintings. He also provided illustrations for a study of Ecuador's biological diversity written by the French naturalist Auguste Cousin and for archaeological texts by González Suárez.[42] Around the same time, Luís A. Martínez, the youngest son of a prominent Highland family who would become an influential Liberal politician, artist, and author, came to Quito. He began writing and painting for public consumption in the 1890s, making a name for himself as an avid mountaineer and amateur scientist along the way. Considerations of indigenous culture infused much of Martínez's work—from paintings of the Incan highway (fig. 10) to photographs of mountain *chozas* (huts) and laments over the rustic state of Ecuadorian agriculture.[43] In other words, even Progressive Era efforts to move outward and establish Ecuador in the world (through export, participation in world's fairs, scientific publication, etc.) meant looking inward for defining features and national character.

During the Progressive Era, Liberal resistance to the national government gradually increased. An economic and political crisis in the 1890s gave the exiled Liberal leader General Eloy Alfaro the opening he needed, and the 1895 Liberal Revolution brought Alfaro into power. That upheaval occasioned dramatic shifts in Ecuador's national climate: the secular Liberals expropriated church property, established civil marriage laws, and began building a secular system of education. Ideologically and politically, Liberals were invested in improving the status of the "miserable" Indian. In service of that commitment, they eliminated the state-enforced tithe that the Catholic Church had demanded of indigenous people; they moved against the debt-peonage system of *concertaje* (though their own interests delayed its demise until the 1920s); and they debated the possibility of extending citizenship to illiterate Ecuadorians (a change that would not occur until 1979). Like their predecessors, Liberals were also committed to establishing a coherent sense of the nation. They pushed through the long-awaited completion of a railway that would connect the Coast to the Highlands.[44] In 1904, at the urging of Luís Martínez, Alfaro's successor founded the Escuela de Bellas Artes (School of Fine Arts) that still exists in Quito today. An aging Joaquín Pinto was one of the school's first professors, and many of the next generation's prominent artists received their training there.

Elite Conservatives, Progressives, and Liberals found themselves at odds over religion, politics, and economics. They shared, however, an overarching goal of national vision and mobilized many of the same tools in service of that vision. They grappled with how to imagine the country's indigenous majority; they built highways and railways to transport goods from the Coast to the Highlands (and back); they engaged the arts, natural science, and history to narrate a national story. Again and again, romantic bourgeois positivism set them in pursuit of a discoverable, measurable, and demonstrable nation defined, as the official closing phrase of Liberal-era missives put it, by order and progress.

Social Realism from Populist Politics to the Artistic Left (1925–1948)

Though it focuses primarily on the 1930s and 1940s, the second period of this study effectively begins with the July Revolution (Revolución Juliana), sparked more than a decade after liberalism's more radical hopes died alongside Eloy Alfaro at the hands of a Guayaquil mob. The twenty-two years between the July Revolution and the coup d'état against President José María Velasco Ibarra in 1947 were characterized by persistent instability: revolving administrations, economic crises, the fission of leftist political parties, and the emergence of populist politics. Artists sought to overturn the romantic aesthetics of the previous century and, in some cases, battled alongside their compatriots in the era's armed conflicts. Throughout the period, Liberals, Conservatives, and leftists struggled to establish authority and draw the nation into their vision of modernity. For all of them, the terms of social realism—starkly focused on the country's problems and possibilities—offered a vocabulary for assessing both national present and national future.

The 1930s and 1940s were particularly fraught with crises. There were constitutional assemblies convened in 1929, 1937, 1938, 1944, and 1946, with new Constitutions produced in 1929, 1945, and 1946.[45] In addition to the destabilizing effects of the global economic crisis of the thirties and the rise of fascism in Europe, internal political struggles and escalating tensions with Peru made for a chaotic era.[46] In the 1930s no president served a full four-year term, and there were multiple brief dictatorships, multiple appointed executives, and multiple coups d'état. The first seven years of the 1940s saw only two governments, but one was overthrown by revolution and the other by coup d'état, and both administrations faced (and suppressed) significant political turmoil. This mid-twentieth-century period featured a socialist president who favored the Catholic Church and export interests—while violently suppressing leftist parties—and a populist Conservative president who briefly sponsored the nation's "Red" Constitution and founded key state institutions that would house the nation's intellectual and artistic Left. It is no surprise, then, that President Galo Plaza Lasso, who took office after a democratic election in 1948, characterized his arrival in power as an "experiment in democracy" that would replace the instability of "twenty-seven chiefs of state, four presidents in one month, six constitutions and innumerable so-called revolutions" with a new era of "social justice, of better times, and of opportunities for work . . . in an atmosphere of peace and liberty and justice."[47]

For white-mestizo politicians, intellectuals, and artists during the mid-twentieth century, discussions about indigenous people almost always engaged the terms of the so-called Indian problem. At its most basic, that "problem" saw unhygienic, uneducated, impoverished, and marginalized indigenous people as a threat to the life of the nation. Where the academic efforts of previous eras had emphasized a mythic indigenous past through historical narrative and archaeology, mid-twentieth-century scholars known as *indigenistas* turned to psychology and physiology to examine the problems of the indigenous present.[48] Though some scholars situated indigenous struggles in light of ongoing exploitation, they still viewed contemporary indigenous people as unfit for active participation in the nation-state.[49]

Indigenismo also came to dominate the arts in Ecuador during the 1930s and 1940s. Like the costumbrismo of the nineteenth century and the romantic *indianismo* of the early twentieth century, indigenismo depicted Ecuador as a nation of Indians.[50] Unlike its earlier cousins inspired by romanticism and positivism, however, indigenismo was grounded in social realism and linked to the expressivist strands of modern art.[51] Starting around 1935, young indigenistas in the Highlands rebelled against the established salon culture and its connections to Quito's traditional aristocracy. They joined or sympathized with the Ecuadorian socialist party and supported leftist political struggles. Some of the indigenistas, including the painter Eduardo Kingman and the critic Benjamín Carrión, became central figures in the new art institutions founded in the 1940s under the aegis of the Casa de la Cultura Ecuatoriana. Some—Oswaldo Guayasamín, Camilo Egas, Galo Galecio, Carlos Rodríguez,

Kingman, and Carrión—gained fame both in Ecuador and abroad. Egas spent most of his career at the New School in New York, while Guayasamín remained in Ecuador but became the international face of indigenismo and its leftist politics. Galecio and Rodríguez traveled to Mexico on government scholarships in the forties; Kingman traveled to the United States through artistic exchanges in the forties and fifties; Carrión lived off and on as an expatriate and sometime diplomat in several European and Latin American countries from the late twenties through the early forties.[52] Indigenista artists painted murals in public buildings, provided illustrations for poems and periodicals, and established new salons and arts collectives. They aimed to alter the scene of Ecuadorian art, making it more profoundly Ecuadorian, more committed to the popular classes, and more visibly modern. In the process, they helped shift the terrain of what "Ecuadorian" looked like, but they also kept that national picture resolutely indigenous.

Between the July Revolution and the ouster of José María Velasco Ibarra very little about the Ecuadorian civil scene can be said to have been stable except, perhaps, change itself. It is compelling, then, that the symbolic role of indigenous people within visions of the nation remained so consistent. There were, of course, fierce debates over the ideological valence of images, over the political purpose behind invocations of the "Indian problem," and over the aesthetic strategies used to depict indigenous people. Yet still the struggling nation remained inextricably and influentially tied to visions of indigeneity throughout those two decades.

From 1852 through 1947, then, projects of nation making occupied a central place in Ecuadorian rhetorical production. They infused artistic media and national development strategies. They crossed ideological, ethnic, and religious lines. They remained consistently present even as political and social circumstances changed dramatically. Images like the rondadors who opened this introduction were central to those nation-making projects, condensing and circulating national vision. Romantic and picturesque in the nineteenth century, hauntingly realist in the twentieth, those images helped the nation imagine itself.

On Public Projects of Identification

The preceding pages developed in light of a driving yet implicit question for the rhetorical study of images like the rondador: what do these repeated, resilient images tell us about how national identity is created and sustained and, in turn, what does such telling reveal about how rhetoric works? My answer to these questions, elaborated over the course of the next six chapters, is this: as scholars interested in how human communities give "emphasis and importance to contested matters," rhetoricians need to pay particular attention to those public projects to which we ascribe powerful emotional attachments, including nationalisms and other politicized identities.[53] Drawing the circle more widely, all scholars interested in nations, publics, and peoples need to understand how strong identifications form, how they change, and how they set the scene for public interaction and decision making. Using the generative case of Ecuador as a catalyst, I argue that such strong identifications are formed and sustained in large part through their circulation in resilient commonplaces that provide a place of return for identification even in the midst of change.

In mapping a history of national common sense and elastic identifications, *Constitutive Visions* both advances and resists a narrative of nation-state formation. It resists that narrative by looking critically at the teleological assertions of national development and new beginnings that so often accompany discourses of democracy and nationalism. It advances it by tracing the interplay of permanence and change within narratives of national identity, showing how resilient commonplaces sustain new arguments about the nation. To maintain a productive tension between such analysis and resistance, the book vacillates between chronological and conceptual development, using three complementary pairs of chapters. The opening and closing sections, chapter 1 and the conclusion, bookend the study with analyses of Ecuadorian constitutions and the rhetorics of permanence and change. The second pair of chapters engages two central nation-founding commonplaces, one that links history, indigeneity, and landscape (chapter 2) and another that holds in tension indigenous labor and national modernity (chapter 3). Chapters 4 and 5, the final chapter couplet, investigate how identifications of the Indian as other and self have enabled arguments about national legitimacy. Engaging a variety of artifacts—images, letters, policies, performances—each chapter of *Constitutive Visions* asks how, why, and by whom such artifacts were created and what work they have done within changing social and political contexts. Taken as a whole, the chapters demonstrate the powerful roles played by resilient commonplaces in the constitution of national identity and emphasize the particular force that elements of visual culture lend to the constitution of strong identifications. They make clear how wide-ranging and multimodal investigations of topoi can foster more robust understandings of national identity and allow us to take better account of the commonplaces and common visions of nationalism.

1

CONSTITUTING CITIZENSHIP

For the citizens of the nineteenth century—meaning, white-mestizo, adult, literate, propertied men—it was unthought and unthinkable that Indians, persons whom they treated as inferiors in their houses, lands, in the streets and markets, could be free and equal Ecuadorian citizens.
—ANDRÉS GUERRERO, "UNA IMAGEN VENTRILOCUA," 1994

The Constitution is in itself a verbal enactment. But in defining a realm of motives for the citizens' acts with regard to the nation's material resources, it constitutes a socio-political *scene* for those acts. Yet all such resources in themselves constitute a non-verbal kind of Constitution-Behind-the-Constitution. And, in the course of time, this scene-behind-the-scene has been undergoing constant . . . changes.
—KENNETH BURKE, "QUESTIONS AND ANSWERS," 1978

In late September 2008, Ecuadorians ratified their twentieth Constitution since their country's founding in 1830. Even before its approval, that new Constitution was the object of much contention, as political leaders, social movements, and members of an active public sphere negotiated the real-world application of the massive document's idealistic vision. From the time of the Constitution's approval, some commentators suggested that it was unlikely to "stand up to the test of time."[1] As one scholar put it, "keeping in mind Ecuador's long history of constitutional makeovers and legal improvisation, analysts would be wise to regard the new constitution as a working draft, not an immutable text."[2] That "long history of constitutional makeovers" includes Constitutional Assemblies that ended without producing valid new Constitutions, other Constitutions that survived less than a year, and Constitutions that lasted only for the terms of their erstwhile progenitors. Though there are many possible explanations for the ongoing instability of

Ecuador's central political document, it is clear that over the nearly two centuries of its existence, Ecuador has been engaged in an almost constant process of national constitution and reconstitution.[3]

This chapter places that long history of Ecuadorian re-Constitution in conversation with a strand of constitutional theorizing within rhetorical studies that has recently enjoyed renewed interest. In the 1960s and 1970s the literary and rhetorical theorist Kenneth Burke seized upon the Constitution as the ideal representative anecdote for his understanding of rhetoric, in which language—and communication more broadly—serves as a means of symbolic action (contrasted, for Burke, with the nonsymbolic motion of purely physical movement).[4] Humans, for Burke, are "symbol-using animal[s]"; for him, all language is symbolic, and, in turn, rhetorical language is "inducement to action (or to attitude, attitude being an incipient act)."[5] Burke examined the U.S. Constitution as an agonistic and hortatory example of such rhetorical symbolic action that played both deliberative (legislative) and epideictic (community-oriented) roles in bringing the nation into being.[6]

After several decades of relative neglect, Burke's version of constitutive rhetoric has come back into circulation, reclaimed by rhetoricians interested in how symbolic action makes and maintains publics. This chapter further extends constitutive rhetoric, informed by the work of rhetorical theorists, by Burke's own treatment of constitutions, and by the rich constitutional context of Ecuador. Ecuador's long history of reconstitution—its frequent shifts, its points of continuity, and its negotiation of a diverse national polity—sheds new light on the terms of constitutive rhetoric and calls attention to the ways in which Burke's choice of the singular U.S. Constitution as representative has shaped the subsequent scope of constitutional theorizing in rhetoric.[7]

As Burke notes of the U.S. Constitution, each new Ecuadorian Constitution has served both as a stance against the perceived errors of previous charters and an idealistic urge toward a new national future. The claims repeatedly staked and undone in those successive documents reveal the contingency of rhetorical constitution. They bring into sharp focus the roles played in nation making by both political Constitutions and the collections of artifacts and acts surrounding those documents—visual elements, political performances, and the material experiences of everyday life—what Burke terms a "Constitution-Behind-the-Constitution."[8] Ecuadorian Constitutions, in their shifting and change, better evince the often contradictory force of national constitution that Burke addresses by means of the U.S. Constitution. The number of new Constitutions and the constantly shifting scene behind them may, at first glance, imply a constitutive process defined primarily by breaks.[9] Viewing the ways that successive Constitutions echo and intersect with one another, however, makes clear that such reimagination draws heavily on existing common sense, creating continuity from the stuff of contingency.

A persistent republican idealism and a repeated (if sometimes implicit) invocation of the nation as indigenous are the most striking elements of that common sense that built national identity through rupture in Ecuador. Working alongside one another over time, political Constitutions and "constitutions-behind-the-Constitution" simultaneously made space for and circumscribed the civic space available to indigenous Ecuadorians. That generative intersection between Constitutions and constitutions is particularly visible in the ways that political processes provoked, responded to, and ran parallel with movements in visual culture. Ecuadorian artists and image makers pictured indigenous people in ways that echoed and legitimized the political roles made available to them in successive national charters. Political texts picked up visions of the nation circulated most widely in pictorial images. Exploring how the simultaneous centrality and marginality of indigenous peoples survived across Ecuadorian Constitutions and was authorized, naturalized, and circulated in visual constitutions-behind-the-Constitution, this chapter sets the scene for the larger study's concern with rhetorical constitution. It begins, though, with a review of Burke's initial work with rhetorical constitutions and of more recent theorizing on the subject.

Constitutive Rhetoric and the Dialectic of Constitutions

Constitutive rhetoric, as treated here, stands apart from the work of previous scholars because it draws a direct connection between Burke's discussion of the U.S. constitutional scene and the constitutional scenes of Ecuador. Placing those distinct contexts in conversation expands and strengthens the study of constitutive rhetoric, and, along the way, it illuminates still-undeveloped possibilities for understanding the messy rhetorical processes of nation making.

The first Burke-influenced scholar to discuss constitutive rhetoric did so, strangely, without reference to Burke's actual writings on the interpretive value of constitutions. Rhetorical theorist Maurice Charland's essay on constitutive rhetoric engages in conversation with Burke but relies on *A Rhetoric of Motives* rather than *A Grammar of Motives* to make its point.[10] Importing Louis Althusser's use of "constitution" to explain interpellation, Charland invokes Burke only to align himself with Burke's contention that identification, not persuasion, ought to be the central term of rhetoric. Focusing on identification (how individuals and groups align themselves with one another), Charland enumerates the ideological and rhetorical processes that convene audience members as part of an addressed group. Linking Burke and Althusser, then, Charland demonstrates how the claim to nationhood is always based on assertions about the existence of a certain kind of subject and therefore "calls [that] audience into being" through rhetorical acts.[11] However, though Charland's constitutive rhetoric brings important complexity to understandings of audience and is widely applicable to rhetorical situations, including that of Ecuador, his focus on Burke's theories of identification and not his discussion of constitutions means that Charland's "people" is primarily constituted through explicit acts of identity-forming speech rather than viewed in terms of a broader constitutional scene, leaving aside the myriad prevalent yet implicit elements that promote membership and identification.

In their recent work, the rhetoricians Dana Anderson and Gregory Clark both address that wider scope of rhetorical elements. They also directly invoke "The Dialectic of Constitutions," making for a more robust application of Burke's own take on rhetoric's constitutive power. However, both scholars continue Charland's rather metaphorical approach to constitution. Their studies use the idea of constitution in its sense of "convening" to pursue questions of identity and identification. Anderson analyzes "the range of constitutive acts by which we . . . transform ourselves and our world," looking specifically at conversion narratives, while Clark examines how symbolic communication "constitute[s] in individuals a sense of shared [national] identity that has the power to shape their beliefs and actions."[12] Charland, Anderson, and Clark, in their mutual focus on identity formation and symbolic communication, provide generative examples of constitutive rhetoric's analytical flexibility. That flexibility becomes all the more pronounced when firmly rooted in the constitutional documents and related theorizing put forward by Burke himself.

What has intermittently intrigued rhetorical scholars about Burke's chapter "The Dialectic of Constitutions" is precisely the utility that Burke himself ascribes to it: considering rhetorical constitutions provides a "generative model for the study of language as symbolic action."[13] In addition, Burke notes, the Constitution is the perfect anecdote for understanding the interaction that lies at the heart of his well-known and much abused pentad: "We are dealing with a word that has to do with matters of substance and motive. . . . And just as obviously, the word covers all five terms of our pentad. A legal constitution is an *act* or body of acts (or enactments), done by *agents* (such as rulers, magistrates, or other representative persons), and designed (*purpose*) to serve as a motivational ground (*scene*) of subsequent actions, it being thus an instrument (*agency*) for the shaping of human relations."[14] Though he seems not to have made the point explicitly, Burke's own discussion of Constitutions suggests the anecdote would work as well for his "hexed" pentad, given that the Constitution establishes an *attitude* toward the nation.[15] Burke makes clear that such a serial articulation of the elements of the pentad is evocative only to the extent that it accounts for cross-pollination among the elements. He explains, "[the] scope (circumference) [of the Constitution] as an *act* [is] so comprehensive that it set[s] up and define[s] the overall motivational *scene*, in terms of which countless personal acts of its citizens [will] be both performed and judged."[16] Instead of a diluted treatment in which act, agent, agency, scene, and purpose serve as individual queries along the lines of who, what, where, when, and how, Constitutions are particularly useful for revealing the pentad as a matter of ratios. The ways that the elements of the pentad overlap and relate to one another are what makes them generative for analytical use.

That attention to ratios and crossings lends itself well to an extension of Burke's own constitutional vision—from the singular U.S. Constitution to the multiple Constitutions of Ecuador. Burke makes clear that Constitutions emerge from interaction with scenes and agents. The contingency and spread of Ecuadorian Constitutions emphasizes that Constitutions are themselves part of that interaction. In this sense, Burkean constitutive rhetoric aligns well with the ecological model for rhetoric outlined earlier. Offering a sense of constant interaction among acts, scenes, agents, and attitudes, it supports an approach to public creation as deeply rhetorical, a quintessential "strategy in situation[s]."[17] That emphasis on strategies and ratios also builds elasticity and complexity into the otherwise unidirectional rigidity of rhetorical interpellation as posed by Charland or the inside-outward model of conversion promoted by Anderson. It reminds us that identification is a matter of both prompt and response and that it is motivated by and situated within a field of interacting scenes and agents.

Constitutions, then, become not merely *acts*, but also purposes, agencies, and scenes (and attitudes) in themselves. In Burke's words, "The Constitution is in itself a verbal en*act*ment. But in defining a realm of motives for the citizens' acts with regard to the nation's material resources, it constitutes a socio-political *scene* for those acts. Yet all such resources in themselves constitute a non-verbal kind of Constitution-Behind-the-Constitution."[18] The constitutional anecdotes offered here follow that tumbling movement from act to scene and beyond. They slide from Constitutions into constitutions-behind-the-Constitution, from texts to contexts and back again, finding invention, identification, and persuasion sprawled among them.

Burke locates what he, in this case, terms the "Constitution-beneath-the-Constitution" primarily in the realm of nonsymbolic motion, even referring to it as the "substance supporting that substance [the Constitution] . . . the nature of existence itself."[19] His invocation of constitutions-behind-the-Constitution as "non-verbal" and as "material resources" and his elaborations on constitutionality in "The Dialectic of Constitutions," however, also leave the door open to a broader interpretation. Such constitutions-behind-the-Constitution can be approached as a range of symbolic actions, not merely the nonsymbolic motion that lies beneath symbolic action. Natural resources and economic trends set scenes and enact constitution, but so do paintings, prints, and poems. Such widely construed constitutions-behind-the-Constitution help authorize the Constitution, making space, for example, for the particular ways that successive Ecuadorian Constitutions imagine citizenship and national identity. They foster a resilient common sense about the national body, one whose circulation and repetition help bring into being the national public that each textual Constitution addresses and convenes. In Ecuador, where between 1861 and 1947 political actors in conflict reconstituted their nation-state every seven years on average, that resilience is particularly striking and instructive.

Constituting the "Shadows of Citizenship" from 1861 to 1946

The Ecuadorian historian Juan Maiguashca argues that Ecuador's 1861 Constitutional reforms—which decreed proportional rather than equal representation among regions, based proportional representation on the entire population rather than solely on citizens, and removed property and wealth restrictions for citizenship—should be seen as the efforts of a generation of elites determined "to succeed where their fathers had failed, that is, in the institutionalisation of a republican order based not on the privileged few but on the majority of the people."[20] Though his research casts light on the ideological commitments of that political generation, Maiguashca's optimistic interpretation of their republican goals must be tempered by an acknowledgment of the fundamental contradiction that lay behind their urge toward universal citizenship. If the majority of delegates in 1861 supported de jure universal suffrage, they also pursued and benefited from de facto limits on participation that kept indigenous people, Afro-Ecuadorians, women, and the lower classes well in what historian Andrés Guerrero terms the "shadows of citizenship" and out of the active scene of the Constitution.[21] They made citizenship possible in theory but used literacy requirements and extra-Constitutional regulations to deny access to all but the most elite Ecuadorians.

The Constitution of 1861 still marks, however, a defining moment of transition, when Ecuadorian elites directly discussed the nature of the nation-state and inaugurated an era profoundly focused on imagining national identity. The next ninety years saw intense rhetorical production seeking to establish a shared sense of national publicity. Many of those arguments relied, at least implicitly, on references to the nation's large indigenous population, using those references to both invoke an inclusive republic and circumscribe access to political power. The next several pages sketch the Constitutional processes through which white-mestizo Ecuadorians came to experience themselves as members of a shared nation and began to justify the marginalization of indigenous Ecuadorians while protecting their ideal of a popular republic.

The political history behind the nine Ecuadorian Constitutions and eleven Constitutional Assemblies between 1861 and 1947 has been characterized as an "agitated progress" of state formation.[22] Those ninety years saw multiple political movements emerge and decline; they were troubled by conflicts; and they were as varied in their political, economic, and quotidian realities as any nearly century-long stretch could be. Yet the entire period from 1861 through 1947 was marked with longing for (and declarations of) new eras of political modernity. Throughout, ideas of popular sovereignty and republicanism were hortatory, admonitory, and, frankly, manipulative tropes belied both by the years' persistent political instability and by the self-evident exclusion of the great mass of the population from democratic participation.

In light of the complexities and contours of those years, the multiple Constitutions and Constitutional Assemblies that struggled to define the national body politic must be recognized as distinct historical events invested in divergent concerns and responding to quite different rhetorical situations. That reality of changing circumstances, however, also makes the resilient consistencies in successive Constitutions of particular interest. It highlights the "motivational fixity" that Constitutions provide and demonstrates a point of stasis on which arguments for the nation could stand. Those consistencies also direct attention toward a submerged, affective process by which a widely shared common sense about the body of the nation emerged and was sustained not despite but through the processes of constitutional contestation.

One of the most powerful pieces of that sustained-through-change common sense was a broad notion of Ecuadorianness that strategically incorporated the nation's diverse population. The nine Constitutions enacted between 1861 and 1947, with only slight variations, declared the Ecuadorian nation to be composed of "all Ecuadorians united under the authority of the same laws."[23] Ecuadorians were consistently defined as anyone born to Ecuadorian parents. That broad scope of Ecuadorianness implicitly but intentionally included indigenous people within Ecuadorian identity. In documents peripheral to the Constitutions, the blanket of national identity falls quite clearly on Ecuador's indigenous population. The abolition of tribute in 1857, for example, was explicitly discussed as placing indigenous people under the same laws as their criollo and mestizo neighbors. While, in practice, the abolition of tribute meant the end of those laws that protected indigenous communities and the continuation of those that exploited them, the official narrative repeatedly emphasized a goal of equality under the law.[24] Similarly, according to Maiguashca, the successful move to base proportional representation on the entire population of Ecuadorian nationals rather than on just the population of citizens came about as an explicit rejection of those who argued that "sovereignty was not born from the masses but from illustration."[25] The broad constitutional definition of Ecuadorian identity was, in other words, a strategic act of incorporation poised to do important work for the idea of a popular republic.

The Constitutions enacted between 1861 and 1947 all give Ecuadorian nationals, including indigenous people, broad responsibilities based on their belonging to the nation. At various moments those responsibilities included respecting religion (prior to 1897), sustaining the Constitution, obeying laws and authorities, defending the country, contributing to funding the state, and conserving public liberty.[26] Participation in the nation-state, in those charters, was granted through obligation and demography, not civil rights. Constitutions consistently housed national sovereignty within that broad demographic sense of Ecuadorianness but emphasized sovereignty's transitive nature. Ecuadorians reflexively delegated their natural sovereignty to the citizens who voted and to the elected authorities who dictated the Constitution and the laws.[27] Sovereignty was, in other words, defined not as an active process of suffrage and election, but as a passive matter of membership in a national body that carried more responsibilities than rights.

Such urges toward universal participation in Ecuadorian identity and in the delegation of sovereignty can be productively understood in terms of what Burke calls the "Constitutional wish." In Burke's formulation Constitutions proclaim the existence of realities that are patently not yet real to bring them into existence. They inherently use an *ought* to reimagine reality, "bas[ing] a statement as to *what should be* upon a statement as to *what is*."[28] Ecuadorian Constitutions beginning in 1861 represent repeated instances of such hortatory assertion. In their inclusive definitions of Ecuadorianness, they invoke a political state that is, in practice, not yet.

Throughout the late nineteenth century, national identity and a sense of the state were inchoate ideals, even among the limited population of criollo elite. It would be a stretch to suggest that those elites saw white-mestizo artisans and traders, let alone indigenous people, as equal partners in the nation. At the same time, the criollos who dictated Constitutions were ideologically invested in notions of republican virtue and popular sovereignty. Their constitutional discussions are rife with concern over the proper practices of republican government: delegates in 1861 spent much of an early session debating whether statues honoring national heroes would smack too much of monarchy, and in 1896 one Liberal delegate published a forty-page treatise on the proposed Constitution that began with the necessary evolution of human societies (including Ecuador) from despotism into feudalism and finally to democracy.[29] Similarly, though mid-twentieth-century white-mestizo elites consistently placed equal citizenship in a future always just out of reach, their Constitutional discussions struggled to make space for indigenous voices. They established (nonindigenous) corporate representatives for indigenous communities in the 1929 and 1945 Constitutions and regularly debated possible paths to future citizenship for their uneducated and miserable compatriots. To align their acts with those ideals, nineteenth-century and twentieth-century delegates pursued constitutional systems that invoked and sustained quasi-democratic notions of sovereignty as well as structures that would mitigate the application of that democracy.

It is that sort of idealistic constitutional imagination that Burke references when he describes rhetorical constitutions as including a "volitional element," where introducing a principle "into a Constitution is to utter a hope that men may [attain it]."[30] Imagining a passive but integral role for indigenous people or aiming toward a distant future when indigenous people would be fully incorporated kept a republican hope alive in the pages of each Constitution as it sought to perfect the polity while simultaneously protecting privilege.

As that simultaneous urge to perfection and protection in Ecuador's Constitutions highlights, there are always failures of representation in public acts of Constitution. Burke claims that such failures are endemic to a "partial world" where the "total act cannot be attained." He invokes the "Constitutional wish" to explain how Constitutions always contain contradictory urges that must be negotiated within the framing of a circumference—a sphere of influence—for the constitutional act. Implicit but untreated in Burke's formulation is the possibility that a Constitution's declarations might be idealistic, even insincere, attempts to cover over the uncomfortable inconsistencies of the *is* with the palliative breadth of a constitutive *ought*. That possibility, visible also in the U.S. Constitution (e.g., the three-fifths clause), underlies much of Ecuadorian constitutional history. Beginning with the initial Latin American efforts at independence that the Mexican José Moñino described as "All for the people, but without the people," the representative republic of each Ecuadorian Constitution has been far more idealistic (or insincere) fiction than functional reality.[31]

The central feature of that fiction is that though the constitutional wish defining "Ecuadorian" intentionally included the majority indigenous population, access to the rights and responsibilities of *citizenship* was carefully exclusive.[32] In a twist on what Michael Feehan notes about Burke's description of the U.S. Constitution, Ecuadorian Constitutions between 1861 and 1947 created "simultaneously both the kinds of citizens [wished] for and the kinds of instruments necessary for sustaining those citizens."[33] Neither Feehan nor Burke means those two clauses to suggest contrary movement. In Ecuador, however, they did.[34] Ecuadorian Constitutions invoked universal citizenship and the topos of the "people" as an elite constitutional wish that covered the actually existing oligarchy with a simulacrum of republican authenticity.[35] Those same Constitutions provided the necessary mechanisms for limiting the republican fantasy of the constitutional wish in a way that sustained the citizenship of a particular portion of the population (relatively educated male criollos) and excluded the majority that had been invoked by declarations of universal suffrage.

Ecuadorian Constitutions from 1861 to 1947 relied on a geographically and ethnically limited education system as the primary mechanism for circumscribing republican action: they made the ability to read and write in Spanish a requirement for citizenship. That literacy requirement—repeatedly contested but ultimately in effect through 1979—functionally retained suffrage and citizenship as a privilege of the lighter-skinned and economically powerful. The common declaration that the government was "popular, representative, elected, alternating, and responsible" (Constitution of 1878) and that all Ecuadorians had the right to "equality before the law and the ability to elect and be elected to public office" was thus highly circumscribed by the simple phrase "always providing that they have the appropriate legal aptitudes" (Constitution of 1861). Considering that voter participation changed from 0.02 and 0.07 percent of the Ecuadorian population in 1848 and 1856 to 3.0 and 3.3 percent in 1888 and 1894 and grew only to 9.5 percent by 1948, it would be inaccurate to suggest that establishing suffrage for all literate males in 1861 and extending the franchise to literate women in 1929 had anything more than a symbolic effect on access to citizenship.[36] For the entire period under consideration here, most Ecuadorians' access to citizenship was highly curtailed, and the gap between "Ecuadorian" and "Ecuadorian citizen" was striking, strategic, and carefully controlled.

Indigenous people, in particular, struggled to escape the "shadows of citizenship" through much of the twentieth century.[37] Even those indigenous people who could (and did) achieve access to citizenship were not widely seen as civic equals. For white-mestizo elites, as Guerrero writes, "it was unthought and unthinkable that the Indians, persons whom they treated as inferiors in their houses, lands, in the streets and markets, could be free and equal Ecuadorian citizens."[38] The image of the nation, in other words, might be popular and indigenous, but the ability to define that nation through active participation was firmly reserved for the few. Every citizen might be an Ecuadorian, but not every Ecuadorian could be a citizen.

That contradiction returns us to Burke's assertion that Constitutions are formed, in part, by the presence of their constitutive exterior: they "proclaim . . . equality *within* the Constitution as a way of counteracting some kind of inequality outside the Constitution (or within the wider circumference of the Constitution-beneath-the-Constitution)." Constitutions necessarily do their hortatory, nation-creating work in the context of an outside or an other. In this sense, Constitutions are "agonistic instruments" that "establish a motivational fixity of some sort, in opposition to something that is thought liable to endanger this fixity."[39] For Burke, that constitutional exterior falls, essentially, at the borders of the nation. The more contested scene of Ecuadorian Constitutions reminds us that circumference drawing can as easily be a tool of internal management as exterior defense (a point discussed further in chapter 4). For white-mestizos to recognize themselves in Constitutions, those documents could not fully incorporate a subordinate, "naturally inferior" Indian. At the same time the nation without indigenous people would be equally unrecognizable to its leaders. Indigenous people may have been fundamentally exterior to citizenship, but such exclusion could not easily be sustained within the idea of the republic so long as it was based on categories of race and culture. Much rhetorical energy was thus expended in efforts to naturalize constitutional visions of the nation as profoundly indigenous, legitimately republican, and fundamentally led by criollos.

In sum, the Constitutions enacted between 1861 and 1947 existed in a constant state of internal tension, resting uneasily between a republican urge and the maintenance of colonial authority. Though there was significant change in Ecuador between 1861 and 1947, the fundamentals of citizenship and national identity were fairly stable. In addition, as Burke says of Constitutions in general, those contradictory ideas of nationality and citizenship became "'binding' upon the future." Even as successive Constitutions sought a truer, stronger, and more modern republic, the long history of their consistency within change encouraged "men to evaluate their public acts in the chosen terms," many of which divided national identity from active citizenship. That established difference built up commonsense understandings of both ideas among elites that served "in varying degrees to keep them from evaluating such acts in other terms" each time they approached a new Constitutional revision. In this way, to again appropriate Burke's language, "constitutions [became] of primary importance in suggesting what coordinates [Ecuadorian elites would] think by."[40] Political Constitutions, however, cannot do that scene-setting, circumference-drawing work on their own. Their instability, seen much more clearly in the Ecuadorian context than in Burke's U.S. context, limits their ability to fully determine the overall scene of the nation. Understanding the full constitutive work done by the split between nationals and citizens in Ecuadorian political Constitutions requires attention to the other sorts of constitutions that aided, underwrote, and contested them.

Ecuadorian Visual Constitutions-Behind-the-Constitution, 1861–1947

Andrés Guerrero demonstrates that in textual records, indigenous people essentially disappeared from central government discourse in Ecuador at the middle of the nineteenth century and only gradually reappeared in the last decades of that century as a "ventriloquist's image" wielded by political elites.[41] However, though Guerrero's assertion of silence and ventriloquism narrates a part of the process by which elites assuaged their constitutional contradictions, the occlusion of indigenous communities' textual presence in government documents does not mean that indigenous people disappeared from national discourse in general. In fact, in literature, in scientific texts, and especially in artifacts of visual culture, images of indigeneity were consistently prevalent over the course of the near-century discussed here. That visibility counterbalanced textual and official omissions. It helped naturalize Constitutions that defined Ecuadorians broadly but retained the rights of citizenship for a select few. Images of indigenous people were important constitutions-behind-the-Constitution that brought Indians before the eyes of elites and the emerging middle class. Such images challenged a certain blindness about the status of indigenous communities. They also, however, provided a clear route to legitimate white-mestizo authority by giving visual warrants for the political distinction between the national public as a whole and a limited sphere of active citizens.

The remaining pages of this chapter treat the contradiction-assuaging work of two artistic genres, one (*costumbrismo*) widely circulated during the second half of the nineteenth century and the other (*indigenismo*) dominant from the mid-1930s through the 1950s. Both costumbrismo and indigenismo emerged from ideological and aesthetic movements that valued realism, attention to the local, and social commentary. They are also both regularly invoked as a definitive genre of their era, in large part because they directly engage questions of national identity. As art historian Diane Elizabeth Hajicek suggests, for the artists who worked in these genres and for contemporary and later critics as well, the canvas became the nation.[42] Matters of significant national concern played out on the surface of those canvases. Though it is easy to distinguish costumbrismo's romantic tendencies from the harsher expressive realism of indigenismo, the two forms share a great deal in their efforts to envision the nation. Primarily focused on Ecuador's indigenous population and the popular nation, both genres circulated images of national identity that matched the more expansive sense sponsored in Constitutions. They also provided justification for the assumption of indigenous marginality from citizenship, first in images of simplicity and then in images of degradation. Close attention to these genres and their rhetorical force demonstrates that the constitution of a shared national public in Ecuador was a matter of *seeing* that public just as much as it depended on establishing textual Constitutions that defined the nation and its citizenship laws.

Costumbrismo and the Image of an Indigenous Subject

The arts played an important role in shaping and circulating the idea of the nation as it emerged in Ecuador starting in the 1850s. In 1852 the group of artists in Quito who founded the Escuela Democrática de Miguel de Santiago announced an artistic mission for promoting democracy, extending the freedoms promised in the Constitution, and extolling the nation. Despite its short-lived formal existence, the Escuela Democrática had a significant impact on Ecuadorian art, and it counted among its members some of the era's most important artists—including the well-known watercolorist and caricaturist Juan Agustín Guerrero. The artists affiliated with the school moved the mainstream of Ecuadorian art from predominantly religious scenes inspired by European styles to resolutely secular images based on national views and histories. A decade later President García Moreno's campaign of national self-definition during his second term (1869–75) bent all available means (political, religious, and artistic) to the creation of a centralized, modern, and Catholic nation. García Moreno provided scholarships for artists to study abroad, promoted art education through an academy of fine arts in Quito, and sponsored foreign visitors who inspired and encouraged local artists. Ecuadorian costumbrismo emerged from and contributed to that context saturated in national identity.

Nineteenth-century romanticism saw the rise of costumbrista-style "customs and habits" painting throughout Europe and the Americas. Those paintings emphasized local traditions, local clothing, and local scenes, partaking of the same spirit that brought the idea of the nation as a particular category of regional identity into wide circulation on both continents.[43] In addition, as Alexandra Kennedy Troya notes, the rising influence of "bourgeois positivism" in Ecuador meant that artists believed in the "importance of approaching nature, or having direct contact with [their] subject or theme and being conscious of the world that presented itself" before their eyes. This orientation encouraged artists to be "subjectively involved with the objects of their painting."[44] Costumbrismo, with its fascination for popular figures and social types, was a perfect genre for negotiating those social and cultural trends in the visual realm. Its development and circulation in Ecuador also point to that emerging political culture that defined republican national identity as distinct from access to citizenship. Costumbrista images participated in normalizing that division, providing a vision of the nation that incorporated popular figures and social types into national identity without implying practices of political citizenship.

Costumbrista artists usually emphasized the external and omnipotent gaze of the viewer and imagined their subjects, especially indigenous types, in terms that descended directly from the previous century's fascination with the noble savage.[45] The main subjects of Ecuadorian costumbrista painting were the urban laborers and rural peasants who populated the streets of Quito and whose descriptions appear in the narratives of travel writers. Costumbrista paintings and illustrations were filled with idealized and generalized popular figures. Those figures usually appeared in isolation, without much in the way of contextual setting, yet they circulated widely as illustrations of the nation. They filled travelers' accounts and the edges of illustrated maps (see figs. 4 and 5). They were commissioned by affluent residents and echoed in contemporary photography. Their circulation, both to foreign visitors and local elites, helped create a vision of the Ecuadorian people that stood in marked contrast to the whitewashed discourse of Ecuadorian citizenship in policy documents.

Many of the costumbrista images examined in this study come from two albums put together by Quiteño artists who compiled images of popular Ecuadorians as part of a specific effort to link viewers to the nation. The first album, a *Libro de pinturas* (Book of paintings) produced by Juan Agustín Guerrero in 1852, was a gift to Pedro Moncayo, a radical Liberal who endured multiple periods of exile during the height of Conservative power in Ecuador. Guerrero's album was meant to give the exiled Moncayo a portable piece of his nation to carry beyond its borders. It is particularly striking, then, that Guerrero chose to include primarily images of indigenous social types alongside his paintings of Ecuadorian mountains and excerpts of popular songs

Fig. 4. *Trajes de Quito (indio de Napo, sereno de Quito, guacicama de Quito).* Lithograph by Simonau and Toovey, 1866. In Lisboa, *Relação de uma viagem.*

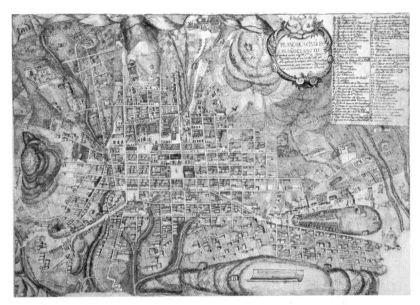

Fig. 5. *Plano de la Ciudad de San Francisco del Quito*, ca. 1800. Collection of the Museo Alberto Mena Caamaño, Centro Cultural Metropolitano, Quito, Ecuador.

(fig. 6 shows one such indigenous figure). The second album, put together fifty years later by Joaquín Pinto, served a similar purpose. Pinto presented that collection to the Cousin family—French in origin, but permanently settled in Ecuador. The bread sellers, festival participants, and rustic vendors that fill this "Album de personajes populares" (Album of popular characters) depict Ecuador almost wholly in terms of its lower classes, though Quito's religious orders also figure prominently in the collection (fig. 7 shows a typical page from the album). Pinto's album served a fixative purpose. It grounded the immigrant Cousins firmly in the Ecuadorian context, just as Guerrero's *Libro de pinturas* had provided Moncayo a tether to his homeland and successive Constitutions had built a sense of Ecuadorianness through repetition.

Though costumbrista artists explicitly valued realism and appropriated a scientific urge to document the local, their images relied so heavily on serially transmitted social types that they should be read as ideologically inflected semifabrications rather than as realistic depictions of the customs and habits of Ecuador's popular classes. The repetition of themes, styles, and phrasings found across these images and related travel narratives suggests that some creators borrowed descriptions wholesale from their predecessors, never having actually ventured beyond the relative comfort of Quito's better

Fig. 6.   Juan Agustín Guerrero, *Yndia que vende fruta en la Plaza Mayor*, 1852.
Watercolor on paper. Reprinted by the Fundación Wilson Hallo, 1981. In Hallo and
Agustín Guerrero, *Imágenes del Ecuador*. Photograph by Jessie Reeder.

Fig. 7.   Joaquín Pinto, *Porquera*, 1900. Watercolor on paper. In Pinto, "Album de personajes populares." Private collection.

lodgings. The fictional realism of these images, however, only emphasizes the force they exerted toward a vision of the nation that served both the needs and the ideals of white-mestizo elites.

Anthropologist Blanca Muratorio suggests that costumbrismo enacted "a romantic search for the national self through the representation of ethnic diversity and local customs." As such, it should be seen within the "larger context of the discourse on Indian-ness and nationalism shared by Ecuadorian cultural elites at the close of the nineteenth century."[46] To return to the terms of constitutive rhetoric, costumbrismo underlined the motivational vision of the national "we" established in successive Constitutions. Just as, according to Burke, Constitutions are "scenic," so also they emerge within a particular scene such that "a complete statement about motivation will require a wider circumference, as with reference to the social, natural, or supernatural environment." The nineteenth-century Ecuadorian constitutional wish toward a national republic, in other words, functioned within and in light of nonverbal, image-based constitutions-behind-the-Constitution that envisioned the people of that republic. Together, they made the constitutional "enactment arising in history" appear natural and given.[47] Costumbrismo, in this sense, allowed white-mestizo elites to convene a romantic image of the national body that called criollo authority into being and authorized a skewed ratio of citizenship and national identity.

According to art historian Trinidad Pérez, the primary way that costumbrista images contributed to that search for a national self was by allowing elites to distinguish themselves from the social types represented and thus imagine a justification for their position of social authority.[48] Costumbrista subjects often do not meet the gaze of the viewer; they are most identified by symbols of office or position; individualizing features are rare; bodies are positioned to invite maximum scrutiny. All these common traits of costumbrismo constitute an external viewer in a position of superiority. This viewer, by gazing at an indigenous subject who does not return the gaze, is able to see what he is not and thus establishes his right to observe and control.[49] In this sense, costumbrista paintings helped naturalize the continued colonial relationship between white-mestizos and indigenous people. Their emphasis on the viewer's superiority and external oversight helped make the basic contradiction of the republic natural and necessary. Indigenous people, in these scenes, *needed* a white-mestizo viewer to make the republic whole and functional. In parallel, the nation as a whole needed white-mestizo elites to serve as the natural recipients of delegated popular sovereignty.

That process of establishing citizenship and authority through disassociation with the image of the passive nation is, essentially, the reverse of the citizenship work that the rhetorical critics Robert Hariman and John Louis Lucaites see being done by iconic U.S. American photographs. Instead of "interpolat[ing] a form of citizenship that can be imitated," Ecuadorian costumbrismo built citizenship from a negation. It interpolated citizenship through the eyes of a superior and responsible viewer. Despite that negative construction, costumbrista images still did citizenship work in the sense invoked by Hariman and Lucaites. They "provid[ed] generic forms of assurance regarding the existence, nature, and legitimacy of the public world and the public media, and also specific validation and infusions of meaning for public action when events [were] chaotic, dangerous, or disturbing."[50] They established a role for white-mestizo viewers vis-à-vis the popular classes that smoothed the potential conflict between an inclusive national public and an exclusive republic of citizens. Such image-constitutions provided a productive vision of republican national identity that, by distinguishing citizen from national, could assuage elite anxiety over democratic practice and reconcile white-mestizo authority with the existence of an indigenous and mestizo majority.

Implicitly carried in costumbrismo was an analogous argument that the body of the nation was to its governance as the indigenous figure was to its white-mestizo viewer, the latter actively gazing and the former passively receptive but both implicated in the national ecology. Costumbrismo thus echoed and made sense of its contemporary Constitutions. Its division between viewer and subject helped naturalize the gap between "Ecuadorian" and "Ecuadorian citizen," between national and civic identity.

Indigenismo, the Indian, and the Nation

Just as Ecuadorian image makers in the late nineteenth century consistently bent their efforts to the service of national identity, the mid-twentieth century saw repeated and concerted efforts to define the nation. Such constitutional efforts freely crossed borders of genre and context. Throughout the early years of the twentieth century, notes anthropologist Mercedes Prieto, "social questions were publicly discussed through a variety of media and expressions: the press, the political essay, painting, photography, poetry, and music."[51] In both the late nineteenth century and the mid-twentieth, all available means were regularly drafted into public dispute over the present and future of the nation. Visual culture absorbed political concerns, and political culture echoed evolutions in image making. Constitutions and constitutions-behind-the-Constitution worked together to envision and enact the nation.

Ecuadorian visual culture made a dramatic aesthetic shift around the second quarter of the twentieth century. That shift was driven by the same scenic complexities that prompted multiple contemporary Constitutional Assemblies: changing economies, rising populism, and foreign intervention. Indigenismo, the new artistic genre that emerged out of that ferment, continued to focus on Indians as national subjects, but it newly emphasized the oppressive conditions that dominated indigenous lives. Using those images of exploitation to stand in for national struggle, indigenismo celebrated a powerful American nationalism rooted in leftist politics, and it identified the indigenous masses as members of an authentic American proletariat.

By that time visions of indigenous people as both central to national identity and exterior to the republic already functioned as a pervasive common sense in Ecuador. It continued to operate in indigenista work, even as those artists sought to destabilize the political dominance of the traditional elite. Working parallel to constitutional debates that struggled to incorporate indigenous Ecuadorians and imagine a white-mestizo nation, indigenista artists set a new scene for national identity but maintained an overarching narrative of *mestizaje*.[52]

For the most part indigenista artists were white-mestizos from the working and middle classes who were aligned to varying degrees with Ecuador's leftist parties. In light of those personal circumstances and political commitments, it is not surprising that indigenista images simultaneously invoked traditions of solidarity and paternalism. Their depictions of indigenous people as downtrodden but brave, as profoundly human yet distorted and dirty, located the possibilities of the nation within indigenous bodies but made clear that the present nation was mired in its own degradation (see figs. 8 and 9). Those visions indexed newly prominent concerns over what political leaders termed the "Indian problem," and they echoed the belief that lifting indigenous people out of oppression into a just and civilized (i.e., white-mestizo) future was of preeminent concern for the nation-state.

Ecuador's was not the first American national art scene to adopt the social-realist style and leftist politics of indigenismo. Funded by revolutionary governments, the Mexican artists Diego Rivera, José Clemente Orozco, and David Siquieros pioneered a Mexican version of indigenismo in the late 1920s and early 1930s. Politically forceful, highly critical of capital's exploitation of the masses, and deeply nationalist, Mexican indigenismo incorporated motifs from Mexico's pre-Columbian heritage and imagined

Fig. 8.   Eduardo Kingman, *Los guandos*, 1939. Oil on canvas. Collection of Modern and Republican Art, Ecuadorian Ministry of Culture, Quito, Ecuador.

present-day workers as supported by the heroes of the past. The style quickly spread as the Left in much of Latin America looked to emulate the example of Mexican political change and cultural action, and Ecuadorian artists and intellectuals consciously echoed their northern counterparts. Looking south-ward, Ecuadorian indigenismo was also linked with similar trends in Peru, especially in light of the cross-border influence of intellectuals such as José Mariátegui. In visual terms, though, Ecuadorian and Peruvian indigenismo were strikingly different, with Peruvian indigenismo retaining much of the romantic spirit of costumbrismo and Ecuadorian indigenismo fully adopting expressive social realism.[53]

Ecuadorian indigenista artists and intellectuals faced a complicated rhe-torical scene as they reimagined the place of the Indian within their nation. Unlike their colleagues in Mexico and Peru who took a stylized and romantic approach to indigenous culture that emphasized its connections to the cul-tural past, indigenistas in Ecuador were not in a position to fully laud their roots in indigenous heritage. The large, visible, and palpably present-day in-digenous population in Ecuador posed a direct challenge to any such efforts. Ecuadorian indigenistas still took up the strong social critique evident in

Fig. 9.   Oswaldo Guayasamín, *La procesión*, 1942. Oil on canvas. Collection of the Museum of the Casa de la Cultura Ecuatoriana "Benjamín Carrión," Quito, Ecuador.

Mexican indigenismo, but they altered it. Where the Mexican artists located resistance in the working class and made indigeneity a source of power for those struggles, Ecuadorian indigenistas made indigenous people themselves into ambiguous protagonists and emphasized the present-day struggles of indigenous communities. That approach, however, still did not move indigenismo beyond the familiar Ecuadorian constitutional divisions. The

Indians of indigenismo remained symbolically linked to the idea of the nation yet hovered threateningly at the edges of citizenship.[54] Indigenista pictures showing Ecuador's excluded, suffering indigenous masses were stark reminders of a nation-state that built itself on the exploitation of its people. They were also powerful visual evidence of a fundamental problem of civilization that dramatized the state of the nation and called citizen-viewers to a new, but still largely paternalistic, relationship with the nation-as-Indian.

The year between Quito's Mariano Aguilera art competitions in 1935 and 1936 marked the emergence of indigenista social realism as a dominant force in Ecuadorian art. In the larger constitutional scene, that year saw an elected, populist president from the Conservative party deposed after he attempted to retain his office beyond the allotted term, followed by the appointment of a reputedly socialist president who quickly moved to repress workers' movements. The liberal national Constitution in effect at the time retained the citizen-national split but also included a "Senator for the tutelage and defense of the Indian race" and evinced special state concern for workers and peasants. That year was, in other words, representative of its era's political tumult and social anxiety over the state of Ecuador's indigenous population.

In 1935 the young artist Eduardo Kingman submitted five indigenista paintings to the Mariano Aguilera. Those paintings caused an immediate stir among the competition's conservative, aristocratic judges, who preferred the romantic Indians of costumbrismo and its successor, early twentieth-century *indianismo*, to Kingman's threatening figures. To avoid the challenge Kingman's paintings posed to their comfortable aesthetics, those judges declared the competition null, claiming that none of the works submitted to the competition that year merited the nation's most important prize. The next year, with new judges, Kingman won the competition using the same five paintings he had submitted in 1935.

In the intervening year, not only had a change in government altered the political scene, but Kingman and his indigenista style had also gained a powerful new advocate, the influential liberal intellectual Benjamín Carrión, who wrote in protest of the rejection: "After seeing, profoundly and emotionally, Kingman's paintings that have been the cause of the Aguilera Prize of 1935 being declared null, I find myself in jubilant and complete certainty and hope that I can announce to the art of America that there has finally been born in this land the strong, the rough, the true painter, whom, with the patience of the Israelites, we have been awaiting."[55] By the 1940s, with Carrión's patronage, indigenismo had become the dominant artistic aesthetic of the Highlands. In 1944 the same Constitutional Assembly that created the leftist

1945 Constitution established the Casa de la Cultura Ecuatoriana (CCE), the country's first omnibus arts and cultural institution, under Carrión's leadership. The indigenistas dominated that institution for the next few decades. Carrión, through his directorship of the CCE and its periodical *Letras del Ecuador*, was also largely responsible for creating a public narrative in which art was a key expression of Ecuadorian national identity. Early issues of *Letras* advanced a new argument about the artistic spirit of the nation and promoted Ecuador's indigenista artists and authors as advancing the country's stature regionally and internationally.

Indigenismo gained prominence at a time when intellectuals and political figures on the Right and the Left shared a set of common concerns about indigeneity and the nation. They debated the proper response to the indigenous community's rustic "backwardness"; they pursued populist politics that both incorporated and avoided the largely indigenous rural masses; they argued over the importance of *mestizaje*—ethnic and cultural mixture—to the national character. Indigenista images were directly and indirectly engaged in those debates. The large oil paintings that are today indigenismo's best-known pieces were often displayed in fine arts contexts such as salons and museums. Indigenista images also, however, circulated to a larger audience in their own moment. Populist governments commissioned murals for public buildings, organizations like the CCE held public lectures, and periodicals adopted indigenismo's stark lines and social message in their cover images and illustrations. Indigenista-style social-realist prints appeared in leftist pamphlets published by indigenous groups. They appeared as well in the pages of right-wing periodicals designed to dissuade workers from communist organizing. As they accumulated, such depictions of indigenous peasants and laborers stood in, visually, for the troubled masses. Whether the concern was hygiene, workers' rights, agricultural reform, education, or cultural heritage, the indigenistas' Indian—thick bodied, large handed, hardworking—figured prominently in both visual and verbal images. Indigenismo tied dominant themes of indigeneity and populism together and gave Ecuador a new picture of itself.

Indigenista images, then, paralleled a constitutional move to foreground the "Indian problem" and lift the nation-state toward new, though still exclusive, visions of citizenship and national identity. The scene of visual culture and the enactments of successive Constitutions informed each other such that the latter moved, as Burke suggests, "*pari passu* with changes in the quality of the scene in which the Constitution is placed."[56] But such change was not simply a question of the scene changing the available forms of enactment.

There was instead a constant negotiation between scene and enactment, one in which the visual scene helped make sense of the constitutional enactment just as much as the act of each Constitution responded to changing visual scenes. It is in this sense that, in a larger application of constitutive rhetoric, Constitution and constitutions-behind-the-Constitution can be seen as being in a fundamentally dialectical relation to one another, creating consistency through change.

Overall, indigenista images, though they challenged the cultural hegemony of the traditional Highlands elite, continued to imagine indigenous people in ways that warranted their exclusion from active citizenship. Like the descriptions of indigenous communities as a national problem woven by political leaders and by social scientists, indigenista images offered an indigenous subject weighed down to the point of brutishness by four hundred years of oppression. In that narrative, even when blame for exploitation was ascribed directly to white-mestizo elites, the necessary conclusion was that indigenous people were ill-equipped to make decisions for themselves, let alone help shape the future of the nation. Changes in the status of indigenous people depended on their education and cultural integration into a mestizo society. Indigenista images asked white-mestizo viewers to identify with their indigenous subjects as compatriots but also called those viewers into a political stance focused on indigenous uplift and improvement as defined from a white-mestizo perspective. The romantic subject of criollo paternalism visible in nineteenth-century costumbrismo looked significantly different from the beleaguered Indians of indigenismo. They had in common, however, a strong implication that though these figures represented the true body of the nation, they required benevolent white-mestizo authority to secure their future.

Over time, through shifting visual and political scenes, Ecuadorian constitutive rhetoric had become "'binding' upon the future." The gap between citizens and nationals, often coded indigenous, became commonplace through its uptake and reinscription across modes and moments. Political Constitutions, undergirded by visual constitutions-behind-the-Constitutions, "centered attention upon one calculus of motivation rather than some other; and by thus encouraging men to evaluate their public acts in the chosen terms, [served] in varying degrees to keep them from evaluating such acts in other terms."[57] Ecuadorian constitutions (in the larger sense) informed, sustained, and reproduced a constrained public of citizens alongside an expansive sense of national identity. The interaction among scenes and acts, as Charland posits of rhetorical identification in general, authorized and naturalized each Constitution and the constitutional whole. It fed a rhetorical milieu in which ideological discourse could present "itself as always only pointing to the given, the natural, the already agreed upon."[58] In Ecuador, constitutions convened a nation with a popular, indigenous body. They also, simultaneously, made visual sense of that body's larger structural divisions.

Permanence and Change

This chapter has argued that between 1861 and 1947, constitutions of Ecuadorian national identity enacted both in textual Constitutions and in visual constitutions-behind-the-Constitution were profoundly resilient and intricately persuasive. Shifting political, ideological, and cultural values stretched the particular terms by which such identities were discussed, but the basic distinction between Ecuadorian nationals and Ecuadorian citizens retained its shape, holding indigenous people simultaneously at the center of the nation and the periphery of the republic. Artifacts of visual culture played important roles in naturalizing that distinction between national and citizen. Their changing visions of indigenous Ecuadorians warranted and sustained a limited sphere of citizenship, while also calling Ecuadorian elites to greater awareness of their indigenous subjects.

That sense of a tenacious historical persistence that kept Ecuadorian constitutions aligned in their treatments of the national body may seem to be primarily an outcome of Ecuadorian history, particular to its political and cultural context. Viewing the scenes of Ecuadorian constitution and rhetorical theories of constitution in light of one another, however, raises a far more evocative possibility. Constitutions of Ecuadorian national identity have been sustained over time thanks to the specific acts and agents on scene there. That resilience, however, should point us to the nature of rhetorical constitution in general rather than merely evoke old paternalistic narratives of Latin American history that see Latin America as stagnant in comparison to its Anglo-American neighbor.

Persistence has been a consistent theme in assessments of Latin American history written from a North American perspective. That theme, traditionally, lauds the progress-oriented United States at the expense of "backward" Latin America. It asserts, as political scientist Jeremy Adelman explains, that "where the United States made perpetual ruptures the hallmark of its history, Latin America forged its historic time lines out of deep continuities. Latin America still bears the shackles of its birth. The past is destiny." Adelman points out that such narratives of persistence have built a "powerful organizing framework" that has served pessimistic and paternalistic purposes with regard to Latin America. He urges scholars to recognize that "accounting for persistence does not preclude admitting change. . . . Continuities . . . have to contend with the indeterminacies of life if they are to mean anything historically."[59] When seen in light of the constitutive theories outlined here, Adelman's arguments for seeing movement within stability are not only apropos for Ecuadorian or Latin American contexts. Instead, they apply far more widely, to every instance of nation making. Persistence is an active feature of rhetoric's constitutive force, a "motivational fixity" perhaps better understood in terms of resilience.

As Dana Anderson writes, "the power of a constitution . . . lies in its power to define substance, and to define it in such a way that those who share this substance then also share in the motives that bear it up." Drawn in the face of changing circumstances and negotiating competing ideological stances and political goals, Constitutions are themselves commonplaces. As such, they undergird commonsense arguments about who and what the nation is. In that way, Constitutions and constitutions-behind-the-Constitution always determine a spectrum of resilient identities. As the case of Ecuador demonstrates, even though Constitutions change or are overthrown, the *ought/is* they invoke establishes a resilient sense of participation in (or exclusion from) the national body. In Anderson's words, "the constitutive act is meaningless unless it effectively motivates people . . . to behave in accordance with the substance that the constitution declares they embody."[60] Constitutions both act and authorize action; they set a scene and an attitude. Put another way, Constitutions simultaneously infuse the national scene with a sense of permanence and shape orientations toward change. They are, in that sense, apt representative anecdotes for the work of rhetoric in general. In Ecuador, the next chapter argues, that constitutive work of crafting permanence and harnessing change for the sake of the nation often began with arguments about the land.

2

GEOGRAPHY IS HISTORY

In what our country has offered us in these days there has been something of the telluric, something immensely profound, more than human
because prior to humanity: the cry of the land, of this land of ours, that
has raised beyond measure the temperature of our blood, beyond measure the volume of our cries.

—BENJAMÍN CARRIÓN, *CARTAS AL ECUADOR*, 1943

Closer to nature, it may be said, than other social groups who have been
exalted by civilization, [the common people] lack the art to express their
ideas and passions in elegant verses; but, in exchange, they feel with
greater intensity and sing with a simplicity that is, often, inimitable.

—JUAN LEÓN MERA, *CANTARES DEL PUEBLO ECUATORIANO*, 1892

Writing in the aftermath of Ecuador's massive 1942 loss of territory to Peru
under the Treaty of Rio de Janeiro, the author and intellectual Benjamín
Carrión issued an impassioned call to his fellow Ecuadorians. He voiced a
shared outrage at the Ecuadorian government's failures, praising his compatriots who took to the streets in protest and encouraging them to further action in defense of their homeland. From out of that anger, Carrión
also imagined the possibility of a new national way forward. Phrasing his
figurative call to arms in the language of land and climate, he attributed
Ecuadorian national character to telluric forces—that spiritual-earthly power
that he called "the cry of the land."[1] For Carrión, the spirit of the land, present in blood and voice, drove everyday Ecuadorians to acts of fervent and
authentic patriotism.

Fifty years earlier, Juan León Mera, the foremost novelist of his day and a
well-known Conservative, opened his paean to popular Ecuadorian song with
strikingly similar language, linking the spirit of the *pueblo* to its proximity to

nature. Whatever those earthy peasants might lack in art and elegance, Mera declared, they made up for in an intense authenticity that demanded both recognition and celebration. Mera, particularly concerned with establishing Ecuador's distinction from Spain, saw popular songs as essential evidence of Ecuadorian specificity. Many were, he declared, "so local, so original to our land alone" that they would be incomprehensible to Spaniards while seeming as natural to Ecuadorians as were the plants and animals that surrounded them.[2] Popular traditions, for Mera, belonged to and thrived within a particular terrain.

When celebrating an Ecuadorian people defined by their proximity to the land, both Carrión and Mera accessed a readily available, well-stocked topos of nationalism. That topos, which ties a common spirit to common land, played a role in defining communities and peoples even before the emergence of the modern nation-state, and it quickly became inextricable from narratives of national identity.[3] In Ecuadorian history its use dates at least from Simón Bolívar's 1822 "My Delirium on Chimborazo," in which El Libertador used a hallucination induced by the thin air on Ecuador's famous mountain (then thought to be the world's highest) to authorize his vision of a Gran Colombia independent from Spain.[4]

In addition to following in that larger tradition, though, the texts by Carrión and Mera quoted here also draw attention to an element particularly common to Ecuadorian topoi of national land: a sense that claims to the power of the land invoked as well an indigenous spirit. In the pages surrounding their descriptions of Ecuador's telluric nature, Carrión and Mera both slip into and out of an assumption that increasing proximity to land coincides with increasing proximity to indigeneity. For Carrión, that meant invoking pre-Columbian indigenous cultures whose greatness imbued Ecuadorian soil. For Mera, it grew from a sense that Ecuador's "simple troubadours in ponchos and sandals" were as authentic and local as "the flowers and fruits of our region, as the hummingbirds and *molle hijos* of our climate."[5] Such appeals to the land as profoundly indigenous and profoundly influential in national culture were not unusual in Ecuador in either the late nineteenth or the mid-twentieth century. They were part of a widely circulated commonplace that assumed indigenous peoples were fundamentally *earthy* and that claimed indigenous land as a principal source of national identity, even as indigenous people themselves were elided from visions of a national future.

Uses of that topos of land and indigeneity moved in two complementary yet seemingly contradictory directions. On the one hand, like Carrión, many Ecuadorian authors and artists called on pre-Columbian cultures to provide a semimythological foundation for their nation-state. On the other, like Mera, authors and artists used the assumption of an intimate affinity between indigeneity and land to activate paternalistic narratives that associated white-mestizos with social and agricultural cultivation and indigenous people with rusticity and natural authenticity.[6] Invocations of those two themes were, together, key to establishing a shared idea of a national territory that was deeply indigenous yet also profoundly white-mestizo.

Of course, as eminently rhetorical material, such visions of land and landscape were never simply neutral mechanisms for forming coherent communities. They were concerned, as Burke says of all rhetorical action, with "classification in its *partisan* aspects," and they defined contested space in ways amenable to particular identities and belongings.[7] The national territory functioned rhetorically in ways simultaneously symbolic and material. It imbued claims to physical land with moral force and in the process naturalized certain sets of claims and definitions to the exclusion of others. Artifacts using references to indigeneity to claim Ecuadorian landscapes invoked what Alexandra Kennedy Troya terms "a notion of belonging in the most profound sense of the term." They were also, however, involved in "distinguishing one [version of the] nation from another, imposing new limits or establishing particular customs."[8] Claims to who belonged in the nation and to whom the nation belonged underlay almost every invocation of the land-indigeneity topos and, more often than not, their use ended up aiding the cause of white-mestizo authority.

Though the commonplace connecting indigeneity to the land was forged most prominently and consistently by white-mestizo elites and generally served their national projects, indigenous communities also accessed the topos and worked within its bounds to gain their own ends. Accounting for both dominant and resistant uses allows a sense of the full persuasive force of the topos to emerge. As Katrina Powell argues in her analyses of Appalachian landscapes, "representing the complex layers of the terrain" about and within which constitutive arguments circulate requires treating elite claims alongside subaltern ones; it demands that the researcher "[dig] up artifacts, both written and material" that unsettle the apparently coherent appearance of the landscape.[9] This chapter does just such digging into Ecuador's symbolic geographies. Sifting through uses of the land-indigeneity topos by different rhetors in different eras, it uncovers overlapping processes by which white-mestizo elites and indigenous peoples imagined and contested the nation. Those layered uses—in art images, political debates, poetry, geography treatises, and land disputes—show how thoroughly the land-indigeneity topos was sedimented into Ecuadorian national discourse.

Though specific data on the circulation of many of the individual artifacts discussed here is difficult to come by, their sheer accumulation suggests that the meaning-making force of national landscape, including its close reliance on terms of indigeneity, was significant, widely available, and implicitly tied to common sense about the nature of the nation. Tracing those artifact conglomerations and their influence, this chapter demonstrates how a thick common sense linking indigeneity and the land developed in Ecuadorian civil society not primarily through the circulation of individual texts or images but rather through the massive accumulation of diverse artifacts. The commonplace, in this sense, gains its force through agglutination as much as circulation. The cumulative force of the land-indigeneity topos, operating in tropes of both rusticity and pre-Columbian mythos and assembled across thousands of artifacts, defined the nation and aided those hoping to contest it. For the most part, however, such topoi worked inexorably, if sometimes indirectly, to authorize white-mestizo understandings of national territory, legitimize white-mestizo control of the land, and authorize a pervasive belief that indigenous people were passive elements of an influential national scene.

Cultivation, Civilization, and the Nineteenth-Century National Landscape

Perhaps paradoxically, the nineteenth-century creation of a particularly Ecuadorian rhetorical landscape owed a great deal to the influence of European and North American artists and scientists who visited the region. Those travelers encouraged a climate of exploration and observation, a fascination with the natural environment, and a proprietary awe for the Andean peaks dominating the highland landscape. Alexander von Humboldt, Gaetano Osculati, Ernest Charton, Frederic Church, Miguel María Lisboa, Alphons Stübel, Wilhelm Reiss, and their many contemporaries helped Ecuadorians see their own country, training young Ecuadorians in mountaineering, landscape painting, scientific illustration, and climate sciences. On his rise to the presidency in 1861, Gabriel García Moreno specially encouraged that trend. He initiated an educational program that encouraged the work of visiting scientists and brought foreign Jesuits to Quito to teach in the new polytechnic institute. The influence of those foreign scientists, artists, and teachers, though not the only force at work in the service of nation formation during the era, helped ensure that the contours of an emerging vision of Ecuadorian identity would be articulated in landscape.

Among their most striking effects, those visitors inspired a pervasive fascination with the wild sublime and with natural resources among the nation's young elite. In the visual realm, that meant paintings, photographs, and prints that featured lush jungles, majestic valleys, and sublime peaks. Scientific texts, for their part, described mountain climates, listed element deposits, discussed navigable waterways, and offered historical narratives emphasizing population development. In turn, political and social discourse featured a pronounced emphasis on exploration, exploitation, and cultivation.

The members of the Escuela Democrática de Miguel de Santiago were among those artists most influenced by foreign visitors. The school itself came into being thanks to the climate of exchange encouraged by the French painter and lithographer Ernest Charton, who set up a painting lyceum in Quito in 1849 that trained many of the school's future members.[10] When those founders later proclaimed a new national emphasis on local scenes and landscapes, they were simultaneously advancing a radical new spirit of nationalism and linking their national art to broader pan–Euro-American trends.[11] Later artists continued that dual move, drawing on the insights of foreign artists to develop a local tradition of landscape art intended to establish and honor the dignity of their national scene.

That desire to establish the contours of a national scene extended to territorial questions as well. In 1858 the first treatise on national geography written by an Ecuadorian (Manuel Villavicencio) explicitly addressed an inchoate national public that needed a sense of its borders and territory.[12] The succeeding decades of the century saw the production of numerous additional texts and countless paintings, all directed toward the creation and maintenance of that sense.[13] Those texts and images used the landscape as "the point of departure for consolidating a specifically [Ecuadorian] identity" around which elites might build the nation.[14] In treatises on geography and history, new maps, accounts of mountaineering treks, and landscape paintings, then, Ecuadorian rhetors did precisely what Gregory Clark suggests their counterparts in the United States pursued in much the same era: they sought to "publicize the potent symbols that prompt individuals to recognize themselves in public images of a common identity."[15] For Ecuadorians influenced by the global trends of bourgeois positivism, the goal of a coherent, modern nation demanded that territory—both land and landscape—be viewed, experienced, mapped, and used. The nation needed a sublime past and a cultivated future. Topoi connecting land and indigeneity served precisely that need.

These elite invocations of land and landscape sought to inspire the territorial vision of literate white-mestizo men; they also worked to marginalize, quiet, and contain other claims to the land. The noninclusive national "we" provided by rhetorical landscapes often made indigeneity distinctly visible, but it simultaneously fomented indigenous peoples' exclusion from the idea of a cultivated nation. In other words, though such landscapes did inculcate a "shared sense of national identity" in Gregory Clark's sense, Clark's hopeful image of national inclusion sets itself too broadly for the Ecuadorian context (and, some might say, for the U.S. context as well). In nineteenth-century Ecuador, not every Ecuadorian was to "feel at home together in the same imagined [nation]" in the same way.[16] Such distinction was achieved, over time, by moving between the two themes of the land-indigeneity topos, emphasizing both the mythohistorical presence of indigeneity within the landscape and indigenous peoples' assumed rusticity and lack of cultivation. Together those two themes allowed nineteenth-century elites to connect themselves to a powerful mythological past and imagine a more modern future in which Ecuador would take its rightful place among the "civilized" nations of the world.

The Territory of a Great Civilization

Nineteenth-century Ecuadorian geography texts frequently included an elaborate discussion of human geography alongside their accounts of physical territory. Such sections, like other accounts of Ecuador's human history, planted the beginnings of national heritage in the grandeur of a pre-Columbian past. Villavicencio's 1858 *Geografía de la república del Ecuador* begins, for example, in the misty days of the Shyris, or Quitus, and follows the rise and fall of empires all the way through the recent independence.[17] In that tale the colonial period received short shrift, dismissed as an era in which the population lived in isolation and darkness, "perhaps even forgetting that there were other men, other events, and other sciences to know."[18] The period preconquest and the era of independence, for Villavicencio, provided the young nation-state with an origin tale worth celebrating and defending. It also defined a national territory separate from the shifting borders of the colonial era. The straight line drawn between pre-Columbian past and independent present secured a coherent narrative of national development in which the cultural richness of the Incan land fed the spirit of criollo independence.

In 1874 Juan León Mera published his *Catecismo de geografía de la república del Ecuador*. That text drew on Villavicencio's tome and early drafts of another geography by Pedro Fermín Cevallos. It was designed specifically for use by schoolchildren and staged a memorizable dialogue between teacher and student to communicate the details of national geography. Mera's textbook built a version of Villavicencio's origin tale into its Socratic dialogue about the shape and extension of national territory. The dutiful student was taught to explain a succession of empires and conquests as evidence of a long process of gradual but interrupted improvement. Mera dwelt particularly on the positive traits of the Incan Empire, having the student explain that Incan religious traditions, "though erroneous, had a certain character of gentility and nobility." The student would go on to note, however, that the brutality of the Spanish colonizers had wiped out the remnants of that advanced culture. The long colonial period had pulled civilization backward and left the surviving indigenous peoples "reduced to the greatest oppression and to the force of tyranny," a condition from which only the progress of an independent Ecuador could rescue them.[19] In Mera's history the armies of independence, not those remaining indigenous communities, were the proper inheritors of Ecuadorian territory and its pre-Columbian indigenous heritage. The noble criollos would rejuvenate the spirit of their Incan predecessors and develop it further through the influence of Christianity, drawing their right from the inevitable progress of civilization.

That origin tale grounded in the pre-Columbian empires was as important in painted landscapes as it was in written geographies. Kennedy Troya notes that in Ecuador's Liberal Era (beginning in 1895), the indigenous inhabitants depicted in landscape painting were "mute figures in a landscape upon which was inscribed grand histories."[20] Her insight applies as well to earlier images, even those that elided indigenous figures in favor of the echo of indigenous histories. The "grand histories" written on the land by nineteenth-century criollo artists often invoked pre-Columbian grandeur. As Matthias Leonhardt Abram puts it, white-mestizos, "in the absence of some other glorious past, sought to make themselves the 'children of the [Incan] earth,' marginalizing its true descendants."[21] The echoing footsteps of the Incas and the Shyris gave the national sublime particular mythological force. Sites where the nation's pre-Columbian predecessors left their prints were obvious and popular subjects for landscape painting.

Luís A. Martínez's 1906 *Camino del Inca* (Incan road; fig. 10) makes that desire to follow in the footsteps of the Incas quite literal, depicting the route of the famous Incan Highway. The painting, done in at least two versions,

Fig. 10.   Luís A. Martínez, *El camino del Inca*, 1906. Oil on canvas. Collection of the Museum of the Casa de la Cultura Ecuatoriana "Benjamín Carrión," Quito, Ecuador.

features a leveled dirt road hewn out of the steep mountainside. The top of road launches itself into the space between the mountains, pointing toward distant and unknown horizons. In one version of the painting, two indigenous men pass each other on the road in the foreground, while another man in a poncho stands at the crest of the hill, perhaps looking back downhill to encourage those below. In another version only the road itself indexes the power of indigenous history, lacking human figures entirely. In both cases, however, Martínez's painting draws attention to the organizing, productive presence of the Incas in Ecuadorian space. In fact, he credits them with a level of success that long evaded criollo Ecuadorians—cutting a navigable path through the rugged Andes.[22] That romantic sublime, invoked by the grandeur of space and the monumental achievement of the highway, invokes the ghosts of the *mingas* (work levies) that built the infrastructure of the old empire. It also projects a new dawn for the present-day nation, one that includes a resurgence of order and progress under the Liberal regimes of the era.

Working several decades earlier, Joaquín Pinto similarly turned to sites of pre-Columbian and Independence Era importance. He used those scenes to paint the natural world and the nation, as he put it, "ennobled, even improved . . . according to the judicious and beautiful conception of the painter."[23] Pinto's historical scenes usually lack human figures but often emphasize indications of humanity, allowing viewers to imagine themselves along a historical line drawn in the land. Those paintings depict ruins and paths or show locations imbued with commonly known historical associations. From his 1875 paintings and prints featuring the sacred *laguna de culebrillas* in southern Ecuador to his 1894 oil painting of the famous Incan ruin Ingapirca (fig. 11), Pinto's images marked the landscape with indigenous features while also making those features fundamentally part of Ecuadorian national territory.

Martínez, Pinto, and their compatriots only occasionally painted actual events from their nation's history. Instead, images of landscape took on history's weight. They allowed, in the process, an elision of indigenous presence by transmuting it into the land. Defining land and claiming landscapes, those artists circulated a powerful social energy that imbued territory with national spirit because of its rich and mythic history. Such heroic visions rooted in the past, however, ran into complications (from a criollo perspective) when they moved into the scene of a national present.

The Problem of the Uncultivated Present

Though the organizing power of a pre-Columbian indigenous past carried significant constitutive and commonplace force for criollo rhetors, the figure of the contemporary Indian played a far more complicated and conflicted

Fig. 11.   Joaquín Pinto, *Una lámina* (paisaje de Ingapirca), 1894. Oil on cardboard. Collection of the Museo Alberto Mena Caamaño, Centro Cultural Metropolitano, Quito, Ecuador.

role in white-mestizo nation building. In fact, Kennedy Troya suggests that landscape painting provided a way for artists to escape the controversial subject of the present-day Indian while still constructing recognizable visions of the national territory.[24] While noble Shyris and Incas were comfortable national icons for nineteenth-century elites, the indigenous peons and laborers of their own moment were at best a source of consternation. Even so, contemporary indigenous people were not merely the constitutive exterior to landscape painting and the national sublime. Indigenous figures and evidence of present-day indigenous life do appear in landscape paintings from the end of the nineteenth and beginning of the twentieth century, perhaps especially in the work of the artists featured here (Pinto, Martínez, Guerrero).

Overall, these figures in landscape painting draw on the tropes of costumbrismo: they provide paintings and photographs with a powerful and picturesque sense of "the local and the autochthonous."[25] They are romanticized and, to some extent, feminized elements of the local and as such are barely distinguishable from the land itself. One of the most famous early twentieth-century landscape paintings, Rafael Troya's *Vista de la cordillera desde Tiopullo*, for example, tucks a young indigenous shepherd into the right-hand foreground of a painting focused on the peaks of the Ecuadorian Andes. The girl and her small flock are utterly dwarfed by the mountain scene around them, almost invisible, but they lend the scene a pastoral tone that softens the sublime of the distant Andes. Such landscape images neutralize the "problem" of an indigenous present using the same strategies as the historical scenes: they blend indigeneity into the land, claiming its romance without granting indigenous people separate agency. To the extent that indigenous people appeared as integral to the landscape yet passively pastoral, both Indians and territory became available for national purposes. Both were open to the active perspective of the knowledgeable white-mestizo viewer. Such romantically populated landscape paintings thus echoed commonplace invocations of the Spanish terms *culto* (both "cultured" and "cultivated") and *inculto* (both "uncultured" and "uncultivated") to distinguish active white-mestizos from passive Indians.

The culto-inculto binary at work in most scenes that incorporated indigenous people into national landscapes resonates with other efforts to justify their exclusion from active citizenship by emphasizing their rusticity and backwardness. That common sense relegated indigenous people to the realm of the uncultured and uncultivated—pastoral shepherds who lived from the land without affecting it. It left them outside the cultivated national public that was a common goal of white-mestizo elites otherwise divided by stark ideological lines. By invoking notions of culto and inculto, land-scapes incorporating indigenous people helped establish a sense of virgin national territory ripe for agricultural and economic cultivation by white-mestizos. Because indigenous people were integrated into the Andean natural world rather than acting on it, they became available to white-mestizo viewers, ready to be exploited for the economic and social development of the nation.[26] Indigenous people, seen as naturally pastoral and premodern, heightened the availability and potential of the rhetorical landscape for white-mestizos.

A small, 1868 black-and-white crayon drawing by Joaquín Pinto titled *Vista al crater de Pichincha desde Capillapamba* (View of the crater of Pichincha from Capillapamba; fig. 12) is illustrative in this sense. The scene of the drawing is set against the southwest flank of the volcano Pichincha—a mountain famous for being the site of the final battle in the wars of independence. In the foreground, a bare-legged man wearing a poncho and hat stands beside a coarsely tiled earthwork building. The land between the man and the mountain stretches away roughly, uncultivated but supporting a few grazing animals. The handwritten title of the drawing notes the location of the scene and the height of the mountain in the background, making no mention of the building or figure in the foreground. The human elements are simply part of the mountain scene. Such a move from uncultured Indian to uncultivated land to sublime national territory attaches indigeneity specifically to land that has been left inculto. It supports, in turn, a national vision in which culture is always provided by white-mestizos who cultivate the valleys and explore the summits and craters of the mountains.

The claim to cultivation and land exhibited in Pinto's single and rather fragile drawing circulated in other visual artifacts as well, perhaps most strikingly in the common series of paintings and prints cataloging the major peaks of Ecuador's Andean corridor. These prints, often copied from one venue to another, frequently supplemented their mountain views with a foreground tableau of rustic Indians. The indigenous figures, set at the center of the image yet dwarfed by the mountain behind them, stood gazing outward from within the wild, untamed landscape (figs. 13–17). In these scenes Indians are just barely human figures, present primarily to give a sense of scale (and romance). Their turn toward the viewer, in turn, invites consideration and authority from the audience. Indigenous figures anchor the scenes, providing a domestic counterpoint to the majestic, dangerous sublime of the mountains. The fact that the indigenous subjects are rustic in appearance—standing on barren ground, often alongside mules or llamas,

Fig. 12.   Joaquín Pinto, *Vista al crater de Pichincha desde Capillapamba*, 1868. Crayon on paper. Collection of the Museum of the Casa de la Cultura Ecuatoriana "Benjamín Carrión," Quito, Ecuador.

Fig. 13.   Juan Agustín Guerrero, *Cotopaxi*, 1852. Watercolor on paper. Reprinted by the Fundación Wilson Hallo, 1981. In Guerrero, *Imágenes del Ecuador*. Photograph by Jessie Reeder.

Fig. 14.   *Vulcane Cotopazi nella grande Cordigliera dell'Equatore ed avvanzo di un antico templo degli Incas*, 1854. In Osculati, *Esploraziones*, lamina 3, fig. 2.

Fig. 15.   *Chimborazo, al sud. est. di Quito, altezza 21.416 piedi*, 1854. In Osculati, *Esploraziones*, lamina 3, fig. 1. Photograph by Jessie Reeder.

Fig. 16.   *Cotopaxi, visto de Callo.* Lithograph by Ferd. Mayer, 1858. In Villavicencio, *Geografía de la república.* Photograph by Jessie Reeder.

Fig. 17.   *Chimborazo, visto de Tapi.* Lithograph by Ferd. Mayer, 1858. In Villavicencio, *Geografía de la república.* Photograph by Jessie Reeder.

dressed as peasants—links them closely to the land itself and, in the process, to a vision of iconic national territory in which white-mestizo viewers wield the potential for cultivation.

One of the most commonly copied of those mountain images invokes both the mythohistorical and the culto-inculto emphases of the land-indigeneity topos (figs. 13, 14, 16). It shows the volcano Cotopaxi with a pre-Columbian ruin and an indigenous figure in the foreground. This image likely appeared first as an illustration in travel narratives produced by Europeans but was directly copied or adapted by several Ecuadorians, including Villavicencio and the costumbrista painter Juan Augustín Guerrero. Setting picturesquely premodern indigenous figures against a massive landscape tinged with a profoundly *past* pre-Columbian heritage shrinks those figures, emphasizing their passivity and blending them into the landscape. Like Martínez's paintings of the Incan Highway, Troya's *Vista de la cordillera*, and Mera's account of historical progress, the scene links pre-Columbian myth and present-day rusticity into a national romance. It grounds Ecuadorian heritage in a grand mythohistorical Incaic period and evokes the need for white-mestizo cultivation.

Such well-circulated, repeated mountain views contributed to a narrative of progress in which indigenous people had forfeited their cultural inheritance to cultivated white-mestizos. The authors and image makers deploying those scenes were not always entirely confident that white-mestizos were themselves sufficiently cultivated, however. Both Villavicencio and Mera warn in their geography texts that Ecuador's leading classes had failed to raise the nation up from its colonial lethargy. Both authors critique the cultivation of their compatriots, warning white-mestizo Ecuadorians that their failures to cultivate the land suggest as well a disreputable lack of culture and, by implication, a troubling proximity to indigeneity.

Villavicencio, for instance, writes that "all the elements of prosperity [so common in this country] are to be found in their state of nature because the hand of man has done nothing to benefit from them." The "degraded character" of the Ecuadorian must be corrected, Villavicencio urges, through government intervention and through education.[27] That this language of degradation and failure to cultivate, so generally indicative of indigeneity, should be applied to the Ecuadorian population more broadly should not be surprising. White-mestizo schoolchildren learned notions of both racial superiority and racial degradation in their classrooms through texts such as Mera's *Catecismo de geografía* and the similar *Geografía universal* taught in schools run by the order of Christian Brothers during the same era. These texts taught that the customs of the Indians were inherently rustic and warned that contact with indigeneity had degraded the otherwise European habits of criollos. Mestizos, in this assessment, were far more inclined toward the backward habits of their indigenous ancestors than the civilization of their European side.[28] The lesson for white-mestizo Ecuadorians, then, was that they must take up their rightful role as those possessing culture and responsibility. They must cultivate the land and care for its less cultured inhabitants to truly claim the national territory. Should they do so, the inheritance of national greatness would naturally become available to them. As Villavicencio so enthusiastically proclaimed, the spirit of entrepreneurship would awaken, rivers would be navigated, roadways and lines of communication would be opened, and "Ecuador [would] quickly become a preeminent nation in all senses."[29]

Several decades later, Luís A. Martínez echoed a similar theme in his treatise on agriculture in Ecuador. He bemoaned the inadequate productivity of the nation's fields compared with more developed countries like the United States and blamed Ecuador's problems on the widespread use of premodern means of cultivation. Martínez asserted that alongside the inaptness of modern farm machinery for use on Ecuador's rugged terrain, the country's troubles could easily be blamed on the uncultivated Indian. He wrote, "the rural Ecuadorian peon [read, indigenous laborer], admirable . . . for his sobriety and resistance to fatigue, is resistant to the meticulous work that one sees described in foreign Agronomy texts."[30] Martínez's intervention adapted the teachings of modern science and agriculture to the particular circumstances of Ecuador, encouraging educated, elite landowners to alter their practices for greater efficiency and productivity. That project implicitly meant learning new methods of administration and control over the rustic, resistant indigenous populations who actually worked the soil. Martínez communicated that point in his paintings as well. His 1909 painting, *Paisaje*, was the first Ecuadorian landscape painting to show cultivated land, and though the scene includes a thatched hut, it is empty of human figures.[31] The careful organization of land and its lush fecundity suggest the positive national potential of fertile indigenous land cultivated under the wisdom of white-mestizo civilization.

In word and image, illustration and painting, textbook and scientific treatise, the terms of cultivation and civilization were widely available to criollos. Like its commonplace counterpart imbuing the land with pre-Columbian mystery, the invocation of culto and inculto provided a flexible and readily accessible resource for elites to imagine the national landscape as both indigenous and available. Those two strands of the land-indigeneity topos were not, however, solely engaged by elites working in oil paint and publishing official texts. Understanding the full spectrum of the social energy carried within the land-indigeneity topos requires a broader scope of inquiry that traces how terms of mythic history and cultivation served the arguments of Ecuadorians who appealed to terms of national landscape in their more quotidian negotiations over land.

Cultivating Topoi

It is nearly impossible to prove that a given member of nineteenth-century Ecuadorian society would have seen a particular painting or read a particular geography text. Evidence that topoi of indigeneity became part of national common sense, then, comes more from the dispersal of patterns than of individual artifacts. Topoi of land and indigeneity move through Ecuadorian symbolic realms not because individual objects had huge audiences but because there were huge numbers of artifacts carrying them. The sheer pervasiveness of images and texts treating the national landscape made the commonplace connecting indigeneity to the land widely available, at least to Ecuador's literate population. The circulating topos, more than any specific image or text, made its way into the everyday rhetorical production of literate white-mestizos, mestizos, and indigenous people and, it seems likely, their nonliterate neighbors as well.

Official records and popular petitions from the municipality of Quito corroborate that sense that the land-indigeneity topos achieved wide, common-sense distribution. In those quotidian documents, we can see white-mestizos and indigenous people negotiating access to local land in the same terms used to establish national territory in more extraordinary rhetorical artifacts. Informed by the affective, nation-building force of land-indigeneity topoi, white-mestizo and indigenous Ecuadorians contesting the use of national terrain on the small scale turned regularly to historical claims and evidence of cultivation to establish the legitimacy of their appeals and influence the actions of the state. Both groups referred to pre-Columbian history and to the historical roles of indigenous people during the colonial and early republican eras to establish claims to land. Even as indigenous people were able to establish ownership using such claims to history, however, their appeals were inevitably indebted to the power of the state as sovereign over all national land. Such appeals subordinated indigenous claims to an increasingly ingrained sense that cultivated (or cultivatable) land was Ecuadorian. Thus those claims to ownership also contributed to the constitution of a centralized *national* territory, even if they simultaneously complicated white-mestizo efforts to occlude indigenous participation in the modern nation.[32]

Soon after García Moreno took office for his first presidential term (1861–65), Quito's municipal council launched an effort to envision the state of the canton in terms both deeply symbolic and fundamentally material.[33] In February 1862 the politically appointed executive officer of Quito, the *jefe político*, ordered the canton's parochial authorities to report on the state of schools, prisons, roads, and municipal and communal lands in their parish.[34] Many of the resulting reports are perfunctory: they characterize in brief phrases the state of schools (miserable), prisons (nonexistent), and roads (deplorable) and give vague assessments of the use being made of municipal and communal land. A handful, however, suggest a more sustained effort by parochial authorities to respond to the underlying concerns of the jefe político's request. In those reports, parochial officials position their community vis-à-vis the nation and, sometimes, offer elaborate commentaries on the state of the land and the people under their authority. Together, the four areas of the reports track the fundamental responsibilities of the republican state as defined by the politics of the moment: offering education to shape the next generation of citizens, providing a system of criminal justice to ensure order and security, building infrastructure to promote commerce and communication, and maintaining control of the national territory to establish the coherence of the central state.[35]

In their discussions of that last area, Quito's leaders evinced a particularly local instantiation of the larger effort to create a modern sense of a coherent national geographic whole. Though at the time that the jefe político requested his reports many Ecuadorians identified more with the *patria chica* (little nation) in which they lived than with the nation as a whole, documents like these make clear how some local authorities used topoi of land and indigeneity to position their local concerns in light of a growing emphasis on the centralized nation-state.[36] In one response, for example, a civil judge from the parish of Cangagua makes clear that he sees the jefe político's request as coming from the state, noting that he wishes he could report the parish in circumstances "conforming to the highest desires of the Supreme Government" and expressing his great pleasure at the recent peace established under the new administration (of García Moreno).[37]

Taken as a whole, the more effusive reports register a basic ambivalence over the status of land they term "municipal and communal." There are at least three sorts of land that might be referred to, used, or contested in terms of "communal land," some of which did, in fact, belong to the state. That land might be part of an urban *ejido*, public land on which any resident could pasture livestock or, in some cases, grow consumables. Or it might be land held (either formally or informally) by indigenous communities who had been given stretches of land by the government for common pasturing and cultivation. Or that "municipal and communal" land might refer to *tierra baldía*: fallow land that, owing to its disuse, would revert to government own-ership and be eligible for sale or rental. The references to municipal and communal land in the 1862 reports seem often to blend these three catego-ries or, rather, to suggest an uncertainty on the part of the municipality as to the extent and character of each of the three types of land within the canton.

It appears that unless they were shown legal titles to the contrary (and sometimes even then), parochial authorities believed that land occupied by indigenous persons in the municipality ought to be considered municipal land. There was a general assumption that indigenous communal land, rath-er than belonging to indigenous people, was a state good provided by the state to indigenous people as a paternalistic obligation and ultimately remained under government control. Though this assumption had a long history and cannot be seen as caused by the naturalized connection between indigeneity and national territory developed in geographic treatises and landscape paint-ings, it should still be seen in the context of the land-indigeneity topos. The easy declaration of state ownership was, in part, authorized by the broad-er assumption that indigenous land always belonged fundamentally to the state both as a rightful inheritance from the mythohistorical pre-Columbian empires and as a primary responsibility of the cultivated for the uncultivated.

In their reports to the jefe político documenting the state of municipal and communal land in the canton, the more thorough parochial authorities regularly refer to the history of indigenous presence on the land. The reports also carry evidence that indigenous people resisted the municipality's claim to their land, often by invoking pre-Columbian or colonial-era history. Both parochial authorities and the indigenous people whose responses appear in the reports regularly used legally (if not culturally) anachronistic titles to refer to *indígenas* and their land rights. Indigenous men seeking to retain author-ity over land are referred to as *caciques* or *gobernadores*, titles that invoked, respectively, pre-Columbian nobility and colonial positions related to the col-lection of indigenous tribute. Citing indigenous men as caciques and gober-nadores in the reports of parochial authorities links current land claims to a long history of indigenous-state relationships based on the administration of people and territory. Such invocations of historical relationship served to establish a sense of continuity in land ownership and responsibility. They also maintained distinctions between indigenous subjects and white-mestizo citizens. By acknowledging and continuing the paternalistic land grants first established by colonial and early republican authorities, the municipality could assert and benefit from racial distinctions proper to an era when indigenous people were legally and categorically distinguished from white-mestizos.

Indigenous people appear also to have invoked those quasi-anachronistic titles and referenced historical land grants to claim privileges connected to eras in which they had enjoyed greater autonomy from white-mestizo authority. In their reports parochial authorities occasionally noted the details of indigenous claims to ownership of land, indicating who provided titles for their land and who claimed ownership but could not produce titles. Some also reported the specific details of those titles, cataloging claims traced back to the colonial period or to the era of Gran Colombia. In one case a parochial administrator simply submitted a list of nearly seventy indigenous men occupying land that they claimed had been theirs "since the time of the Incas." Other parochial authorities indicated that indigenous gobernadores established their ownership with reference to having been given the land by the republic in payment for assistance with the collection of tribute. In 1862, appealing to laws that had governed indigenous-criollo relationships during the late colonial and early republican periods, a group of indigenous people in the parish of Quinche objected to the municipality's attempted sale of communal land by suggesting that indigenous communal land could not be sold by the state, could not be owned by a private individual, and could not pass into white hands.[38]

These and similar claims to history by indigenous communities appear to have allowed some indigenous individuals and groups to retain control of land they occupied, at least in the short term. However, those appeals, in their reliance on topoi that connected indigeneity to the land and land to national landscape, often simultaneously catalyzed the authority of the state over national territory. By appealing to previous land grants, service to the state, and republican laws reserving land for indigenous use, indigenous petitioners necessarily acknowledged that the state had ultimate claim to the land. They also contributed to a sense of historical legal continuity for the national territory through their invocation of claims dating from the pre-Columbian and colonial periods. Such claims based on history and the authority of the state were, of course, among the only means available for indigenous petitioners seeking to retain their land and were, as such, both important and effective. But their assumption of legitimate state authority also placed indigenous appeals at risk, allowing others to challenge those claims based on their anachronism.

Challenges to indigenous control of land based on charges of anachronism regularly accessed terms of cultivation to devalue indigenous ownership. Where appeals to a history of indigenous connection to land were sometimes effective for nineteenth-century indigenous petitioners seeking to retain access to land, the theme of cultivation was more often used by white-mestizos hoping to undermine those claims. Just as landscape painting offered viewers a visual elision between uncultivated land and uncultured indígenas, white-mestizo efforts to usurp indigenous land often activated the land-indigeneity topos through terms of modern efficiency and indigenous backwardness to establish a superior claim to make use of national land.

Appeals to white-mestizo cultivation and indigenous rusticity engaged commonsense assumptions about indigenous lack of cultivation even in the face of evidence that indigenous landholders were, in fact, actively working their land. Disputes between indigenous people and their white-mestizo neighbors (or government authorities) often included the charge that land belonging to indigenous communities had been left inculto or underutilized. In 1862, Rafael Brito, a resident of the parish of Conocoto, wrote to the municipal council to request that he be allowed to rent land previously ceded to the area's indigenous communities. Brito began his petition by undermining the historical argument for indigenous access to land, arguing that there were very few indígenas residing in Conocoto at that point and emphasizing further that those who did live in the parish no longer paid the "contribution of their class" (i.e., tribute). Still, he wrote, they had been allowed a large "egido" [sic] for their use. The historical claim by indigenous communities that provided that ejido, he suggested, should no longer be active. The old state-indigenous relationships had been replaced and the indigenous population itself had begun to fade. Here, Brito is tapping into another widespread assumption about indigeneity: that it would eventually disappear due to natural population decline and be replaced by a whiter, more civilized population. Progress was not a matter of displacement—of white-mestizos usurping indigenous land—so much as an evolutionary reality in which the new and energetic gradually overtook the old and used up.

Brito did not, however, rely solely on his negation of the historical argument. He also emphasized the commonplace assumptions of indigenous rusticity and lack of modernity with regard to the land. He complained that because the ejido belonged to the indígenas in common, "it remain[ed] *uncultivated* and [wa]s barely serviceable for pasturing a few animals."[39] Brito, in contrast, would cultivate the land efficiently, making it productive and providing valuable income to the municipality so that it could pursue its "important and growing responsibilities." His argument, in other words, contrasted indigeneity and cultivation and then tied cultivation to the health and advancement of the state. The white-mestizo *citizen*, cultured and cultivating, stood as a necessary precondition to progress. The communal, rustic Indian was inefficient by nature, characterized by a complete failure of cultivation.

Other white-mestizo petitioners of the era made similar use of the culto-inculto binary, and the records of their exchanges with the municipality demonstrate that the charge of inculto was regularly made even of land that was solidly in indigenous hands. In an October 1862 dispute from the parish of Tumbaco, for example, the white-mestizo petitioner used terms of cultivation to support his claim to "abandoned" tierra baldía that was, as further documents in the dispute demonstrate, actively cultivated by indigenous people. There, the white-mestizo citizen, Rafael Lopez Conde, informed the municipality of several pieces of tierra baldía that had slipped past its attention, costing Quito's government needed income. Lopez requested that he receive title to rent the land, thus correcting the loss and bringing the land back into cultivation. However, an appointed parish official, the *teniente político*, responded to Lopez's request by indicating that the land belonged to a group of indigenous people (a fact that the teniente político had learned by completing the report requested by the jefe político earlier in the year). The accompanying documents for the case list the history of land ownership, in several cases referencing participation in the collection of tribute.[40]

In a similar case from March 1871, Manuel Quesadan, a resident of the parish of Lloa, informed the municipality that a piece of land previously rented to "the *indígena* Manuel Chauca" was abandoned and uncultivated because Chauca had indebted himself as a *concierto* (debt slave) on a nearby hacienda. Quesadan asked that he be given title to the land instead. Quesadan's request, however, was followed closely by a letter from Lloa's civil judge. The judge urged the council to deny Quesadan's request on the grounds that Chauca had not made himself a concierto and had simply been traveling to a nearby town.[41] Here, Chauca's right to remain on the land he had rented was established by the fact that he had been making good use of the land and was a good subject to the central government, not merely on the basis of his having a preexisting rental contract.

These examples suggest a significant level of rapacity among white-mestizos in their efforts to usurp indigenous land. The spaces they claimed were likely not uncultivated, given the quick negative responses of indigenous renters and parochial authorities. Those responses, which often countered the inculto charge with references to history, suggest that the issue at play in these disputes was not that the land in question itself lacked cultivation but that the commonplace of indigenous rusticity, of the uncultivated Indian, made indigenous-held land immediately inculto by association. It is interesting that in each of these examples where the official response is extant, the government, despite its usual investment in the "problem" of indigenous rusticity and barbarity, was required (by indigenous petition) to defend the prior claim of indigenous people, thus interrupting its own push toward white-mestizo modernity and national territory. In general, however, as the larger histories of white-mestizos encroaching on indigenous land suggest, invoking modernity and the mechanisms of efficient cultivation allowed white-mestizos to undermine indigenous claims to land because those invocations tapped into the belief that indigenous people could never be modern: they were of the land. Contrasting white-mestizos' assumed action on the land with indigenous peoples' status as *of* the land provided a powerful commonsense claim both to particular parcels of land and to the broader symbolic geography of the nation.

Though the terms of argument over communal land in the nineteenth century usually show white-mestizos foregrounding terms of cultivation and indigenous people responding in terms of historical claim, these two lines of argument share two fundamental features: they assume a special indigenous connection to land and they emphasize the fundamental right of the state to benefit from and give claim to that land. One final example brings these underlying assumptions about national territory and indigeneity into the foreground. In a set of cases from the parish of Tocachi, three separate indigenous men occupying municipal land appealed to Quito's municipal council for formal titles (it's not clear whether these were titles of rental or of ownership).[42] The indigenous men's appeals were made verbally; the written records of those appeals took the form of a parish panel decision that was forwarded to the municipal council, supporting the land grants. In each of the cases, the referral was phrased in what were clearly formulaic terms. Invoking the sense of indigenous dependence on the land, the referrals characterized the land as the petitioners' "only means of survival." The referrals established the major force of the claim to formal titles in terms of residence on the land "since time immemorial," tracing that connection to the land into a misty history. Closing the referral and offering a clear glimpse of the subject-making force of claims to land, the members of the panel emphasized that the indigenous men petitioning for titles were loyal subjects of the government and faithful children of the Catholic Church. If they were positioned as dependents insufficiently culto for the titles of citizenship, the men and their families still fulfilled the constitutional obligations of nationals, being presented as proper, but passive, citizens through their dependence on the land.

Culture, Conflict, and Progress

At the end of the nineteenth century, artists, intellectuals, politicians, and petitioners all engaged topoi of indigenous land to shape the contours of the national landscape and the nation itself. In the mid-twentieth century appeals to the land gained renewed exigency. They appeared again and again, used to address national and international conflicts that posed new challenges to the fate and future of the nation. As in previous eras, when the state of the land was tied strongly to the state of the nation, those commonplaces of indigeneity played central and contentious roles in defining the stakes of conflict. The disputes of the mid-twentieth century were not new; often their roots lay in the nineteenth century. In the tumult of midcentury, however, a confluence of political, economic, and artistic factors brought new attention to land as a source of conflict. The resilience of the land-indigeneity topos allowed a new generation to link those conflicts, large and small, to the possibilities of the nation and its future development.

By the late 1930s, a new generation had gained prominence in Quiteño intellectual and artistic circles. Unlike the old municipal aristocracy, the members of this new generation largely came to Quito from the provinces and the middle class. Eduardo Kingman, the young man whose social-realist paintings, discussed in chapter 1, caused an uproar at the 1935 Mariano Aguilera competition, arrived in Quito from the southern city of Loja by way of coastal Guayaquil. The influence of the Coastal literary group now called the "Generation of the Thirties" filtered up to the Highlands by the mid-1930s with the migration of figures such as Kingman and the author Alfredo Pareja Diezcanseco, sparking a greater social consciousness in the work of visual artists. That consciousness inspired left-leaning Highlands artists to develop new, independent venues for artistic exploration. Those venues included a syndicate (the Union of Writers and Artists), periodicals (e.g., *Revista del Sindicato de Escritores y Artistas* and *Revista del Mar Pacífico*), and an art competition and exposition (the Salon de Mayo), all intended to challenge the Quiteño art establishment. Over the next thirty years indigenismo came to dominate not only Ecuador's art world but also its academic spheres, where a new generation of young scholars advanced the social sciences as the premier means for understanding the state of the nation.

This new generation of artists and intellectuals had been shaped, politically, by a brutal massacre of protesting workers in Guayaquil in 1922, by the 1925 July Revolution—which attempted to reinstall the promise of Liberalism—and by the economic and political turbulence of the 1930s themselves. Though Catholic conservatives still held a great deal of sway in the Highlands, these emerging artists and intellectuals were influenced by the secular Left and aligned themselves with liberal, socialist, and communist groups. If today's sense of history imagines those actors working in the midst of a long period of political instability stretching from 1925 to 1948, their own writing suggests that they saw themselves as perpetually embarking on a new moment of stability, progress, and democratic rule. Their work was consistently directed toward the redemptive promise of the new era they imagined was beginning.

In almost all the groupings of this new generation, finding a solution to a version of the "Indian problem" was of great concern for achieving goals of stability, economic progress, and democracy. These white-mestizos imagined the Indian problem as a rural issue and regularly relied on commonplaces that tied indigeneity to land to formulate the problem and imagine its solution. In many ways the land-indigeneity topos had changed little from the nineteenth century. The uncultured indígena, lacking education, living communally, and degraded by years of colonization and exploitation, was a commonsense figure whose features were well established in resilient commonplaces. The "places of return" established around indigeneity and land meant that the familiar indígena returned repeatedly in mid-twentieth-century appeals. At the same time the investments of the moment and the context of political and economic upheaval did occasion some shifts in the ideas and issues that intersected within the topos. In particular, while the appeal to history remained relevant, this era saw greater emphasis on terms of culture and cultivation, including in arguments advanced by indigenous communities.

The force of pre-Columbian mythohistory, particularly its ability to authorize a narrative of long-term territorial coherence, diminished in the twentieth century. Turn-of-the-century debates among historians called into question the accuracy of Padre Velasco's 1789 *Historia del Reino de Quito* (History of the kingdom of Quito), which had been the accepted source for claims that there were advanced, organized states in Ecuador prior to the arrival of the Incas.[43] The influential, aristocratic Quiteño politician and archaeologist Jacinto Jijón y Caamaño was a foremost critic of Padre Velasco's tale.[44] His work rewrote the familiar pre-Columbian history of Ecuador, downplaying the story of great empires in favor of a more consistent history of indigenous rusticity and backwardness. In that history the Incas were outside conquerors whose brief period of authority over the primitive indigenous communities of Ecuadorian territory was quickly succeeded by that of the conquering Spaniards and then by the criollo elite of the early republic. With the rise of Jijón y Caamaño's argument, pre-Columbian mythos no longer provided white-mestizos with a stable sense of noble connection to the land.

The force of historical narrative in the land-indigeneity topos also declined because of changing investments and foci among artists and intellectuals. An increasing interest in social-realist literature and art meant that the struggles of contemporary popular classes had more attraction for artists than did their predecessors' romanticized visions of the past. Similarly, the rise of the social sciences meant that sociological and psychological studies of contemporary Indians were very much in vogue for the emerging scholars of the day. For the new generation, historical studies of indigenous culture belonged largely to the folkloric romanticism of an earlier era.

Still, history did retain a certain force for the generation coming of age at midcentury. Though the debate earlier in the century interrupted any easy assumption that the narratives of pre-Columbian greatness were solidly historical, the romance of an Incan past continued to capture the imagination of white-mestizo elites. After all, as Mercedes Prieto puts it, "the polemic about the native past was, in fact, a discussion about contemporary Indians."[45] In that context the force of mythohistory shifted, so that whether it contributed to a narrative of ongoing rusticity or one of a fall from civilization, it buttressed the terms of cultivation that had become dominant. Rather than remaining separate and sometimes competing strands of the land-indigeneity topos, history and cultivation merged in the twentieth century. Historical narratives served assertions about cultivation and its lack. Ecuadorian indigenous people had been part of a primitive civilization either for millennia or for the past four hundred years. Either way, a long history of rusticity and alienation from the benefits of culture meant to white-mestizos that the integration of indigenous people into national society required a cultivated intervention.

Culture and cultivation, then, became the primary locus for disseminating the land-indigeneity topos and advancing an idea of the nation. As before, indigenous people also used the commonplace to articulate their claims and mediate their relationships with white-mestizo neighbors. By this time, thanks in part to years of organizing by leftist groups, indigenous people themselves engaged terms of cultivation in their arguments about the land and painted white-mestizo *terratenientes* (large land-holders) as backward and inefficient in contrast to the consistent cultivation pursued by indigenous communities.[46]

The coherence that topoi of indigenous land lent treatments of territorial conflict operated at multiple levels. They are visible, then, both in discussions of the national future prompted by Ecuador's 1942 loss of territory to Peru and in local disputes over land reform. Despite their differences in purpose and scope, such appeals became allied with one another, thanks to their common invocation of land-indigeneity topoi. Claims to national territory drew implicitly on the history of indigenous resistance to land appropriation. Indigenous efforts to secure land reform echoed national arguments for development. In the process, visual depictions of land struggle wound up blending the two levels, making local struggles for land synecdoches for the defense of national territory.

Great Nation, Great Land

Though in exile from his homeland for portions of the 1930s and 1940s, Benjamín Carrión wrote regularly to his compatriots during the territorial crisis of the early 1940s. A series of his letters was published in Quito's liberal newspaper *El Día* as the crisis unfolded, and the letters were quickly republished as a single volume in 1943. In those letters and in his broader criticism, Carrión rejected what he termed a sterile history of dates and events. He believed that the land endowed nations with "spiritual and professional vocations" and shaped history as well.[47] Ecuador, he wrote, had a spiritual vocation for liberty and a professional vocation for the arts. Those values defined the country's past and would drive its future development. His homeland could become a great nation if it would cultivate liberty and artistic expression. Such greatness, he suggested, was inevitable. Invoking a theme prevalent across the Americas—particularly in the work of the Mexican José Vasconcelos and the Chilean Gabriela Mistral—Carrión argued for the centrality of tropical America.[48] He declared, "the great civilizations began between the tropics and the last [great] civilization will return to the tropics," giving Ecuador a grand future based primarily on the influences of its geographic location. "We are *tropicales*," Carrión wrote, "and we should be so courageously, proudly. Because that is our physical reality. Our biological

reality. Our economic reality. Our whole reality."[49] For Carrión, geography
was history, present, and future.

According to Carrión, Ecuador's physical geography determined its national vocations. The land, straddling the equator, rich with flora and fauna,
profoundly verdant and rugged, had shaped the peoples who had come there.
It made them Ecuadorian above all else. Turning away from what he saw
as an unnecessary focus on the exact origins of the Ecuadorian population,
Carrión wrote, "Here we are now . . . in this land that is situated in the center
of the great terrestrial ball. Like the wise men, we have come from all parts"
with the vocation to build that last great civilization.[50] Place, for Carrión,
catalyzed national potential. Even so, Carrión still went on to consider some
origins for the spirit being refined by Ecuadorian terrain. Despite his mostly
privileged audience, however, Carrión emphasized the subaltern in his catalog of Ecuadorian spirit. Nodding first to characteristics provided by Spain's
marginal groups—the Basque, the Catalan, and the Arab—Carrión then
turned to the Americas, writing, "The Maya [gave us] a sense of the artistic.
. . . The Incan, love for the land and the sun."[51] Not coincidentally, those two
traits drawn from the Americas provided the foundations for the spiritual
and professional vocations that Carrión offered his compatriots: love of the
land provided the impetus for liberty; a sense of the artistic fed the professional inclination toward the arts.[52]

Given the wide circulation of commonplaces linking land, nation, and
indigeneity, Carrión's argument that national vocation emerged in part from
indigenous land would have resonated as both natural and evocative. His
words point as well to the array of modes and forms in which those topoi
circulated: not only political texts and newspaper columns but manual and
fine arts as well. In other words, the white-mestizo arguments about agriculture that regularly represented indigenous people as "physically connected to
and immersed in their landscape, rather like geographical features" partook
of the rhetorical milieu visualized in strikingly similar terms within artistic
and intellectual circles.[53] Land-reform arguments grounded in a sense of indigenous people as "rather like geographical features" echoed the pens and
brushes of the indigenistas who produced image after image of "swollen
Indians . . . that can sustain themselves above the earth only because their
enormous fleshy legs emerge from her themselves, as if they were something of hers, shaped and cooked pieces of earth."[54]

Degenerate Land, Degenerate Nation

In mid-twentieth-century discussions of the "Indian problem," the connection between indigeneity and the land was seen as both cause of and possible means of escape from a conundrum often described in terms of national life or death. Terms of cultivation provided a powerful commonplace to articulate the stakes of "providing" culture and civilization to indigenous communities. Constitutional Assemblies posed improving the culture of indigenous communities as a fundamental requirement for national progress. For elites from across the wide spectrum of ideological persuasions, failure to provide Indians with education and a place in the nation carried dire consequences for the nation as a whole. As the journal *Previsión Social*, published by the Ministerio de Previsión Social (Ministry of Social Welfare), put it in a 1946 article, "this problem . . . has been addressed in every tone and by diverse elements of the national culture since the early days of independence until our present moment." If the "Indian problem" was not solved and the "indigenous race" was not "incorporated into the national culture," it would instead "degenerate such that [Ecuador] would have to sustain within itself a living corpse."[55] Such desperate assessments of the risk facing the nation-state make striking and consistent use of the terms of culture and cultivation. Their efforts at solutions did the same. As Victor Gabriel Garcés, a prominent indigenista social scientist, put it, "I am convinced that the Indian will continue as an agriculturalist and that his ancestry is much stronger than any longing for a change in the conditions of his labor, because the land is maternal, even in a biological and ecological sense, for the Indian."[56]

These concerns, running parallel to efforts aimed at assimilating indigenous people into a vision of white-mestizo national culture, meant that indigeneity was a strangely suppressed, yet omnipresent, term in elite discussions. During the mid-1930s, for example, *El Día* featured regular articles about Ecuadorian agriculture and land reform, suggesting consistent interest in legal reforms and the state of the rural population. In those articles, however, indigeneity was often referenced implicitly or subsumed beneath the category "rural." A 1935 response to President Velasco Ibarra's rural reform plans laments the difficulty of making real change among "that degraded majority [of the population] that vegetates—because it vegetates more than lives—in the agrarian [portion] of Ecuador." Only later in the column does it become clear that the cause for concern is particularly indigenous: "For *campesinos* and for the Indian especially, it will be painful to change . . . his promiscuous home and his animalian company and move to new homes whose conditions would be appropriately hygienic."[57] Though it takes until the second column for the article to invoke a specifically indigenous subject, the terms of moral and physical degradation and of proximity to the land (a population "vegetating" rather than "living") prepare the reader for the eventual admission of indigeneity.

Such indirect reference to indigeneity through the terms of land was not unusual. In her study of two statistical projects carried out in Ecuador in 1934 and 1950, historical anthropologist A. Kim Clark notes that elites sought to understand the Indian problem as social and moral rather than as economic and racial. In practice, though, elites continued to understand the problems they identified as *Indian* issues: "There was resistance to raising their [indigenous peoples'] agricultural wages . . . because in many cases large landowners perceived that as *Indians* [indigenous peoples'] work was not worth higher pay. Similarly, as *Indians* they encountered difficulties in gaining legal title to lands."[58] In this context the multivocal terms of cultivation allowed the simultaneous erasure of and emphasis on indigeneity. To be "Indian" became increasingly a matter of location and lack of culture, as well as a biological trait.[59] The uncultured Indian was responsible for the inefficient cultivation of land, and thus the rustic, uncivilized, uncultivated land remained referentially indigenous.

Related discussions of land and indigeneity reveal a similarly contradictory tendency within white-mestizo efforts to solve the Indian problem. Rafael Brito's 1862 objection to the "inefficiency" of indigenous communal land had been prescient of the next generations' concerns. Half a century later legislators debated new laws for communal ownership that, they hoped, would eventually pave the way for individual ownership and a sense of private property among indigenous people. Prieto documents multiple instances in which white-mestizo legislators discussed laws protecting indigenous communal land in terms of promoting eventual individual ownership of that land. Those arguments regularly assumed a particular indigenous connection to the land, hoping to capitalize on that "natural" affinity and direct it toward more cultured ends. Only a strong sense of private property, argued politicians and social scientists, would transform the Indian's love of the land into a modern sentiment appropriate for the progress of the nation.[60] Such arguments depended on a pervasive assumption that indigenous "cultivation" required a desire for private property.

At the same time those elites became skittish when it came to allowing indigenous people to own the land on which they lived and worked. They placed the possibility of indigenous uplift in a vague and indefinite future that would require several generations of indigenous education and evolution and ignored indigenous people's potential as landowners.[61] In a February 1935 column in *El Día*, the columnist Juan Fernández announced (and critiqued) the inaugural edition of the communist periodical *Nucanchic Allpa* ("Our land" in Kichwa). Fernández argued that the new periodical could not possibly be a "voice of the indigenous masses" as it claimed, because Indians lacked literacy and culture. Instead, he warned, the periodical was taking advantage of indigenous people's natural love of the land by promising them eventual ownership of it. That promise, Fernández claimed, was bound to fail because indigenous people lacked the necessary culture for sustained, efficient, and productive cultivation on their own.[62] Notably, the terms of culture and cultivation play a central role in Fernández's utterly circular arguments.

Though elites tried and failed to promote agricultural land ownership and colonization by white-mestizos and European immigrants, indigenous people were largely unsuccessful in their direct efforts to secure legal titles for land.[63] The terms of cultivation were the mediating force between these two seemingly contradictory tendencies (the stated desire to promote indigenous private ownership and the consistent failure to do so in practice). As long as indigenous people remained "uncultured," they were both fundamentally associated with the "uncultivated" land and seen as singularly incapable of appropriately modern sorts of ownership. Even those laws and policies designed to promote indigenous access to land evince considerable white-mestizo anxiety about the capabilities of indigenous people and promote systems of administration that make access to land a means of establishing parallel sorts of citizenship and participation.

Organized Cultivation

Indigenous organizing during the 1930s and 1940s made use of terms and arguments that ran parallel to the emphasis on the Indian problem in more dominant spheres. White-mestizo leftists, particularly communists, actively engaged indigenous communities, and some of Ecuador's prominent communists over the years were themselves indigenous.[64] Those activists—from both within and outside of indigenous communities—encouraged indigenous people to organize as rural laborers alongside their urban, working-class compatriots. Doing so, they tied terms of cultivation to terms of labor (for more on the labor front, see chapter 3). These organizing projects often focused more on class (on campesino identity) than on ethnicity (on indigeneity). Even so, the commonplaces eliding ruralness and Indianness meant that organizing peasants often meant organizing indígenas. Indeed, the pan-Highlands organization that first formed out of that leftist activity, despite billing itself as a campesino organization, was named the Federación Ecuatoriana de Indios (FEI, or Federation of *Indian* Ecuadorians; emphasis mine), and some of the strongest support for the FEI came in areas where indigenous people were already actively organizing themselves as indigenous communities.[65]

Ironically, white-mestizo elites regularly identified such planned and structured activity in indigenous communities in terms of an indigenous lack of cultivation. Juan Fernández's article about *Nucanchic Allpa* based its doubts as to the periodical's indigenous audience not only on the assumption that Indians were "illiterate [and] unlettered" but also that they were "without elements of culture but disposed to fierce and tenacious struggle" in "natural" defense of "the land that feeds them."[66] Just a few years earlier, in 1931, a proposed "Congress of Campesinos" that would have brought together Highlands indigenous communities and Coastal campesino groups to discuss land conflicts was canceled under pressure from government officials who argued that the congress "in reality could never have had this character [of a congress], given the ignorance of the participants—thousands of individuals completely lacking in culture."[67]

Despite these pervasive assumptions about indigenous cultural failings, indigenous communities also turned the arguments of culture against white-mestizos. Starting in the 1930s, according to Clark, indigenous communities regularly argued that "*campesinos* were the real producers of agricultural wealth in Ecuador," emphasizing their key role in cultivating the land.[68] In these claims, indigenous people positioned themselves as modern and productive, while landowners were backward inhibitors of national progress. The bilingual periodical *Nucanchic Allpa*, which Fernández so roundly dismissed, began appearing in 1935, organized by members of the groups that eventually formed the FEI. Though most issues of the periodical have been lost, the five known issues show a consistent concern with land, regularly articulated in terms of indigenous labor and cultivation.[69]

Later examples of the paper, from 1944 and 1946, include a woodblock-style header that places the title above a stylized, pre-Columbian geometric pattern meant to mimic textile and alongside a small, indigenista-style print of a poncho-clad man raising his left fist and grasping a traditional hand plow in his right. The group to whom the "our" of *Our Land* belongs is, here, firmly asserted in language (the choice of Kichwa), image (the indigenous farmer and his tools), and symbol (the textile pattern). "Our Land" is indigenous land. From the top of each page, then, the commonplace connection between indigeneity and land does important claiming work. It establishes indigenous people not only as *of* the land but also as the primary means of cultivating that land. The theme continues in the pages of the paper, where articles emphasize the plight of indigenous peons and *huasipungos* (sharecroppers), whose cultivating labor was exploited by affluent, white-mestizo Highlands landholders.

Beginning at least in the late 1920s, indigenous and campesino organizations critiqued the intentional blindness of terratenientes and state officials who were happy to exploit indigenous agricultural labor while denying indigenous people access to the fruits of that labor. As the authors of a resolution sent to the 1928 Constitutional Assembly noted, "the bosses and terratenientes have considered the producers of wealth as a part of their fields," as much their *property* as the land itself. Those authors fault the system of indigenous exploitation not only for the degraded state of indigenous people themselves but also for the larger poverty of the nation:

> The vast accumulation of land [by terratenientes] can be defended only by a specious and barbarous mentality, given that the biological needs of the terratenientes are the same as those of the great mass of dispossessed workers and for [those workers] only a parcel of productive land is sufficient. [It is because of] the enormous extensions of land covering unlimited virgin mountainsides where private property plays no role other than obstructing cultivation that there exist great masses of unemployed peasants in situations of anguish. . . . Not only does *Latifundismo* [the system of massive land control by a few affluent elites] fulfill no social mission of production, as some formerly believed [it did], it is a negative force in the common effort toward an improved economic condition for the entire country.

Savvy of the rhetorical and physical risks of their position, the authors of the resolution were careful to place their claims to indigenous cultivation in the service of national advancement. The backwardness of the latifundio system and the virgin land left uncultivated by the greed of the terratenientes are thus threats not only to indigenous people but to the country as a whole. Land left inculto by elite landholders leaves the nation inculto. The anguish it causes in the lives of indigenous peasants is socially immoral; the damage it does to the nation is economically and spiritually stunting. Part of the solution offered by this 1928 letter (and extended in later critiques and in elite arguments as well) was the formation of agricultural communes. In those communes, the authors argued, rather than "divid[ing] the land in order to enrich [them]selves," they would "work under a system of order [. . . to] stimulate greater production."[70] Common cultivation would lead to national improvements.

Similarly, in 1943 a group of indigenous people from Cayambe (north of Quito) requested that the state sell them two hundred hectares of land by suggesting that they were the ones who had tilled the "impenetrable and resistant mountain." They and their ancestors had turned that barren land into an "appreciable extension of tilled and cultivated land" and had "contributed, by [their] own hands, to the improvement of agriculture, the increase of national wealth, and the very progress of the nation."[71] In a 1945 manifesto supporting indigenous uprisings in Cayambe, the executive committee of the FEI described indigenous people as "the sustenance of the country's agriculture," declaring defiantly, "Our spirit has not died and our race is the productive majority of the country." Indigenous organization and resistance, they asserted, would not separate indigenous people from the land; rather, it was "the open road that will lead to us being powerful factors in the greatness of the nation."[72] Indigenous people, in other words, presented themselves as *the* source of national cultivation thanks to their stronger and longer-lasting relationship with the land, melding once again the two tendencies of the land-indigeneity topos. They also linked that cultivation to the broader idea of the national territory, using tilled land as a marker of national progress. Modern cultivation, in these arguments, came from and depended on the self-directed action of indigenous communities.

Defense of the Land

Given the images and texts they produced, it is clear that the artists and image makers of the mid-twentieth century were paying attention to the arguments advanced by indigenous communities and by their white-mestizo peers. They accessed activist, academic, and journalistic versions of the land-indigeneity topos and used them to envision more abstract themes of national territory and national identity. Such invocations of the topos for the sake of the nation appeared in their artwork and in the articles and reviews they wrote for one another. A representative article, written in 1945 by Gilberto González y Contreras, traces the origins of social-realist art in Latin America to indigenous soil. González y Contreras's "Aclaraciones a la novela social americana" (Clarifications to the American social novel) argues against the popular assumption that such art was fundamentally Marxist (and therefore externally imposed rather than born of the nation itself). Instead, it locates the origins of what González y Contreras calls "social art" in the emergence of a truly *American* identity and the rejection of colonial classicism. Modern art's concern for social issues, González y Contreras asserts, is fundamentally telluric: "Art became an art with American sentiment the day that it began to pose problems of existence, acquiring a human quality and aligning itself profoundly with the land." Here, González y Contreras's emphasis on the "profound sense of the land" bleeds easily into an emphasis on the people, particularly the popular classes: the telluric is "made up of the landscape and the soul of the people [*pueblo*]."[73] Art defended the land, and, in so doing, it offered a defense not only of exploited indigenous people but of the nation as a whole.

The nation's foundation in the land allowed midcentury image makers to claim both their content and their style as authentic to their place. An interview with the young Ecuadorian artists Galo Galecio and Carlos Rodríguez, originally published in Mexico and possibly reprinted in Ecuador, advances exactly this claim.[74] In it, the interviewer suggests that the similarities among Mexican and Ecuadorian art arise not from Mexico's direct influence but from common ground, saying, "it is simply that they all have been fed by the same American roots." In other words, the similar aesthetics at work in the two countries developed because a shared American soil inclined far-flung artists to produce similarly themed, profoundly social, indigenista work. The land, referentially indigenous, fed American identity and gave Ecuadorian art a profoundly autochthonous character.

Benjamín Carrión took that generalized focus on American landscape and narrowed it to the scope of Ecuadorian territory when he argued that the pre-Columbian peoples of Ecuador had left vocations for the arts and for liberty behind in the land itself. Similarly, the novelist Jorge Icaza argued for a particularly Ecuadorian identity drawn from the land in his speech at the opening of the first national salon of fine arts in 1945. Quoting an unknown source (possibly Carrión), Icaza declared that it was common knowledge that "our destiny is tied to the acts of those who came before us on the road and to the very structure of the land on which we were born."[75] In this narrative a truly popular Ecuadorian art emerged from the land, cultivated the earth, and drew its nourishment from the soil. That telluric character formed the basis of indigenismo's argument for the nation.

Such profound reliance on the land spoke to a particularly strong vein of left-leaning nationalism that appeared in the wake of the 1942 crisis and was intensified by the 1944 Revolución Gloriosa (Glorious Revolution), in which a populist coalition of leftist and conservative forces ousted the president responsible for the disastrous capitulation to Peru. The Casa de la Cultura and its periodical, *Letras del Ecuador*, were born out of that upheaval, and art and nationalism went hand in hand in its pages. In an early issue, the speech by Icaza referenced earlier appeared alongside an excerpt from a speech given by President José María Velasco Ibarra at the same event. In his speech Velasco Ibarra extolled the arts as essential to crafting the "sensibilities" and the "spiritual emotions" of a nation, noting, "just today I have seen . . . a painting that in just one viewing was more valuable than reading several volumes of social economics."[76] Ever a populist, Velasco Ibarra's words likely reflect the mood among the left-leaning intellectual and artistic elite to whom he was speaking, though he was certainly exaggerating well beyond his own beliefs.[77] The members of that audience, Quito's leading artists and intellectuals, saw their paintings, their prints, and their texts as directly combating the problems facing the nation and as offering a powerful sense of national identity during a decade of crises.

Through topoi of land, indigenista artists linked images of indigenous struggle with a narrative of national struggle. Such a move is clearly visible in the woodblock prints of Eduardo Kingman's 1937 album *Hombres del Ecuador* (Men of Ecuador). Fifteen of Kingman's twenty-four prints feature clearly indigenous subjects, and many move implicitly from indigenous use of the land to the national struggle for development. Every one of the album's thirteen rural images features indigenous people. Eight of them show indigenous people directly involved in cultivation (see figs. 18 and 19), three capture moments of rest from cultivation, and another two invoke communal action related to the land (the celebration of the harvest festival of San Juan, or Inti Raymi, and a land rebellion) (see fig. 20). As they plant and harvest, Kingman's indigenous figures seem to echo the land—hunched like the hills behind them. Their heavy bodies, broad hands and feet, and wide stances make them part of the land, visually, and suggest that they draw sustenance from it. Kingman's title makes his album explicitly a depiction of the nation: his images of indigenous people on the land are meant to make a statement about national identity and national territory.

Though most of Kingman's images of cultivation depict indigenous people using traditional means of cultivation, thus emphasizing indigenous rusticity, they also clearly imagine indigenous people as tied to the land through cultivation and mark the agricultural production of the nation as indigenous. In this way Kingman appears to align himself more with the arguments of indigenous communities than with those of his white-mestizo compatriots.

Fig. 18.   Eduardo Kingman, *Los huachos*, 1937. Woodblock print on paper. In Kingman, *Hombres del Ecuador*. Collection of the Fundación Posada de las Artes Kingman.

The means of production may suggest significant rusticity, but the cultivation of the land appears dignified.

This constant move from indigenous land to national land suggests that though *Hombres* was published five years before the 1942 crisis, it is still possible to read the second-to-last print of the album, titled *Defensa de la tierra* (Defense of the land), as both a commentary on land reform and a larger allegory for the defense of national territory against more powerful neighbors (fig. 20). The print features a crowd of indigenous men engaged in a land action, defending a highland field from an unknown assailant. Wielding cudgels held over their heads, the mass of men surges from the right margin of the page toward the left, using common action to defend the land. Though

Fig. 19.   Eduardo Kingman, *Sembradores*, 1937. Woodblock print on paper. In Kingman, *Hombres del Ecuador*. Collection of the Fundación Posada de las Artes Kingman.

the print's immediate subject is the violent struggle for agrarian land reform, its vague invocation of "defense" and its lack of a specific, pictured enemy also links it to a long-standing national narrative that envisioned the country as a whole beset by greedy neighbors looking to invade its territory. Peru's successful annexation of Ecuadorian territory in 1942 was preceded by border conflicts dating from at least the late colonial period. During the second half of the nineteenth century, Peru made several efforts to claim Ecuadorian territory, and the exigency around mapping national territory expressed in Villavicencio's 1858 *Geografía de la república del Ecuador* explicitly invoked the rapacious incursions of neighboring countries, especially Peru.

Fig. 20.   Eduardo Kingman, *Defensa de la tierra*. Woodblock print on paper, 1937.
In Kingman, *Hombres del Ecuador*. Collection of the Fundación Posada de las Artes
Kingman.

Though Kingman's *Defensa* predates the quotation from Carrión's letters that opens this chapter, it partakes of the same national spirit. It imagines the urgency of conflict and the spirit of the nation as heightened by
the land itself. Echoing the themes carried across time and genre by the
land-indigeneity topos, Kingman's rebelling indígenas and Carrión's telluric *pueblo* are profoundly of the earth and directly inspired by it. Defense of
the land is tied to defense of the right to cultivate the land. Cultivation and
defense of the land are, in turn, linked to the cultivation and defense of the
nation, of national territory, and of a sense of national culture.

A Nation Built on Solid Ground

From the nineteenth century to the mid-twentieth, the land-indigeneity topos provided both white-mestizos and indigenous people a powerful means for advancing claims to land. It gave them a flexible and resilient place of return in changing circumstances. In both eras that topos also authorized the extension and defense of territory as national concerns. Though it was engaged in contradictory ways by indigenous people and white-mestizos, the land-indigeneity topos tended overall to buttress national visions that advanced white-mestizo versions of progress and modernity. The rhetorical landscape that Gregory Clark introduces (for the U.S. context) as predominantly oriented toward the symbolic experience of national identity should be understood as having force in material terms as well. If landscape is defined as the symbolic experience of the land, its interpretive and definitive power still should not be divorced from its effects on the material experience of land. The functioning of land-indigeneity topoi in the Ecuadorian context demonstrates this simultaneously symbolic and material effects of rhetorical landscape. Assumptions about the peculiar connection between indigenous people and the land underlay symbolic geographies that fostered and encouraged key forms of Ecuadorian nationalism. Those symbolic geographies, in turn, authorized policies and practices that frequently disenfranchised indigenous landholders but that also facilitated specific opportunities for resistance (always, of course, within the dominating narrative of the state).

The land-indigeneity topos, like the topoi analyzed in coming chapters, gained much of that constitutive force from its ability to index and shape Ecuadorians' experiences of the nation over time. It was deeply integrated into the national imaginary, into artistic and intellectual understandings of national society, and into policies governing agriculture, citizenship, and property. Though the particular terms of the topos shifted from the end of the nineteenth century to the middle of the twentieth, its commonsense explanatory power remained remarkably consistent. If the narrative of national history became more complex after the first decades of the twentieth century, the resulting discussions of indigenous peoples' long history of rusticity were easily accommodated within the topos' twin emphases on history and cultivation.

The next chapter considers how images of indigenous labor expanded the narratives of progress and modernity introduced here. Because so much of indigenous labor was imagined as rural and agricultural, many of the commonplaces of land coexist with those invoking labor. Chapter 3 demonstrates, however, how an emphasis on labor was intended not only to tame the uncultivated, unproductive land but also to build and reform the greatness of the nation.

3
BURDENS OF THE NATION

[In Ecuador] while horses and mules are called *bagajes mayores*, asses
and Indians are called *bagajes menores*; that is to say, as a beast of burden,
the Indian is considered below the horse and the mule, and on a level
with the donkey.

—FRIEDRICH HASSAUREK, *FOUR YEARS AMONG SPANISH-AMERICANS*, 1868

The Indians of Ecuador reflect the environment in which they live: they
are poor but hardworking and strong.

—VICTOR GABRIEL GARCÉS, "CONDICIONES DE VIDA," 1946

From the supply lines for the wars of independence to the *conscripción vial*
(road conscription) of the mid-twentieth century, indigenous people literally
carried the burdens of Ecuador as it pursued regional integration, modernization, and republican stability. Indigenous porters carried equipment for
the travelers who arrived to summit mountains, tour cities, and establish
schools during the nineteenth century. Sometimes, they carried the travelers themselves. Indigenous *peones* helped lay the track for the railway from
coastal Guayaquil to highland Quito, not only for the successful effort completed in 1908 but also for several previous, aborted attempts.[1] Indigenous
conciertos, huasipungos, and *comuneros* (debt slaves, sharecroppers, and
communal farmers) worked the land, providing subsistence for themselves,
foodstuffs for the residents of nearby towns, profit for white-mestizo landowners, and tax income for the national coffers. During the nineteenth century indigenous people disproportionately paid taxes in money and labor
and supported the Catholic Church through the *diezmo* (obligatory tithe).
Directly and indirectly, during the near century between the presidencies of
Gabriel García Moreno (1861–75) and the period of democratic stability under
Galo Plaza Lasso (1948–52), indigenous people provided much of the labor

that brought to fruition Ecuadorian projects of infrastructure improvement and modernization, especially in the Highlands.

Yet if the arguments circulated by white-mestizos throughout that period are to be believed, indigenous people also bore the brunt of responsibility for years of slow national progress and underdevelopment. They were—according to those arguments—brutish, slow to adapt, fractious, and dull. The modes of production they employed were primitive and inefficient. Because of their poverty and communal insularity, they failed to participate in the nation as modern consumers. In that national story, if Ecuador tarried in its journey toward greatness, it was because indigenous people were a "dead weight" that dragged it down, no matter that their labor made the projects of modernity possible. There was a flip side to that narrative that ascribed responsibility for national failure to indigenous people, however. In it, indigenous workers—properly educated, properly docile, properly organized—could provide the solution for all that ailed the country, if only they would accede to the authority of white-mestizo culture.[2] Those projects and narratives of modernity consistently kept a troubling, constitutive pattern in the national foreground. In it, the road to modernity was paved, physically and symbolically, by the labor of Indians.

This chapter approaches that pattern of indigenous labor as a nation-making topos. Rather than tracing how indigenous labor itself sustained projects of national modernization, it examines how commonplace depictions of that labor provided, as Robert Hariman and John Louis Lucaites say of U.S. iconic photographs, "generic forms of assurance regarding the existence, nature, and legitimacy of the public world," especially "when events [were] chaotic, dangerous, or disturbing."[3] This rhetorical history of indigenous labor demonstrates how consistently arguments providing "generic forms of assurance" about national development relied on visions of indigenous labor—as rustic, as threatening, as essential, and as fundamentally available. In shifting but overlapping ways the Indian worker stood in, synecdochally, for national problems, national resources, and national potentials.

Indian laborers hammered out a leitmotif of effort beneath the exhortative melodies of modern progress. Their participation in public works projects was omnipresent, and their depiction in visual and textual images of the labor required for national life was ubiquitous. Scenes of indigenous labor consistently served as places of return in the arguments over national modernity that recurred throughout the nineteenth and twentieth centuries. Such topoi worked differently at the beginning and the end of that long period—in the nineteenth century they emphasized labor over laborers, and in the twentieth, they emphasized workers more than work itself. Throughout both centuries, however, those topoi consistently mediated among conflicting visions for the national future and provided a sense of stability that obscured the fissures transecting efforts at nation building. As the pages ahead demonstrate, from costumbrismo, labor evasion, and hortatory images of progress during the late nineteenth century to indigenismo, communist organizing, and developmentalism in the mid-twentieth, images of available but resistant, essential but problematic Indian workers inextricably linked indigenous labor to the construction of a modern nation.

If the commonplace connection between indigenous people and the land explored in the previous chapter allowed white-mestizos to claim the national territory, topoi of indigenous labor authorized a corollary narrative of nation *building*. They provided a place of return in changing circumstances that accounted for the nation-state's dependence on its indigenous population for modern progress without necessarily incorporating that population *as indigenous* into the modern nation. The next two sections track the different but overlapping uses of laboring topoi in the nineteenth and twentieth centuries. Each section opens with a visual example and then looks in more depth at the ways that political elites, indigenous communities, and artists engaged those familiar patterns in generative ways. The chapter's conclusion unravels the cumulative effects of such topoi, particularly their corroboration of the idea of a white-mestizo nation.

Available Means of Production

In the last years of the nineteenth century, the artist Joaquín Pinto began preparing an album of costumbrista watercolors for his friend Francisco Cousin, the son of a French naturalist who had employed Pinto as an illustrator. The resulting "Album de personajes populares" (Album of popular characters) contains forty-four pages depicting eighty-three separate paintings, each signed and dated by the artist. The album represents the height of Pinto's costumbrista skill, showing the exquisite detail that emerged from his commitment to realism and painting "from life." These watercolors also evince Pinto's fascination with popular figures, especially the indígenas, whose labor was both marginal and integral to Quito's existence as a city. The album's depiction of Quito's popular characters, its attention to detail, and its sympathetic portrayal of its subjects exemplify why Pinto is considered one of the first Ecuadorian artists to paint the nation through truly local eyes.[4]

The "Album de personajes populares" features many scenes of Quito's popular classes laboring at the daily activities of urban life: bringing food to market, selling basic necessities, providing products and services.[5] Of the album's eighty-three scenes, at least half show figures whom Pinto's contemporaries would have automatically recognized as indigenous because of their occupations, dress, or physiognomy. Several of those images show indigenous laborers whose occupations would have signaled to Pinto's contemporaries the labor obligations established between urban Quito and its outlying indigenous communities—lamplighters, road builders, and masons conscripted to work on the construction of the new basilica.

Pinto's *Nayón que pone el alumbrado* ([Indian of] Nayón who sets the lighting), for example, invokes the men from the nearby indigenous community of Nayón who were responsible for maintaining Quito's streetlights for much of the nineteenth century (fig. 21). The Nayón of the title appears alone in the scene. He wears his community's typical garb: a soft hat, long tunic, short pants, and, instead of a poncho, a swath of fabric draped over one side of his body and tied at the opposite shoulder. The young, barefoot man stands gazing away from the viewer, toward the empty space above his left shoulder. Along with his indirect gaze, his open stance—turned just slightly from the front—makes the figure available to the viewer's observation. It instills as well a sense that the man was caught in the midst of motion and extracted from a more complete city scene. That sense of abstraction invokes the surrounding city through its absence, an impression emphasized by the ruddy glow thrown onto the lamplighter's body but not the surrounding page by the lantern he holds in his right hand. Appearing on a blank page, this Nayón lamplighter is in one sense very much out of time and context. Yet he is also clearly placed within the city by the detail of Pinto's brush and by the title that invokes a shared knowledge of where, why, and under what circumstances this Nayón "sets the lighting."

The Nayón, with his basket of wax tapers meant for lanterns around the city, was an incipiently anachronistic figure in Quito when Pinto painted him in 1901. A system of electric lighting was inaugurated there on May 24, 1899. That first extension of electricity was limited, though, so outlying neighborhoods and private homes likely still relied on the lamp-lighting labor of men from Nayón.[6] Pinto may also have been painting from a photograph or sketch done earlier in the century. The risk of anachronism, however, only aids the underlying message of the image, in which the always amodern Indian acquiesces to work in the service of enlightenment. Images like Pinto's *Nayón* placed indigenous labor in willing subordination to modern

Fig. 21.   Joaquín Pinto, *Nayón que pone el alumbrado*, 1901. Watercolor on paper. In Pinto, "Album de personajes populares." Private collection.

life. In the process they helped authorize narratives of national progress that left those rustic Indians behind. If such images made visible the systems of labor exploitation that underlay development, they also naturalized and romanticized them, depicting compliant Indians serving the needs of the white-mestizo city.

Though many turn-of-the-century white-mestizo elites expressed chagrin at their nation's lack of modernity, they regularly engaged "uncivilized" indigenous labor such as that of the men from Nayón to achieve an appearance of progress (lighting, clean streets, etc.). The arrival of modernity in Ecuador, in fact, depended on systems of labor conscription and exploitation inherited from colonial practice.[7] Those neocolonial labor relationships haunted elite conversations about the creation of a modern city. The minutes of city council meetings from the eras preceding the installation of electric lighting in Quito, for example, show regular discussions about modernizing the city's lighting. Those minutes, however, never refer directly to the current system of lighting, leaving the labor contributed by Nayónes just outside the margins of official discussion.[8] Such omission reveals a deep preoccupation with progress that tied the idea of a more modern city to its literal enlightenment but could not admit that such a system was dependent on indigenous labor. The nighttime labor of the Nayón rendered in Pinto's watercolor was both required to achieve modernity and omitted from discussion, owing to its assumed fundamental lack of modernity.

Though art historians generally agree that all costumbrista images should be seen in terms of an emerging national identity, images of conscripted laborers like Pinto's *Nayón* are among the clearest examples of artists' linking indigenous labor and nation building. Pinto was not alone among costumbrista artists in his depiction of such labor. In fact, his album leaves out one of the most commonly reproduced figures: the street sweepers from Zámbiza who were responsible for maintaining urban hygiene (fig. 22). Showing the indigenous men recruited to build roads, clean streets, and light lamps linked costumbrista artists' work to larger projects of infrastructure creation—projects designed and carried out to promote national well-being in symbolic and material senses. Such images, then, contribute simultaneously to a semblance of national modernity and a romantic vision of pastoral rusticity. Such romanticized versions of indigenous labor and urban enlightenment worked alongside hopeful plans for national infrastructure development to circulate narratives of progress and modernity. Those narratives covered over a more contentious history of indigenous exploitation and resistance. The remainder of this section unearths those buried scenes in three

Fig. 22. Juan Agustín Guerrero, *Yndia de Sambisa á quien la policia hace barer las calles*, 1852. Watercolor on paper. Reprinted by the Fundación Wilson Hallo, 1981. In Guerrero, *Imágenes del Ecuador*. Photograph by Jessie Reeder.

layers, digging more deeply into the rhetorical work of nineteenth-century laboring topoi as they appeared in elite narratives of labor and progress, in indigenous resistance to forced conscription, and in the mediating images of costumbrismo. It reveals, along the way, the firm yet fractured commonplace foundations on which the nineteenth-century nation built itself.

Building Toward Modernity

For much of the nineteenth century, regional and local identities trumped national ones, and many Ecuadorians saw minimal benefit in the idea of an integrated national whole. Infrastructure, or rather its lack, played a significant role in that sense of regional division. The routes of communication among Ecuador's major cities and regions were treacherous and in poor repair. Within the Highlands, the rugged terrain limited interactions even among neighboring valleys.[9] As a consequence, when governments at midcentury began to see the economic and political benefits of national integration, their attention turned quickly to the problem of infrastructure construction. Beginning in the 1850s and continuing through at least the 1910s, Ecuadorian governments across political spectrums advocated infrastructure improvement and the civilizing benefits of labor as key to establishing a truly modern and fully integrated nation-state. Though each new political era announced itself as a break with the past, administration after administration used strikingly similar, labor- and infrastructure-inflected language to imagine a hopeful future emerging from the struggles of the present.

An 1862 letter to the Municipal Council of Quito, for example, extolled the "dawn of national progress" under the new García Moreno administration, praising especially the president's proposal to build a highway from the capital to the coast. That project and the labor it demanded, the letter writer argued, would encourage not only industry and commerce but also good character and improved civilization.[10] Similarly, in a Progressive Era volume commemorating Ecuador's role in the 1893 Chicago World's Fair, President Luís Cordero and his ministers offered a hopeful vision of the developing nation that praised the labor of those pursuing "the definitive triumph of liberty and justice" through infrastructure development. Because of that "incessant labor in favor of progress," the national laws "are liberal and humanitarian . . . public education gains each day greater extension . . . the Treasury is scientifically reorganized . . . [and] Public Works progress. . . . In a word, Ecuador is today a rich, progressive, and honorable nation that enjoys the greater part of the principal elements of modern civilization."[11] Writing three years and one revolution later, the Liberal politician José Mora Lopez used the same language of infrastructure and progress as his Conservative and Progressive compatriots. He praised the Liberal triumph as the culmination of an inevitable story of progress, depicting the proposed railway connecting Guayaquil and Quito as "that powerful resource belonging to all the peoples of the world [that] will be for us not only a source of wealth but a resource for social progress." He continued, "Steam and locomotive represent not only the change of production and industry, they will in turn carry with them . . . the civilizing ideal. . . . [They will] carry generous blood to share with all the members of the great human family." The Liberal Ministry of Public Instruction, in its 1900 report to Congress, further imagined national greatness as flowing from work: "Labor is the basis of social morality and of the betterment of peoples. . . . Manual labor must necessarily be united with the other elements of education, if we want to secure the foundations of greatness and prosperity for the Republic."[12]

As those sentiments drawn from distinctly different political contexts suggest, labor, mobility, and progress were watchwords whose force transcended ideological position. Such claims to the benefits of labor and infrastructure improvement also coincided in their strange abstraction. *Labor* ennobled and improved. *Laborers* were conspicuously left in the background. That indirect treatment of the men and women whose effort built modernity can likely be traced to the fraught social status of those who labored. No matter which party held political power, their plans for development and public works consistently relied on the efforts of indigenous people for their fruition.[13] Even Liberals, whose rise to power brought a dramatic increase in explicit discussions of the exploited status of indigenous people, turned repeatedly to a conscription system that disproportionately drew unwilling indigenous labor. Local and regional authorities directly responsible for public works rarely strayed from traditional labor relationships like those visible in Pinto's album and other costumbrista images.

The much-vaunted projects of modernization and national progress, in other words, depended on labor relationships inherited from the colonial era in which indigenous people were drafted, sometimes forcibly, for public works that rarely benefited their communities.[14] It is not surprising, then, that references to labor proliferated while discussions of laborers did not. White-mestizo political elites summoned their white-mestizo compatriots to identification with a vision of national progress and modernity, but achieving that vision depended on the labor of indigenous people. Drawing attention to the national reliance on supposedly premodern workers would only undermine the project of elite identification. Instead, labor might ennoble, but those laboring and those being ennobled were decidedly not the same.

Evading Modernity

Not surprisingly, those colonial labor relationships became sites of significant conflict as the contradictions between modern progress and neocolonial
exploitation played out at the local level. Public documents from Quito in the
second half of the nineteenth century show that conscripting *peones* from
the municipality's indigenous parishes for public infrastructure projects was
common practice. Those public documents also, however, demonstrate that
the acquisition of indigenous labor was a contested and conflict-filled matter.
Local authorities resisted the municipality's efforts to draw labor into the city,
sometimes by invoking the prior claims on indigenous labor made by the
central state and sometimes by explaining that those laborers were already
involved in local projects. Likewise, indigenous communities consistently
sought to evade public works conscription. They disappeared into the mountains when the local police arrived to "recruit" them, and they established
debt obligations with local hacienda owners that disqualified them from
municipal conscription. Especially after the beginning of the Liberal Era (in
1895), indigenous people around Quito petitioned the government to protest
the illegal use of force in recruitment, pitting the state against local authorities and thwarting the progress of public works projects.[15]

In Quito's municipal archives, indigenous resistance to public works conscription usually appears between the lines of reports written by parish-level
authorities—*tenientes políticos* (political lieutenants) and *jueces civiles* (civil
judges). Those reports sent to the *jefe político* (appointed executive of the canton) or the *cabildo* (municipal council) most often reference indigenous peons' direct strategies of evasion, such as traveling to the coast in search of
work or establishing contractual relationships with neighboring haciendas.
Sometimes, however, reports from local authorities reveal the more explicitly
rhetorical strategies used by reluctant indigenous laborers to avoid conscription. Indigenous recruits most often raised practical objections or appealed to
the charity of white-mestizo authorities in their evasion efforts. Two tenientes
políticos, writing in 1870 and 1897, for example, informed their municipal
superiors that they could not find any unmarried indigenous men to work
and implied that indigenous men with families had objected to being conscripted away from their responsibilities as heads of households.[16] Similarly,
potential peons apparently argued that they were too infirm or aged to contribute the heavy labor required for infrastructure improvement, given the
extensive discussion of age as a factor for recruitment in an 1870 letter from
the parish of Alangasí and a January 1895 letter rejecting a peon based on

infirmity.[17] A missive from Cumbayá in the spring of 1894 suggests that indigenous communities might also have used religious obligations to excuse themselves. That letter explains that local authorities could not provide peons because the free indigenous people in the parish had "many occupations" for which they were responsible during Holy Week and therefore could not work.[18] Perhaps most commonly, indigenous people in Quito objected to the conscription of able-bodied men during the harvest, pointing to the risk of losing their primary means of survival.[19] A. Kim Clark notes that indigenous communities in the province of Chimborazo similarly resisted conscription during the height of the agricultural cycle with arguments that their absence could result in the loss of crops and the means of subsistence.[20]

All these intimations of resistance, filtered through the voices of local authorities, suggest that indigenous people were not content to be the available laborers whose efforts benefited the plans of the white-mestizo elite. They objected using the means available to them. Though we cannot know the specifics of those arguments, mediated as they are by reports written by white-mestizos, the frequency with which parish authorities reported trouble with labor conscription suggests that indigenous people found many ways to resist conscription, even during the Conservative and Progressive Eras, when indigenous objections were of less concern to the state.

The arrival of the Liberal Era did, however, make new arguments available for indigenous peons in their battles over labor conscription. Notably, those available means of persuasion included new appropriations of the terms of labor, modernity, and nation building that were circulated by Liberal elites. As Clark demonstrates of indigenous communities in Chimborazo, indigenous communities around Quito appear to have used allegations of illegal recruitment and appeals to renewed national ideals as means of arguing against conscription.[21] The ideals that white-mestizos pursued by exploiting indigenous labor were also useful for indigenous petitioners as they contested that exploitation.

Such strategies are clear, for example, in a three-way exchange between the indigenous leaders of Zámbiza, the cabildo, and the landowner Carlos Larrea G. In a letter dated July 1897, Larrea alerts the council to the bad state of the road that connects Zámbiza, Nayón, and "other diverse [locales]" by passing through his hacienda.[22] Drawing on commonplaces of indigenous misery and white-mestizo paternalism (discussed further in chapter 5), Larrea notes that a bridge on the path is especially treacherous and has led to the deaths of some indigenous people. He continues, "This has moved me to propose that I take on the improvement of said path." Though Larrea offers to fund those improvements, he requests that the municipality provide him with peons for the labor. Invoking civic duty and the ideals of modern efficiency and infrastructure improvement, Larrea notes that his project would cost "the Municipality absolutely nothing and . . . [will benefit] her greatly, owing to the public use of [the road and bridge]." In Larrea's terms the use of indigenous labor is justified both by the fact that the project would avoid the further loss of indigenous life and because the public would benefit from the project. It is an added plus that the project would cost the municipality nothing, but "benefit her greatly." Larrea, in other words, situates his proposal in terms of paternalistic concern and civic duty, emphasizing that it is in the interest of the modern municipality to accept his offer.

Responding a few days later, the indigenous leaders of Zámbiza and Nayón tell a different story.[23] They submitted a long letter to the municipality "expounding the just reasons that we present for why we are not able to contribute our personal labor" to the project. Their objection covers several topics, including the communities' preexisting labor obligations for the city of Quito. The primary force of their refusal, however, lies in their suggestion that Larrea's investment in the project is self-interested. According to the indigenous petitioners, the bridge caused very little trouble for their communities, but its bad state of repair prevented Larrea from driving his cattle to market. Where Larrea invokes the public good, in other words, his indigenous respondents claim private interest.

Both sides of the exchange engage topoi of indigenous labor and national modernity to present their positions and mediate the conflict. Larrea draws on the misery of the uncivilized indígena and the assumption that indigenous laborers ought to contribute to the improvement of the nation. The indigenous people of Nayón and Zámbiza present themselves, instead, as exploited laborers who need the aid of the council to protect them from a rapacious landowner. Both parties word their petitions so that the terms of state intervention are predicated on the topoi of indigenous labor and its connection to the state of the nation. Their arguments rest on a shared assumption that it was expected, maybe even appropriate, for indigenous laborers to contribute to nation building. Infrastructure improvements and the demand for urban hygiene were compelling, modern needs for which conscription was justified. Problems arose, then, not because of labor conscription itself but because Larrea's aim was private gain, not public progress.

Over the course of the late nineteenth century, the evolving, sometimes piecemeal rhetorical tactics employed by indigenous people to resist public works conscription frequently made use of the terms of laboring topoi even as they contested white-mestizo authority. They sought to bend the contradictions of the modern/amodern nation-state to indigenous benefit and limit opportunities for elite white-mestizos to exploit indigenous labor. Clark's observation with regard to the Liberal Era in Chimborazo holds true in Pichincha (Quito's province) as well: "Repeatedly, Indians appropriated the discourse of the central state, and rather forcefully and cogently argued that they were timid and ignorant and thus deserved protection from the state, particularly in relation to labour issues."[24] By necessity, however, such arguments accepted the commonplace terms of debate. Indigenous labor remained a public good in service to national progress.

Costumbrismo and the Available Laborer

State and municipal officials glorified labor and positioned public works projects as part of a coherent narrative of modern progress; indigenous resistance called attention to the laborers who made public works possible and interrupted the claims of infrastructure improvement for common benefit. For their part, costumbrista images played a middle role between the hortatory exclamations of political leaders and the conflicts of actual labor conscription. They revealed yet constrained the means of production. From Juan Agustín Guerrero's 1852 watercolor of a man from Sambisa (Zámbiza) sweeping Quito's streets (fig. 22), to Pinto's 1901 painting of an indigenous peon shoveling a pile of earth (fig. 23), costumbrista images made visible the nation-building project's reliance on exploited indigenous effort. At the same time, those images showed indigenous workers as fundamentally *available* to white-mestizo observation and conscription. In costumbrismo, indigenous laborers—though exploited—were mostly docile. Their labor still stood in for the projects of modernity, and they still remained outside the progress they provided.

It is, of course, possible to argue that these costumbrista paintings merely depict reality. Despite resistance and evasion, nineteenth-century white-mestizo elites were generally successful in securing the labor of indigenous people for public (and private) projects of maintenance and construction. In the case of the bridge on Carlos Larrea's land, for example, the communities of Nayón and Zámbiza did evade conscription. Other documents suggest, however, that the municipality simply turned to another indigenous community to recruit laborers. That inescapable claim to labor was enacted sometimes through physical force and sometimes through other, seemingly softer means of coercion, but it did mean that indigenous laborers were common

Fig. 23.   Joaquín Pinto, *Longuito peon*, 1901. Watercolor on paper. In Pinto, "Album de personajes populares." Private collection.

figures at work on the roads and bridges of the canton. Yet the depiction of mere reality is never an ideologically neutral activity.

The chosen point of view in costumbrista images and their attendant framing of reality tell us a great deal about the patterns that give them force as suasive objects. In the case of Pinto's work, it is worth noting the difference between a sketch of a landscape "where there was an indigenous rebellion in the time of García Moreno" and the *Nayón, Longuito peon,* and *Albañil* (mason, bricklayer) images from his album (figs. 21, 23, and 24). All four images reference the history of public works labor. The rebellion mentioned in the title of Pinto's sketch began as an attack on two officials responsible for drafting labor and another who collected the *diezmo.*[25] Eduardo Kingman Garcés, Ana María Goetschel, and Cecilia Mantilla note that the increase in indigenous rebellion during García Moreno's administration can be tied directly to his expanded programs of forced labor conscription for national infrastructure construction.[26] Despite the clear invocation of indigenous agency in the title, however, Pinto's scene of that rebellion is depopulated. The indigenous rebellion of the title has faded into the land and been washed over by the passing decades of white-mestizo dominance. Pinto's costumbrista figures, on the other hand, are engaged in the tasks set for them by elites, and it is those power holders whose influencing hand is markedly absent. The Nayón carries his tapers and lantern; the indigenous peon drives his shovel into the ground; the poncho-clad albañil spreads mortar on an invisible wall. If these images of indigenous people as available means of production are strategic framings of reality, they are also part of the available means of persuasion for white-mestizo elites who would have been simultaneously aware of indigenous resistance and deeply invested in imaging a nation-state in control of its corps of indigenous labor and en route to national development.

My suggestion that costumbrista paintings bring a political charge to questions of indigenous labor is supported as well by the social messages the artists themselves left behind. Guerrero, for example, offers a less-than-subtle critique of Quiteño social relations in his painting of a street sweeper from Zámbiza, captioned "Indian of Sambisa [*sic*] whom the police make sweep the streets" (fig. 22). Guerrero produced other sardonic depictions of the relationship between white-mestizo elites and indigenous people, including a painting of an indigenous shepherd pleading with a Franciscan priest who, "begging" for alms, demands several sheep from the shepherd's flock.

Pinto, though his political leanings were more conservative than Guerrero's, similarly integrated commentary into his costumbrismo. He used fragments of popular songs to caption some of his paintings, engaging

Fig. 24.   Joaquín Pinto, *Albañil*, 1900. Watercolor on paper. In Pinto, "Album de personajes populares." Private collection.

Fig. 25.   Joaquín Pinto, *Indio cargando un bulto*, 1900. Pencil on paper. Collection of Modern and Republican Art, Ecuadorian Ministry of Culture, Quito, Ecuador.

their light social critique to question Quito's labor relations. On the reverse of a sketch titled *Indio cargando un bulto* (Indian carrying a bundle; fig. 25), for example, Pinto wrote,

> Dos pantalones me han dado
> Ambos p' amor de Dios
> Con el mas ancho me quedo
> El angosto es para vos;

Los pobres comen moyuelo
Y los ricos comen ave
Para los pobres hay cielo
Para los ricos Quien sabe!

[I've been given two pairs of pants
Both for the love of God
I'll keep the larger pair
The smaller is for you;
The poor eat grits
And the rich eat fowl
The poor go to heaven
The rich, Who knows!]

Pinto drew these *coplas* from a collection of popular songs compiled in 1892 by Juan León Mera. The Conservative Mera shared Guerrero and Pinto's concern for the "miserable Indian," seeing indigenous laborers as a source of obligation for white-mestizo elites. Mera was also deeply concerned with establishing the nation, and he regularly invoked popular traditions to create a sense of national particularity.[27] Pinto's use of Mera's songs to caption his paintings and sketches thus positions Pinto's work in conversation with both the social critique offered by the songs themselves and the folkloric project essayed by Mera. The combination of those moves suggests that Pinto wanted his viewers to see the subjects of his paintings as typically Ecuadorian and as meriting national attention. Pinto, Guerrero, and Mera, in other words, used commonplace images to call attention to indigenous labor. Their sights, however, were set on national vision.

In its effort to picture the nation, costumbrismo practiced what Margaret LaWare calls "visual epideictic": it forwarded "claims about the community it addresses, [and] about how [that community] should view itself" in ways that encouraged that community to "witness the present" and that "make visible the previously invisible."[28] In this sense of national praise and blame, the mild social commentary of costumbrismo overlaps significantly with its portrayal of the available laborer. Making visible the means of national progress, these images called white-mestizos not so much to a changed vision of indigenous laborers as to an appreciation of the full national scene. They did call attention to laborers, in a way, but their images still reduced laborers to their occupations, to social types. These social types then provided an exhortative moderation for white-mestizo viewers. They deemphasized indigenous resistance in favor of an appeal to elites' own paternalistic intervention. The topoi of indigenous labor circulated in costumbrismo identified the problem of exploitation but altered the terms of conflict. They placed laboring social types in the service of the nation and invoked a corollary responsibility in elites based on that labor.

When wielded by white-mestizos, nineteenth-century topoi of indigenous labor emphasized labor—the building of roads, the sweeping of streets, the possibility of modernity—rather than the workers enacting that labor. In visual contexts such visions of labor placed more emphasis on the type and nature of the work done (the lamplighter, the street sweeper, the bricklayer) than on the needs and actions of the workers themselves. Indigenous communities, in their petitions, sought to interrupt the omission of laborers. Their petitions called attention to the effects of conscription on daily life, and their successful work-avoidance strategies made clear that labor required laborers. That push and pull between work and workers shows both how essential indigenous laborers were to national modernity and how fraught the reliance on indigenous labor was for elites. The ways that costumbrismo and other images of indigenous labor kept a focus on work rather than workers helped elites subordinate indigenous objections to the pressing labor of modernization. It eased the otherwise problematic contradiction in which the modern nation was made by amodern laborers.

Popular Labor and National Development in the Mid-Twentieth Century

By the mid-twentieth century the commonplace connection between indigenous labor and nation building began to take greater account of workers. That shift had several sources: indigenous resistance and organizing began to spread and more profoundly shape the national scene; leftist parties were increasingly successful in organizing working-class and peasant movements, such that in the 1930s Ecuador saw its first truly populist politics; and the new generation of image makers emerging in Quito at that time had been spurred to political awareness by incidents of governmental violence against workers, including the massacres of striking workers in Guayaquil in 1922 and in the Highlands in 1929.[29] Many left-leaning members of that young generation joined the Partido Socialista Ecuatoriana (PSE, Ecuadorian Socialist Party) when it was founded in 1926 and were critical of governments, both Liberal and Conservative, in their failures to improve working conditions and provide land rights for the marginalized and oppressed.

During the 1930s and 1940s workers became a matter of concern across the political spectrum and began to stand in for the people as a whole. In turn, use of the topoi of indigenous labor shifted to emphasize workers rather than work. Such topoi drew less attention to the specific tasks that workers would accomplish (building roads, cultivating fields, etc.) and more attention to their status as members of a *class* whose participation in efficient production and commercial consumption was essential to national well-being. The health, hygiene, and education of workers, especially indigenous campesinos, became of heightened concern to political elites and social scientists envisioning the modern nation and to indigenous communities and leftist groups seeking to refashion it. As before, the analyses that follow begin with a visual anecdote and then work through the uses made of laboring topoi by white-mestizo authorities, by indigenous communities, and by artists. Like those in the nineteenth century, twentieth-century artistic commonplaces frequently served as a middle ground. They corroborated an elite sense of the "Indian problem" yet challenged the exclusive, aristocratic underpinnings of that Highlands elite, all with an eye toward imagining the shape and potential of the nation.

Imagining an Autochthonous Proletariat

In 1952 the printmaker Galo Galecio provided illustrations for a four-volume *Historia del Ecuador* (History of Ecuador) written by Alfredo Pareja Diezcanseco, a well-known author and critic affiliated with the Socialist Party and Quito's indigenista artists. Diezcanseco's book, published by the Casa de la Cultura Ecuatoriana, retold the history of Ecuador from a modern leftist perspective. Galecio's line drawings, lightly scattered through the *Historia*, occasionally depict indigenous people explicitly, each time accessing topoi of national landscape or labor. In the fourth volume, as Diezcanseco's tale moves into the twentieth century, Galecio invokes topoi of indigenous labor in an illustration addressing the outcomes of the July Revolution. That illustration, *La nueva legislación social* (The new social legislation), references the postrevolution government's failed efforts to establish more progressive policies toward laborers and the popular classes. Galecio's drawing uses the commonplace of the indigenous laborer to both illustrate that earlier historical moment and allude to questions of labor and nation that continued to be relevant for his contemporaries.

The illustration shows an urban street corner (fig. 26). On the right side stand three figures: a businessman in coat and tie, a farmer dressed in a poncho and round hat, and an urban laborer wearing overalls and a billed cap. The ethnic identity of that third figure is ambiguous because his back is turned completely to the viewer, but his short, wide body and round head suggest that we are not meant to read him as white-mestizo. The other two figures are clearly situated in ethnic terms. If the poncho and round hat worn by the agricultural worker were insufficient to indicate his intended indigeneity, the traditional hand plow he carries and his long, braided hair would be. The businessman's features also encourage a racialized reading: his short hair and long face with its aristocratic nose and prominent chin suggest criollo heritage and place emphasis on the *white* of white-mestizo.

The three figures are positioned mostly facing away from the viewer and toward the wall that dominates the left side of the small image. On that wall, a large sign announces new *leyes de trabajo* (work laws) and features a raised fist clutching a torch. In his relation to that sign, the indigenous campesino is clearly the focal point of this illustration. Alone among the figures, he turns his head away from the poster and looks out of the illustration toward the viewer. In the flattened triangle of men, he stands at the apex, pointing toward the poster. The fact that more of his body is visible, that his grip on the hand plow echoes the fist on the poster, and that he turns toward the viewer all emphasize his importance to the scene. The indigenous laborer becomes the axis around which efforts to reform labor must revolve.

Galecio's drawing nicely illustrates how the topoi of indigenous labor functioned at midcentury. As in previous eras, such images of the laboring Indian spoke both to the national urge toward modernity and to a lingering anxiety about the nation's backwardness. Like their counterparts at the end of the nineteenth century, mid-twentieth-century white-mestizos identified indigenous labor as the source of the nation-state's lack of development but also imagined that labor, if properly modernized, as the foundation of national progress. What changed in the mid-twentieth century was that the terms of discussion began increasingly to conceive of indigenous labor in terms of *workers*. Indigenous campesinos became part of a larger working class, though a particularly anxiety-producing part, and the specificity of social types in costumbrismo fell by the wayside. In their studies of Ecuadorian workers, social scientists did sometimes categorize workers into different types to analyze their aptness for acquiring hygiene, health, and integration into the nation. More widely available discourse, however, evinced a fairly homogenous concern with "our workers" or "our workers and peasants" that folded indigenous people into the larger political, semiscientific category of "laborers."

In the mid-twentieth century discussions of workers as a plural force always invoked the specter of socialism. Leftist artists and activists used the

"La Nueva Legislación Social".

Fig. 26.   Galo Galecio, *La nueva legislación social*. Illustration after woodblock print, 1952. In Diezcanseco, *Historia del Ecuador*. Reprinted with permission from the family of Galo Galecio and the Casa de la Cultura Ecuatoriana "Benjamín Carrión," Quito, Ecuador.

existing link between indigenous labor and the nation to forward a new vision of a socialist nation-state led by its workers. Similarly, leaders on the Right, as part of their campaigns to maintain the authority of the church and the traditional elite, tapped into fears that indigenous laborers would rebel violently. Both groups encouraged new engagement with indigenous campesinos and new forms of public administration to encourage indigenous Ecuadorians to buy into the white-mestizo nation-state. Resistance and organizing by indigenous groups, for its part, challenged the common sense that subsumed indigenous labor to the benefit of the white-mestizo nation.

Indigenous Resistance and Its Discontents

Starting in the early 1930s, according to historian Marc Becker, direct exchange between white-mestizo communists and indigenous communities led some Ecuadorian leftists to abandon paternalistic goals for integrating indigenous communities into a white-mestizo nation and instead see contemporary indigenous cultures as valuable in themselves. In turn, involvement with the radical Left "helped trigger a shift in Indigenous strategies from reacting to local and immediate forms of exploitation to addressing larger structural issues." They "pushed protest from the private sphere of negotiated relations with individual landholders and church officials into the public sphere of engaging and ultimately influencing the nature of state formation." Thanks to those partnerships, class-based organizing in indigenous communities sometimes successfully threatened the control of landholders and altered the national scene.[30] In their petitions, protests, and organizing, indigenous leftists and their allies challenged the prevailing assumptions that indigenous labor belonged to white-mestizo patrons. They opened space for indigenous agency and resisted narratives of indigenous passivity.

As those arguments for and by indigenous communities drew on topoi of indigenous labor, however, they also tied the good of indigenous labor back to the good of the nation-state. A 1931 strike declaration by indigenous peons on two haciendas in Cayambe, for example, repeatedly invoked the Constitution and related labor laws to highlight abuses perpetrated by *terratenientes*, the national police, and the Ministry of Social Welfare. It argued that indigenous laborers worked the land for the sustenance of others and therefore should be protected by the state. Noting the government's recent pledge to consider indigenous land claims, the declaration asked how long the government would "continue considering the Indian as less than a beast of burden" rather than treating him as an integral part of the nation.[31]

Similarly, the pages of the indigenous periodical *Nucanchic Allpa* frequently made careful use of the state's legal commitments to workers as they called for indigenous organizing, transmitted strike demands, and outlined the mission of the Federación Ecuatoriana de Indios (FEI, or Federation of Indian Ecuadorians). Articles highlighted contradictory behavior by political elites and put forward the assumption that workers ought to be protected because of their integral role in national development. They also argued for state support in creating rural schools and literacy programs to advance the culture, efficiency, and health of indigenous workers. Such appeals to state authority allowed indigenous arguments new legitimacy on the national stage. They extended and altered the commonplace terms of Indian labor that had been so often used to exploit indigenous communities. Along the way such use helped extend the pattern of national vision to which those topoi returned. Doing new and apparently contrary work with the links between indigenous labor and nation building, those arguments also contributed new points of intersection to the national patterns driving laboring topoi.

Those new patterns were, in turn, reappropriated by the media outlets, academic texts, and state-level discourse that responded to indigenous demands. Though portions of Ecuador's radical Left worked alongside indigenous communities, a larger body—including the intellectuals and political leaders whose views circulated in the national press—used indigenous resistance as a foil for paternalistic arguments about indigenous degradation. Juan Fernández, the columnist for *El Día*, voiced a common assumption when he scoffed in one 1935 column, "Yes, [the Indians] rise up; but for an irate and violent protest. Brusquely erupting against repression and [land] takings. They don't rise up for anything greater."[32] Indigenous rebels were not, Fernández tried to make clear, organized activists guided by well-developed ideological aims. The idea of "Los Indios 'comunistas'" was, in Fernández's eyes, preposterous. In one sense Fernández was sympathetic to indigenous workers. In multiple columns he urged attention to what he saw as "a complex economic and social question" troubling the status of indigenous laborers and critiqued the rampant exploitation of indigenous campesinos. His writing emphasized, however, that the problems facing indigenous communities required an expert and scientific solution that lay beyond the capacities of degraded indigenous people.[33]

Fernández's approach, viewing indigenous resistance under the same "Indian problem" heading as indigenous oppression, was paradigmatic of elite white-mestizo response. Indigenous organizers, in fact, noted this rhetorical problem, and they essayed specific arguments against it (e.g., profiling local leaders and indigenous-led education projects). Still, that common sense that could not see indigenous people as the authors of their own advancement remained dominant. In general, white-mestizos dismissed indigenous-led organizing as improbable based on circular assumptions about indigenous incapacity for self-directed action. They argued that outside activists were misleading or riling up a credulous indigenous population that had been oppressed for too long to be capable of envisioning its own liberation.[34] Though intellectuals and politicians on the Left were, to some extent, interested in undermining widespread assumptions about indigenous people as "dead weight" and "passive," their arguments often exacerbated a sense of indigenous people's inherent difference from white-mestizos and reinscribed their status as laborers who built but did not participate in the nation-state.[35]

Reinforcing a sense of paternalistic responsibility within topoi of indigenous labor, Ecuadorian intellectuals advocated state-led programs of education, hygiene, and worker training that would incorporate indigenous people into the white-mestizo nation. The editors of the 1930s periodical *Los Andes*, for example, argued that if the state made honest, just work available to the peasant classes, they would be smoothly incorporated into the national economy: "Only work, but work whose fruits entirely benefit the Ecuadorian and create in him a consciousness of his value as a social element, the consciousness of his significance as the elemental economic producer and a sense of civic and democratic affirmation, can conserve social harmony and structure nationalism and fortify the fundamentals of the state."[36] These sorts of assertions suggest that equitable labor from which peasants received just rewards ought to be the broader goal for political and social reform. But they positioned the benefits of that reform in terms of white-mestizo leadership and indigenous acculturization. The Indian, in these terms, continued to serve primarily as an element of nation building and only secondarily as a protocitizen.

Mid-twentieth-century Ecuadorian beliefs about the inherent marginality of indigenous citizenship conditioned the actual possibilities for integrating indigenous laborers into the nation. Though elites sought to transform indigenous people into productive worker-citizens for the sake of the nation, such productive participation was constantly positioned just out of reach for contemporary indigenous people.[37] Mid-twentieth-century indigenista social scientists consistently located the possibility of indigenous equality somewhere in the future, after the passing of several generations erased centuries of inherited degradation.[38] White-mestizo political leaders similarly cited indigenous lack of education as a fundamental block to their success as workers and allocated funds for indigenous education while simultaneously preventing the realization of those projects.[39] White-mestizo landholders who, in theory, sponsored rural public schools to improve worker productivity, in practice actively undermined indigenous-led literacy programs and intimidated, injured, and drove out the leaders of those projects.[40] Business leaders and industrialists, for their part, anxiously promoted the transformation of indigenous people into consumers whose participation in the national economy would secure white-mestizo wealth. One industrialist of the time reflected that he would know modernity had arrived in Ecuador on the day that he saw Indian women dressed in patent leather shoes rather than handmade sandals.[41]

Development and modernization were central themes in national discourse, and their advocates "aggravated the political tensions inherent in the concept of ethnic identity by claiming that the fundamental obstacle preventing Ecuador from modernizing lay in the 'backwardness' of its indigenous and nonwhite citizens."[42] If, on the one hand, elites assumed that obstacle would be removed by absorbing indigenous peoples into a white-mestizo national culture, they were also invested in notions of indigenous peoples' fundamental difference from white-mestizos to explain national problems. Indigenista images were one of the major venues in which that contradictory vision of the indigenous worker as protocitizen moved toward synthesis. They helped smooth the simultaneous urges toward incorporation and dissociation, tying depictions of worker unrest to the idea of a struggling nation and to the Left's broader efforts to reorganize Ecuadorian political society in a more egalitarian frame.

Visualizing Indigenous Workers

Starting in the 1930s, young visual artists in the Highlands who had been influenced by literary indigenismo, by social and artistic revolutions in Mexico, and by political upheaval in their own country turned their attention to the struggles of Ecuador's popular classes, especially indigenous people. The elaborated and reappropriated topoi of indigenous labor dominated those indigenista images. They used depictions of indigenous laborers— downtrodden, noble, rebelling—to envision the larger scene for national improvement. The ideological commitments of the indigenistas and their desire to redefine the terms of Ecuadorian national identity resulted in frequent images of indigenous struggle that served as commentaries on what it meant to be Ecuadorian in the mid-twentieth century (see, e.g., fig. 8). The indigenistas both identified with and distanced themselves from indigenous workers, and the cumulative effect of their image production can be seen in parallel terms: indigenista artwork profoundly challenged national vision and gave urgency to reform projects; it also tethered the struggles of indigenous workers tightly to the concerns of a mestizo nation-state.

Chapter 5 offers more sustained reflection on the politics of mestizaje in Ecuador and their relation to topoi of indigeneity. The ways that midcentury leftists engaged mestizaje also bear some brief treatment here, though, as they affected how indigenista artists figured indigenous workers. The artist Eduardo Kingman's reflections in "Nacionalismo en arte" (Nationalism in art) from May 1951 neatly illustrate that intersection between indigeneity and mestizaje in indigenista claims about the nation. Kingman quotes an uncited author to argue that social realism began in the Americas: "América [is] the world in which this art with social content was [first] propagated. . . . In so far as América [is], in a cosmic and primordial sense, wider and more free, [it] is essaying the rehumanization of art through [this social sense]."

Explicitly connecting the nationalism of socially conscious art to its indigenous roots and mixed heritage, Kingman continues, "By saying América, we have to differentiate: [we refer to] Indian América . . . those places where the great collective tradition of Indian origin was incompletely absorbed by the ferocity of Spanish individualism. For, the América without an Indian tradition is nothing more than a prolongation of Europe without any signs of a greater impulse."[43] Kingman's point here is to emphasize the national character of work by the artists of his day. He contrasts his contemporaries with an earlier generation that believed in artistic universalism and echoed European aesthetic trends. For Kingman, the new generation of Ecuadorian artists was reclaiming the role of art in society: art is tied to nation, and the artist carries significant social responsibility. Fulfilling that responsibility means seeing indigeneity, because the centerpoint of nationality is the encounter between "Spanish individualism" and "Indian tradition." In Kingman's narrative the commonplaces of indigenous labor take central stage as defining arguments for national identity. Focusing on "incomplete" absorption, however, Kingman also suggests that incorporating the Indian into national identity paves the way toward a future national greatness embodied in the figure of the mestizo.[44]

The assumption of indigenous people's essential collectivity, seen most emblematically in shared labor, was key to this idea that the image of the Indian could stand in for the mestizo nation—indigenous communal spirit was an essential check on the "ferocity" of Spanish individualism. It eased the slippage between images of collective indigenous effort and images of collective national effort. Such movement is visible throughout Kingman's *Hombres del Ecuador*, which, with one or two exceptions, depicts indigenous labor in collective terms. Even in his print echoing costumbrista images of men from Zámbiza sweeping Quito's streets (fig. 27), Kingman shows a pair of men at work on the cobbled streets rather than the single figure traditional to nineteenth-century paintings (see, e.g., fig. 22). Those scenes in *Hombres* that show indigenous people in rural contexts emphasize indigenous collective labor even further. *Defensa de la tierra* (fig. 20), examined in chapter 2, an image of communal ritual (*Un San Juan*), and five prints showing indigenous people working the fields (*Los huachos, Cabe de papas, Sembradores, Segadores,* and *El trigo*) all feature groups of indigenous people engaged in common work (see figs. 18, 19, and 28).[45]

Fig. 27.   Eduardo Kingman, *Huangudos al amanecer*, 1937. Woodblock print on paper. In Kingman, *Hombres del Ecuador*. Collection of the Fundación Posada de las Artes Kingman.

That communal labor invokes the "great collective tradition of Indian origin [that] was incompletely absorbed by the ferocity of Spanish individualism" that Kingman described in text some fourteen years later.[46] Read in light of Kingman's later discussion, those rural prints show the nation *because* they show indigenous community. Yet the connections that Kingman draws between the nation as a whole (the titular *Hombres del Ecuador*) and the collective, traditional effort of indigenous people authorize ambiguous interpretations of the place of indigenous laborers in the modern nation. Those communal workers are clearly foundational to the idea of the nation,

Fig. 28.   Eduardo Kingman, *Cabe de papas*, 1937. Woodblock print on paper. In Kingman, *Hombres del Ecuador*. Collection of the Fundación Posada de las Artes Kingman.

but if the modern nation is a place of mechanized agriculture, patent leather shoes, and education, the future of the Indian as *Indian* remaines uncertain.

That tenuous status of indigenous culture—both active and absorbed—allowed the indigenistas to identify with indigenous people yet engage their struggles for broader ideological claims. Envisioning indigenous campesinos as part of an authentic, Ecuadorian proletariat, they connected indigenistas and indígenas through the common theme of marginalized work. The indigenistas imagined themselves as workers and used that identity to connect themselves to the marginalized masses. The indigenista artists had arrived in Quito from middle-class, provincial families; they were unable to survive on their painting alone; and they were engaged in a constant struggle against the conservative aesthetics and politics of Quito's old aristocracy. They saw the fraught conditions of their labor as echoing those of indigenous workers, and they attempted to reimagine the body of the Ecuadorian nation in that image.[47]

The artists' leftist sympathies made a labor- and class-based sense of affiliation natural. In 1936 they formed the Sindicato de Escritores y Artistas del Ecuador (SEA, or Union of Writers and Artists of Ecuador), hoping to "confer on the literary and plastic expressions of the moment a dimension of social revindication and a [connection to the] popular [that had been] unrecognized prior to that point."[48] That connection was elaborated in both text and image, and it imagined a very particular role for the indigenista artists vis-à-vis the working classes. A xylograph by the indigenista Leonardo Tejada, used as the cover image for the first issue of the Sindicato's monthly magazine, provides a telling example. It makes clear that the artists meant to inspire and lead the people. In the illustration two burly, shirtless men—arms upraised and hands clutching pencils and brushes—stand above an indistinct mass of faces. The two artists-as-workers encourage the people forward, giving them direction and energy. The artists and authors of SEA, in other words, imagined themselves as image makers for the proletariat. They were leaders in solidarity with the broader class of Ecuadorian workers, and their artistic production would bring into being a national identity weighted toward the popular classes.

The artists affiliated with the SEA placed their struggles to alter Quito's cultural landscape in the context of the deeper indignities faced by indigenous people. Their art sought to challenge the status quo and goad a local aristocracy that viewed the popular and middle classes with disdain. Eduardo Kingman's brother, Nicolás, tells, for example, of an indigenista mural that Kingman painted in the Ministry of Agriculture. The mural, "more a panoramic landscape with figures than a typical mural," depicts "industry (or rather, indigenous artisanship), agriculture, and tourism in the Coast and the Highlands."[49] It shows indigenous people at work sustaining the nation (fig. 29). The mural, however, was quickly neglected and damaged by ministry employees either uninterested in the artwork or offended by its subject.[50] Similarly, murals Kingman painted for Benjamín Carrión were erased when Carrión sold his hacienda. The wealthy Italian buyer, Nicolás Kingman reports, "refused to enter the old rustic house while there were Indians on the walls."[51]

Fig. 29.   Eduardo Kingman, detail of *La industría de la sierra*, 1944. Mural in the former Ministry of Agriculture. Photo by author.

In that sense indigenista artists placed their efforts alongside those of indigenous communities and used both to encourage a changed national vision. Those arguments did not suggest that the indignity of having one's art defaced was equivalent to the exploitation faced by indigenous communities. They did, however, evince a strong sense of connection, of parallel forms of injustice operating at different orders of magnitude. For some indigenistas, that common link as workers allowed the artists to become advocates for the cause of indigenous labor. The critic Ignacio Lasso called Kingman the "Painter of the Worker's Drama" in 1940, arguing that he and Diógenes Paredes (another indigenista) had "taken on the tremendous responsibility of expressing the collective inquietude of the proletariat masses of Ecuador, which is to say the yearning of the people, of claiming rights for the humble, of empathizing with the terrible results of hunger, lack of clothing, misery, and opprobrium." Similarly, in 1945 Humberto Vacas Gómez described Kingman as, "in reality, the painter of the drama of the suffering and exploited man of the high plateau." Introducing an exhibit by Carlos Rodríguez and Humberto Estrella in 1940, the critic Enrique Terán suggested that the artists had struck a blow for workers. Their pictures, starkly portraying the

exploitation of indigenous campesinos and urban workers, were "accusa-
tions against the medieval Ecuadorian reality, sustaining the organized action of young workers that aims to create a new vital rhythm in the old and
decadent Ecuadorian *patria*."[52]

Kingman himself made similar arguments about artistic responsibility
for the circumstances of the masses and the force such artwork would carry.
He declared in a 1949 lecture that "the artist of today also knows when his
moment has arrived to suffer because it is the moment in which [suffering]
has touched the collective. When hunger and injustice have struck their mor-
tal claws into their familiars, . . . the nerves of the artist irritate themselves
to the point of total exhaustion." The artist's response to such injustice was,
of course, to paint, and that painting was an active force, bringing about
new awareness and a new reality for the nation. It created justice and was
what Terán called "the art of the truth and the truth in art."[53] Artists were to
make images of the nation that would call toward solidarity, action, and a
new vision of the collective. The indigenistas demonstrated their ideological
commitments and advanced their arguments for a more just society, then,
by laying new claim to the topoi of indigenous labor. Speaking for and about
the image of the true Ecuadorian—the laboring Indian—the indigenistas advanced a new nationalism.

Though the indigenistas used their art to communicate solidarity with
indigenous people and alter how their contemporaries imagined the nation,
their work originated and circulated primarily in Ecuador's urban centers,
and their arguments were aimed toward an urban, middle- and upper-class,
white-mestizo audience.[54] Drawing on the modernist, social-realist aesthetics
that influenced artists across the Americas and building on the existing common sense that connected indigenous labor to national identity, Ecuador's
indigenistas brought the miseries of indigenous labor into galleries to shock
and displace elite viewers. Those images did critique and destabilize the cultural, political, and economic hegemony of the white-mestizo minority. At
the same time they also thickened the social patterns in which images of
indigenous labor served as images about the nation-state.

During the 1930s and 1940s the publications and organizations in which
indigenista artists and intellectuals participated were closely affiliated with
those strands of political and social thought that viewed indigenous communities as simultaneously a font of cultural energy and a problem that
required outside intervention. Thus, even if the indigenistas themselves
professed radical visions of indigenous action, their art moved in an intellectual climate that emphasized cultural integration and imagined a national

future in mestizo terms.[55] Moreover, it circulated within a broader society that saw uncivilized, rebelling indigenous people as a threat to the national future, not as its source. The commonplaces of indigenous labor that the indigenistas promulgated may have carried a variety of meanings for their producers and viewers, but their rhetorical force lent itself to national visions that imagined the interests of indigenous communities in mestizo terms. Kingman's Ministry of Agriculture murals are paradigmatic of this fact. They emphasize indigenous laborers as central to the industry and agriculture of the Highlands, infusing their work with dignity and using it to picture the nation. Yet the murals are located in the Ministry of Agriculture—a space reserved largely for the official classes. The viewers for these images, those who need to see anew to change the national direction, are not the same subjects as the workers at the center of the paintings. Kingman's paean to workers, in other words, uses familiar topoi of indigenous labor to spark new national possibilities through the action and vision of urban mestizos.

Like their costumbrista predecessors, then, indigenista topoi of indigenous labor mediated between the commonsense assumptions about indigenous incapacity that circulated in newspapers, academic texts, and elite political discourse and the radical arguments about indigenous vindication advanced by indigenous syndicates and their supporters. By connecting images of organized, resistant indigenous labor to the idea of the nation, indigenismo highlighted the intentional action of Ecuadorian indigenous workers but envisioned their liberation as a part of the liberation of the nation as a whole. Those artists imagined the figure of the degraded, rebelling Indian not on its own terms, but as a synecdoche for the larger nation. In the process, indigenismo, like costumbrismo, built on and infused new social energy into the topoi of indigenous labor, helping "bring before the eyes" a pervasive common sense about nation building and modernity. Images of indigenous workers struggling against oppression, then, carried arguments about the present and the future of the nation by linking indigenous effort to the creation and maintenance of a modern Ecuador.

Indigenous Labor, White-Mestizo Nation

Commonplaces of indigenous labor have wielded varied and complicated yet pervasive force in Ecuador's rhetorical history. They have marked conflicts over the character of the nation and called attention to exploitative labor conditions. They have also made certain that such conflicts and conditions were framed in national terms, eliding the specificities of indigenous resistance. From the second half of the nineteenth century through the first half of the twentieth, artists engaging topoi of indigenous labor have played mediating roles in that history of marking and omission, consistently calling their compatriots to awareness of exploited indigenous labor but also contributing to a powerful common sense that imagined that labor in terms of the nation.

At the same time there has been a gradual, inconsistent, but real evolution in Ecuadorian common sense about indigenous labor and in the possibilities available to indigenous laborers. The narratives of populist paternalism in costumbrismo and imperfect solidarity in indigenismo track changes not only in white-mestizo awareness of their indigenous compatriots but also in increasing political intervention by indigenous communities. As recent histories of Ecuador's indigenous movements suggest, the local uprisings of the nineteenth century and the class-based organizing of the mid-twentieth century led to the emergence of powerful, plural, and autonomous Ecuadorian indigenous movements in the late twentieth century.[56]

Through their arguments imagining Ecuador as a plurinational state, those indigenous movements could be said to have attained the rhetorical upper hand in the twenty-first century, altering not the topoi of indigenous labor so much as the meaning of the nation-state to which those topoi refer. *Plurinacionalidad* is now Ecuadorian national ideology, at least in formal documents such as the Constitution. The idea that labor will play an integrative role and that modernity is inherently mestizo has ceded some ground to a cultural pluralism in which indigenous people, Afro-Ecuadorians, and mestizos all simultaneously define the nation. The effort to live plurinacionalidad in reality has led to new struggles over how Ecuador will practice its commitment to distinct nations within the singular state, especially in the face of economic difficulties and a long history of mestizaje. Topoi of indigenous labor continue to resonate in that conflict, both allowing recognition of the contributions made by indigenous workers and undermining indigenous claims to modernity. Those topoi allow new work to be done with national identity, but their pattern-bound nature also makes them constant reminders of the scenes and values of earlier eras.

In that spirit, conflicts over the contributions that indigenous communities make to the national economy, including discussions of migrant remittances from abroad and of foreign tourism, continue to return to the familiar pattern in which the image of indigenous labor is tied to national development yet imagined as thoroughly amodern. The echo between two articles, one an art review written in 1941 and the other an academic essay written in 1997, is illustrative. The review, published in the magazine *Mar Pacífico*, notes a tension between the romantic images of indigenous workers that might appeal to outsiders and the harsher tones of the artist Camilo Egas's social realism: "The Indians painted by Egas in all their dramatic expression are not the delicate and beautiful Indians necessary for national propaganda [designed to] attract tourism. But, unfortunately, they are the real Indians, the only ones we know around here."[57] Writing more recently, Carlos de la Torre notes a continued, contemporary fondness for images of the folkloric Indian worker among tourists and mestizo Ecuadorians. Underlining the problematic ambiguity such romanticism introduces into Ecuadorian realities, he writes, "this interest in rescuing the popular is ambivalent since the *pueblo* doesn't [mean] the actual nation; the *pueblo* is seen as something premodern that has to be incorporated into modernity. Those who seek out the popular also assume the elitist role of educators and civilizers of the primitive energies of the *pueblo* that has to be led to the correct road in order to reach the longed-for modernity."[58] The commonplaces of indigenous labor, in the late nineteenth century, the mid-twentieth century, and today consistently allow for assumptions about modernity and the nation-state that serve the interests of white-mestizos and grant them particular claim to civilization. Two larger, apparently contradictory patterns lie beneath those divestments from and appropriations of indigeneity. Those patterns picture indigenous people as either entirely "other" or as deeply "self," and they are the subject of the next two chapters.

4
DEAD WEIGHT

The Indian race is an ethnic, economic, and social dead weight that
drags the country [backward]. Either we acculturate the Indian through
primary instruction and the encouragement of white immigration or the
country will retrograde into an inferior state of civilization. The dilemma
is fatal.

—FEDERICO PÁEZ, "MENSAJE," 1937

We present here a collection of views that largely avoid the defects
that . . . mar . . . the photographs of the capital taken by foreign tourists that have circulated in the exterior. . . . [Those foreigners] have presented us as an almost savage country awaiting conquest; indeed, where
they have tried to show our buildings, where they have chosen popular
customs, landscapes, and so on, the indigenous element has been their
dominant if not exclusive [theme], making everything ugly and giving an
impoverished idea of our population and our culture.

—J. ROBERTO CRUZ AND JOSÉ DOMINGO LASO, *QUITO A LA VISTA*, 1911

There is no question that nineteenth- and twentieth-century nonindigenous
Ecuadorian rhetors—criollo politicians, white-mestizo artists, and mestizo
peasants alike—found repeated opportunities to distinguish themselves from
their indigenous compatriots. From the 1843 uprisings by rural mestizos
who argued that paying the "personal contribution" (tribute) would make
them into Indians to a 1943 article that acknowledged indigenous people as
an integral part of the nation yet described them as "distanced from society
[and] deprived of the elements of culture," Ecuadorian texts and images predominantly imagined indigenous people as profoundly other.[1] Indigenous
people were "dead weight," and their presence made "everything ugly"; they
were savage and drunken, dirty and backward. Indigenous people, in this

sense, represented everything that nonindigenous Ecuadorian rhetors pursuing national greatness and modern progress sought to repudiate. Often, then, Indians figured as fundamentally exterior to Ecuadorian civilization and, in that exteriority, constituted the cultural and political limits of the nation-state. Such strategies of constitutive exteriority, however, coexisted with another rhetoric of otherness, one that placed indigenous others at the center of the nation and, in so doing, highlighted the divisions that marked and made Ecuador's civic world.

Recent scholarship examining narratives of indigenous otherness in Ecuador has largely approached those narratives through the lens of constitutive exteriority, producing good results. Such work brings to light the integral role that indigenous others played in historical processes of national identification. It shows how both the legal distinction between "indígena" and "citizen" prior to 1857 and the "shadows of citizenship" that fell on most Ecuadorians between 1857 and 1979 grounded disenfranchisement on widespread assumptions about indigenous peoples' cultural and racial otherness.[2] Scholars of Ecuadorian national identity have noted that rhetors who did incorporate elements of indigeneity into their sense of the national body often relied on visions of a noble, pre-Columbian indigenous heritage and imagined contemporary indigenous communities as trapped in the past, making indigenous people other through temporal distance.[3] Highlighting how strategies of otherness helped picture the nation, visual-culture scholars have emphasized the exoticism, romanticism, and degradation prominent in images of indigenous people, and scholars examining Ecuadorian modernization projects have pointed toward the intensive administration of difference that infused plans for national development.[4] In all these cases analysis of the construction and maintenance of indigenous otherness makes clear the extent to which indigenous people, positioned outside the idea of the nation, have provided the foil against which white-mestizos imagined that nation.

Often, then, framing rhetorics of indigenous otherness in terms of a constitutive exclusion has provided sufficient analytical insight: nineteenth- and mid-twentieth-century nonindigenous Ecuadorians repeatedly refused identification with indigeneity and located the nation either by negating the value of indigenous culture or by making indigeneity temporally distant from the present-tense nation. And yet, frequently enough to merit attention, intriguing narratives of otherness that exceed the explanatory power of the constitutive exterior have emerged in Ecuador's national rhetorical ecology. Occasionally, Ecuadorian practices of othering have enacted a complex, conflicted, constitutive, and *interior* politics. In such moments, when

Ecuadorian rhetors mark their indigenous compatriots as fundamentally other than themselves, they set *themselves*—not the Indians they describe—apart from the nation.

In the epigraph from Federico Páez, the Indian other appears as a fundamental problem, a burden that pulls the country toward oblivion. On the first read Páez's depiction of that indigenous problem appears to place the Indian as exterior to the nation; Indians are a "dead weight" that the country has to carry. They "drag" the country, an action that implies that Indians exist in an outside position. At the same time Páez's solutions for that Indian problem do not treat his indigenous other as fully exterior. Instead of arguing that the country loosen its indigenous burden, Páez urges his audience to heal and activate it. Doing so, Páez suggests, would make the *nation* right and healthy.

Indigenous people were clearly others for Páez, but their fatal influence moved *within* the nation, not outside it. In this sense, we might read in Páez's assessment an implication that the nation itself was a dead weight. Rather than picturing the Ecuadorian nation as carrying the weight of an indigenous mass, Páez hinted—perhaps unintentionally, yet still provocatively—that another figure shouldered the burden that was the nation. Given Páez's audience (the members of the 1937 Constitutional Assembly), his purpose (to position himself as a leader among leaders), and his proposed solution (new policies of education, hygiene, and European immigration), it is reasonable to imagine that Páez was positioning himself and the elite criollo members of his audience as the unfortunate beasts of burden responsible for hauling the nation forward. Only by reviving the inert national body could Ecuadorian leaders free themselves from the onerous nation they were otherwise obliged to shoulder.

So, yes, Indians were profoundly other and deeply problematic in Páez's speech. They remained, as well, outside the bounds of civilization. Yet the solution Páez announced betrayed an underlying sense that the nation—including both its current problems and its future possibilities—was something slightly other than the white-mestizo officials gathered to form a new Constitution. The nation itself dragged Ecuador down, despite the best efforts of its leaders. The elite, in this formulation, were not entirely of the nation. The nation was, first and foremost, Indian. And that nation, as Indian, was in turn troublingly other.

Like the claims advanced in Páez's speech, arguments in which nonindigenous Ecuadorian rhetors strategically made the nation other by making it indigenous generally enacted the larger constitutive strategies outlined in earlier chapters: legitimizing elite authority and absolving elites of responsibility for national trouble. Those strategies, however, had a particular edge to them: though aimed toward shaping national identity, they emphasized division far more than identification, suggesting that republican life was as marked by distinction as by cohesion. While commonsense assumptions about cultural and racial difference often symbolically exiled indigenous people from the nation-state, they also, sometimes, shifted responsibility for national struggle more firmly onto the shoulders of indigenous Ecuadorians. Along the way such othering moves positioned aristocratic strategies of government as integral to popular sovereignty. Making the nation itself strange, elites recognized but distinguished themselves from the demographic majority. They authorized their permanent leadership. And they dissociated themselves from the causes of intransigent economic troubles. Strategies of nation othering, then, made the republic work for elites whose interests often foreclosed claims to participation in the popular nation. They provided tactics that distinguished elites from the nation while further salving the resulting representative contradiction.

The processes of othering and identification in Ecuador during the late nineteenth and mid-twentieth centuries took varied forms in different regions and moments. This chapter sketches one located history of such othering, focusing on the specific and symbolically rich spaces of Quito from the mid-1800s through the mid-1900s. Suggesting that the other-invoking, nation-making work done by Quito's elite civic institutions—political alliances, religious organizations, and academic institutes—is visible in official texts produced by institutional figures and in paintings and photographs that depict public spaces, it analyzes the symbolic and material work done by Quiteño rhetors making the nation strategically distant from themselves.

Over its course the chapter uses Ecuadorian rhetorical histories to trace how republican polity writ large is haunted by otherness. Working within a recent tradition of scholarship documenting actually existing democracy, it begins with an analysis of oligarchy and representation, then examines how Ecuadorian rhetors working across expressive forms engaged rhetorics of otherness to dramatize and mitigate the underlying contradictions of popular sovereignty.[5] The texts and images engaged here envision an ideal national society and bemoan its failures; they situate indigenous people within a national scene and attempt to erase them from it; they indict practices of exclusion and provide justification for them. In each case an indigenous other takes center stage in the nation while white-mestizo rhetors and audiences stand slightly apart.

This chapter is thus about the confluence of two rhetorical strategies of nation making in Ecuador: one that uses indigeneity to figure the national body and the other that exiles indigeneity from the self. Sometimes, the chapter suggests, notions of self and other are not directly analogous to notions of national and foreign. The nation is not always "self"; the other is not always foreign. In light of that strange disjuncture, the following pages reevaluate the rhetorical implications of narratives of national otherness, arguing that we miss something of the complexity of identification and division when we assume that because the other is the self's constitutive exterior, that other is equally and always the nation's constitutive exterior. Instead, the chapter asserts, encountering and making strategic sense of internal others are important elements of actually existing republican polity, essential rhetorical tools for negotiating the disappointments and sacrifices of civic life.

On Others and Oligarchies

Since its earliest Western inception, rhetorical study has often depended on theories of otherness to understand the work of persuasion. Traditionally, as Diane Davis notes, rhetoricians have understood otherness primarily in terms of division: humans are primordially divided from one another and rhetoric exists because of a deep urge to cross that difference. That assumption of original separation appeared in Greece at least as early as the fourth century B.C.E., when Isocrates, in the "Hymn to Logos," asserted that the ability to communicate with and persuade otherwise-distant others is what allowed humans to "come together and [found] cities, [establish] laws, and [discover] arts." Working in that same general tradition, Kenneth Burke asserted that division—in the form of a fundamental experience of distinction between self and other—is what drives humans to desire identification and makes rhetoric necessary. Jacques Derrida, credited with coining the idea of the "constitutive exterior," made the ontological experience of division from the other fundamental to the creation of not only community but also the self.[6] In that trajectory, then, the existence of otherness not only calls into being a need for rhetoric but also shapes the exigency for forming its opposites, both selfhood and community.

Writing against the grain of those assumptions in which ontological distinction defines human experience, Davis, channeling Emmanuel Levinas and Sigmund Freud, argues that rhetoricians ought to approach identification, not division, as the original human state. That reorientation positions the creation of the self as a series of jarring encounters with uncontrollable difference that dissolve a previously unitary experience of the world.

Davis's reassessment of ontological difference brings to light a preexisting, extrarational identification and rhetoricity, "an obligation to respond that holds the 'I' and the other in an extreme proximity." Within that proximity, Davis explains, "'I' am only inasmuch as I respond to the Other."[7] A sense of self then relies entirely on the proximal other.

For all these theorists, however, whether identification or division is the original state, the eventual experience of distinction becomes constitutive of both the self and the other. In their analyses, whether we seek to return to a lost state of identification or strive to overcome fundamental division, it is the yearning toward communion, toward touch, that makes community happen. Isocrates, Burke, Derrida, Levinas, Freud, and Davis all position the other as, eventually, constituting the meaning-making edge of the self, both exterior and essential. Those scholars then extrapolate from their understandings of the boundary-forming other to explain broader relations, particularly those between self and community. Such extrapolation, however, must be made with some caution. It must move out of the bright glare of ontological theorizing and into the historical or anthropological shadows of everyday experience to capture the contradictory ways that invocations of self and other underlie communal arguments and identifications. The originary relations between self and other sit relatively comfortably in the philosophical realm; the more social questions of self, other, and community demand a social context.[8]

Treading in those social shadows of everyday life, this chapter adds to existing rhetorical treatments of otherness another way of conceiving the force of distinction. It analyzes otherness in the interstices of republican practice and stresses how the social and political divisions of representation rely on notions of a proximal other and a distant self. The pages that follow, rather than attempting an ontological treatment of the other, examine instead a particular society-centered manifestation of otherness. This analysis, in other words, is less invested in discerning the ontological primacy of identification or division in individual relations with others than in illuminating the roles played by otherness within the messy, lived processes of civic encounter. Those everyday processes point toward applied practices of othering that are repeatedly enacted in the context of representative democracy but for which no existing tool allows sufficiently contradictory nuance. In practice the status and use of others both exceeds and fails to achieve the coherence of philosophy's other. Working from that practical spirit, this analysis of how otherness haunts republican practice begins by theorizing from the matter of particular artifacts and their historical moments.

Republican Oligarchy and the Other of Representative Democracy

During the presidential campaign of 1891, Liberals critiqued the leading Progressive candidate, Dr. Luís Cordero, as just another aristocrat in republican clothing put forward by a thoroughly oligarchic party (and, honestly, they were right). One pro-Progressive Quito newspaper, *El Ecuatoriano*, took that Liberal objection head-on, positing oligarchy as the functional principle of republicanism. In an article titled simply "Oligarquía" (Oligarchy), the editors pointed out that only a select portion of the population could achieve Ecuador's basic requirements for citizenship. A smaller part of that body rose to minor political office. Yet another culling occurred when electing members of the national legislature or the executive branch. That process was necessary, they asserted; far from conflicting with the ideal of popular sovereignty, it actually allowed such republican spirit to thrive. At each electoral stage, the editors implied, the best and brightest rose up to lead the republic.

That oligarchic process allowed the nation-state to enact the ideal republic. In it, the better few took on the task of representing the common many: "To elect Senators, Representatives, President, and Vice President of the Republic, one has to consider the aptitude of the individuals, [seeking] guarantees of talent, enlightenment, social and political position, and even historical and familiar precedent. Elections that have [brought to power] subjects without the aptitude to carry out the responsibilities assigned to them have in all times and all places resulted in disgrace. . . . The conditions that we would call superior are not common among all; from there emerges in practice a permanent *oligarchy* that even the most advanced civilization cannot make disappear." The editors further asserted that such admission of permanent oligarchy need not undermine the Constitution's assertion of Ecuador's republicanism: "though the Government of Ecuador is Popular, Elected, Representative, Alternating, and Responsible . . . it has been and is *oligarchic*." Thus, they argued, the Liberals who decried Luís Cordero as an "oligarch" were correct in identifying the situation, but completely wrong about the implications of their accusation. Oligarchy was the only way to ensure freedom, the ultimate good of republican polity. Only oligarchic republican government could "improve the links of fraternity among men, give to each one the greatest measure of well-being possible, and reach that state of social perfection called *civilization*."[9] Representation, in this sense, was an oligarchic form. Liberty and social progress relied on a naturally oligarchic republican system by which the best of the nation, filtered by elections and the franchise, guaranteed the freedom and success of the whole. Oligarchy confirmed the capacity of the elect and, ultimately, the existence of the republic.

There is an explicit assumption of republican otherness within *El Ecuatoriano*'s assessment of representation as an oligarchic system. Simply by virtue of rising to power, the elected (and electable) were distinguished from the mass of the nation by the action of the franchise. Representation confirmed the relationship between an already *elect* leader and the mass of others who formed the reservoir of popular sovereignty. That relationship of elite self to popular other, rather than marking the edge of the nation at the outside border of hegemonic power, instead set elites at the edge of the nation, even as they were fundamentally connected to it. The elite were also the elect, drawn out of the nation to represent it.

It may be odd to take theory lessons from the aristocratic self-justifications of a periodical thoroughly in the pocket of late nineteenth-century bankers and agroexporters. Yet the theory of representation elaborated on *El Ecuatoriano*'s front page does rather effectively identify the practice of actually existing representative democracy, both in its own moment and today. Those editors writing in 1891 were more inclined to celebrate the status quo than is rhetorical theorist Ralph Cintrón writing in 2010, but both recognize that, to some extent, "All contemporary governance . . . is a ratio of these two terms, these two forces [democracy and oligarchy]." Cintrón, whose account of twenty-first-century, post–Berlin Wall democracy resonates as well with the republic of the Progressive oligarchs and with those advanced by their Conservative and Liberal compatriots, notes that "power has always tampered with the demos by resisting, via laws and other means, equitable distribution of resources while allowing, as a kind of escape valve, the discourses of liberty to foster its distracting ideology." Representative democracy, in other words, is no more free of power's machinations and restrictions than any other system; it merely legitimizes such controls through different rhetorical means. Cintrón explains that oligarchy haunts democracy because of an inevitable "disjunction between the limitlessness that democratic subjectivity implies, through rights talk and all other mobilizations of democratic rhetorics, and the limitedness that material life represents."[10] Cintrón's analysis here is primarily concerned with limits in resources—the capacity of any individual or group to access the fundamental elements of bare life. His insight, however, applies more broadly as well: to the material conditions of actually existing representative democracy and the effacement inherent in representation. The uneven distribution of representation is endemic to republican polity.

Cintrón emphasizes the limitedness of rights in a material sense—the *stuff* of republican life is, or appears to be, in short supply. In a parallel argument focused on U.S. citizenship after *Brown v. Board of Education*, Danielle Allen notes that sacrifice is the quintessential experience of democratic citizenship: "Democratic citizens are by definition empowered only to be disempowered. As a result, democratic citizenship requires rituals to manage the psychological tension that arises from being a nearly powerless sovereign." Citizens have, but cannot hold, republican power. While seeking out new citizenly rituals that might spread the experience of sacrifice more evenly across sectors of the polity, Allen recognizes as well "the old bad habits" that "dealt with the inevitable fact of loss in political life by assigning to one group all the work of being sovereign, and to another group most of the work of accepting the significant losses that kept the polity stable."[11]

Such rituals for negotiating the losses of democratic representation are not, however, only a matter of "bad habits." As the editorial in *El Ecuatoriano* implies and Cintrón asserts directly, those rituals are inherent to republican experience and political processes. Representation—in both political and image-making rituals—elevates a few through the sacrifice of the many others. That privileging may be articulated particularly baldly in *El Ecuatoriano*, but the rhetorical force that legitimized the "bad habits" of uneven representation circulated and infused social relations in Ecuador well beyond the 1891 presidential election. To enact their justifications of actually existing practice, such republican rhetorics relied on a messy sense of otherness in which indigenous people were simultaneously positioned as the nation's constitutive exterior and as its internal republican other. Efforts to visually organize the nation, in particular, vacillated between excision and integration, making indigenous others visible as distinct from the viewer yet profoundly (if problematically) of the nation. Distinction and order thus become the operative principles of republican life. They establish subordinate positions that authorize a sense of elite leadership. In those representative moves the *elect* (the chosen, the upper echelon) are naturally the *elected* (the politically enfranchised) by virtue of the existence of an internal republican other.

Imagining a Nation of Others

Perhaps nowhere is this late nineteenth-century approach to order and otherness in terms of representation more visually present than in a set of four anonymous paintings showing Quito's Plaza Grande (figs. 30–33). Those images, painted in the 1860s, depict the buildings on each side of the capital city's

Fig. 30.   *El Palacio de Gobierno de Quito,* ca. 1860s. Oil on canvas. Collection of Modern and Republican Art, Ecuadorian Ministry of Culture, Quito, Ecuador.

Fig. 31.   *La Catedral de Quito,* ca. 1860s. Oil on canvas. Collection of Modern and Republican Art, Ecuadorian Ministry of Culture, Quito, Ecuador.

Fig. 32.   *El Palacio Arzobispal de Quito,* ca. 1860s. Oil on canvas. Collection of Modern and Republican Art, Ecuadorian Ministry of Culture, Quito, Ecuador.

Fig. 33.   *Casa Municipal de Quito,* ca. 1860s. Oil on canvas. Collection of Modern and Republican Art, Ecuadorian Ministry of Culture, Quito, Ecuador.

central square: the presidential palace (Carondelet), the cathedral, the archbishop's palace, and the municipal building (Municipio). In these paintings visual representation and aesthetic organization interact in much the same way that political representation and oligarchy commingle in *El Ecuatoriano*'s argument, and to similar effect. They structure the republic and justify its hierarchies through visions of the nation made distant from its leaders.

Each of the canvases is anchored by an iconic building tied to national identity, and the name of the building forms the title of the painting. The building, in each case, stretches almost the entire width of the canvas and sits heavily in the middle of the painting's lower third. Above each building (except Carondelet), an open expanse of sky just touched by mountain foothills fills the upper two-thirds of the painting (the quickly rising slopes of Pichincha shrink the sky in the Carondelet canvas to just half the image). Below each building the Plaza Grande stretches toward the viewer, though its open expanse is broken in each canvas by the fountain standing in the middle of the plaza. For a viewer the effect of that combined use of space—massive sky, narrow buildings, wide plaza, and fountain—is to suggest the experience of gazing across the plaza toward each building while standing on the second-floor balcony of the building directly across the square. Thus, we see the cathedral from the perspective of the second floor of the archbishop's palace, Carondelet from the balconies of the Municipio, and so on. With the exception of the cathedral entrance, which was public, the second floor of each of the plaza buildings would have been protected. Access would have demanded elite status, membership of one sort or another in the national elect. The viewer, in other words, is placed in semiprivate or restricted space to take stock of the national scene. In addition, the opportunity to stand idly gazing across the square required a leisurely assumption of authority that suggests a distanced relationship between the viewer on the balcony and the cross section of Quito in the plaza below.

For the plaza is indeed filled with national life in these paintings. A religious parade emerges from the archbishop's palace and heads toward the cathedral (or perhaps Carondelet?). Soldiers in uniform, men in suits and top hats, and women wearing full skirts and shawls cross the square and pass through the porticos of each building. Indigenous (or perhaps mestizo) women and men stand barefooted among their more prosperous compatriots. And indigenous water carriers cluster around the fountain, filling urns and heading out into the city. Interestingly, the poorer, lower-class figures in these paintings seem to cluster toward the front and center of each canvas. They are most available to view and placed in the middle of the national scene.

The paintings are small enough that it is difficult to discern identifying details for the diminutive figures walking along the cathedral's promenade or passing through the porticos of the Municipio and the archbishop's palace. Those details that are visible suggest that the figures are more likely meant to be middle- and upper-class white-mestizos than indigenous or mestizo laborers. Despite how the paintings bring indigenous figures toward the center of the plaza, nonindigenous figures dominate the paintings in numeric terms. These paintings, in other words, are not properly seen as paintings of or about indigeneity. They are, instead, paintings about the nation: its iconic buildings, its central spaces, and its varied population. What is particularly interesting for the purposes of this analysis, however, are the ways that these paintings organize national space and, in the process, invoke the polity.

There is a fundamental sense of distinction at work in the four Plaza Grande paintings, and it is closely tied to questions of representation. Each painting enacts representation, depicting the order of the nation within an iconic national space. Its figures, drawn from costumbrismo's pantheon of romantic types, represent the various strata of the republic. The viewer, however, stands apart from that national catalog, claiming access to positions of authority and the right to represent the nation both visually and politically. The paintings, then, call attention to both political and visual representation and to the twin structures of aestheticization and oligarchy that authorize such representation. If political representation fits oligarchy into republican clothing, legitimizing the presence of otherness and distinction within democratic practice, visual representation aestheticizes the republic, picturing the relationship between a viewing self and a represented other in terms of a natural civic order.

Making distinctions, in this sense, forms the foundation of the republican community. That is the *Ecuatoriano* editorial's point: republics work through election and representation, both of which require distinction between the "elect" and "electors" (and, in the case of nineteenth-century Ecuador, between the popular masses who transmit sovereignty and the enfranchised minority that receives it). The sacrifice of rights and power constitutive of political consent thus simultaneously marks divisions in the body of the nation and ties it together.

Representative Responsibility

The aristocratic Progressives of the late nineteenth century were not the only Ecuadorians who advanced a theory of republican polity that separated the uneducated, problematic nation of others from its leaders, nor were they the only ones who imagined those ordered divisions in both textual and visual terms. Mid-twentieth-century writers and image makers reviewing Ecuadorian polity might have been less inclined to align themselves with the oligarchic elite than their predecessors, but the legitimizing act of internal othering continued to undergird their civic criticism. In fact, the moves that twentieth-century leftist authors and artists made to distinguish themselves from both the nation's leaders and indigenous communities show even more clearly how otherness haunts republican life.

Writing almost sixty years after *El Ecuatoriano*'s authors and from a left-leaning and academic perspective, the indigenista social scientist Carlos Andrade Marín elaborated a similar assessment of Ecuadorian civic life in which a republican elite separated itself from a troubled nation of others. Unlike the late nineteenth-century Progressives, however, Andrade Marín critiqued those elites for not adequately carrying out their responsibilities to the struggling nation-other:

> The leading forces of the country, and among them the youth, have the primary obligation to remember that they are a minority, a fearsome minority facing a national mass of indigent Indians and mestizos. And [they must remember] that such a minority, however cultivated it believes itself to be, does not have the right to play political games. The Ecuadorian *pueblo* is fundamentally that mass of two and a half million Indians and mestizos, of illiterates, of seminaked inhabitants of the highland plains or the jungle, that waits with indolent hopelessness for the Patria to call it and integrate it into its columns.

Andrade Marín repeatedly, in this text, marks the popular classes as the nation. His assertion that the *pueblo*, the people-nation, is "fundamentally that mass of . . . Indians and mestizos" is matched, a page later, by a lament that "we must radically transform the Ecuadorian national mass in order to transform Ecuador." Andrade Marín negotiates the oligarchic nature of Ecuadorian republicanism by naming the nation in terms of its masses but distinguishing that nation from the Patria (the fatherland). In such use the paternal undertones of Patria come clear: the nation of children cries out to its father-leaders who guide their children into national adulthood. Andrade Marín was not alone in his assessment that a distinction existed between the nation's leaders and its people nor in his sense that such distinction carried responsibility. Writing in *El Día* in 1935, the pseudonymous columnist Tupac

Amaru argued that "the defense of the poor" was "the defense of the nation-ality."[12] Ecuadorian leaders who failed to heed the calls of the indigenista social scientists and pursue real reform were failing the nation.

Lambasting the elite minority—from the nation but not *fundamentally* the nation—for its willingness to sacrifice the interests of the national majority, Andrade Marín and Tupac Amaru enacted a form of republican othering. They called Ecuadorian elites into republican responsibility for the nation of others. For Andrade Marín, that meant weighting the nation with a heritage of pathology: "If we do not redeem from misery, sickness, and ignorance the Ecuadorian mass majority, uncultured, miserable, and sick, the daily political transformations of our national history will serve for naught." In that move Andrade Marín made the national majority into a needing other, refusing identification with the nation to draw attention to the urgency of its plight and jar elites into generous action. Tupac Amaru, for his part, used the urgent need for reform to destabilize elites' own place in the nation: "When we have achieved a fruitful balance [in society], we will be true citizens. While the ignominious neglect of the Ecuadorian [lower] classes continues, we may be politicians, professionals of all types, literati, illustrious men, but we will not be Ecuadorians. We will be lacking [the necessary] love of the national soil."[13] So long as elites denied their republican responsibility to create a balanced so-ciety and raise up the oppressed and neglected national other, Tupac Amaru asserts, they lost their own Ecuadorianness. The nation could not be the self.

The critique of elite neglect offered by Andrade Marín and Tupac Amaru echoed as well, though more harshly, in the work of two young Marxist artists—Carlos Rodríguez and Humberto Estrella—who exhibited a series of paintings and caricatures in a 1940 exhibit titled *Quito Colonial*. The cata-log from that exhibition reproduces several of the artists' works alongside the speeches presented at the exhibit's opening. Naming their presentation of twentieth-century images *Quito Colonial* and explicitly invoking the city's colonial-era title, Mui Noble i Mui Leal Ciudad de San Francisco de Quito (Very noble and very loyal city of San Francisco de Quito), Rodríguez and Estrella tied their criticism of the contemporary national order to a long his-tory of representation and exploitation.[14]

In many of the images reproduced in the catalog, especially Rodríguez's paintings, indigenous figures press up against the page, threatening to over-flow it. Behind them the modern colonial city haunts and hovers, an inescap-able presence. The contrast between these images of Quito and those of the four nineteenth-century Plaza Grande paintings is stylistic, of course, but it is also spatial and rhetorical. The earlier paintings emphasize distance.

The architecture and the sky were the paintings' protagonists and the people moved across the square without disturbing it. The aesthetic order of representation was discrete, solid, and natural. In Rodríguez's paintings, the viewer is uncomfortably close to the suffering, exploited nation. Though not quite *of* the nation, that viewer is quite distinctly present as the paintings' subjects shoulder their way into iconic space, pushing it aside and rupturing its clarity.

The position of the viewer in these paintings is ambiguous. Very close to and entirely implicated in the circumstances depicted, the viewer is not *quite* part of them and stands instead at an oblique angle to the action. This sense is particularly strong in Rodríguez's painting *Primicia* (First fruits). *Primicia* illustrates an ongoing tradition of colonial origin in which indigenous communities gave the first fruits of their harvest to the Catholic Church (fig. 34). In the painting, a bloated, tonsured priest with a face like a slab of stone fills the left third of the canvas. His great, rounded chest and enormous right arm squeeze four indigenous petitioners into the remaining two-thirds of the canvas. Only the head of the fourth figure fits in the image. A sacrificial lamb takes center stage in the painting, mediating between the parties. The domes and steeples of Quito above that crowded tableau are almost pushed off the canvas by the five adults in the foreground. A baby carried on the back of one petitioner appears lifelessly draped over a church roof, sacrificed to the church along with the lamb. There is no room at the inn.

The claustrophobic atmosphere of this painting presses the painting's audience into relation with the depicted scene. One cannot help but recoil from the priest's arm and his accusatory finger pointing directly at the hat grasped submissively in the hands of the foremost indigenous supplicant. Yet the audience is viewing a public problem and is positioned neither as an additional indigenous petitioner nor a clerical oppressor. The scene of exploitation pushes itself into view, but it is not quite our scene. Instead, the invading scene obliges responsibility to and for the visually marginalized indigenous other and demands as well that viewers distinguish themselves from the exploiting classes represented by the priest.

That experience of being obligated by the paintings but not quite participating in them resonates neatly with Estrella and Rodríguez's own description of their position within the nation. They launch harsh attacks on Ecuador's elites, making a clear division between themselves and an elite other they describe as parasitic. They also, however, set themselves just slightly apart from the national masses, expressing leftist commitment to exploited workers without entirely identifying with them. Rodríguez and Estrella open

Fig. 34.   Carlos Rodríguez, *Primicia*, ca. 1940. Oil on canvas. In Rodríguez and Estrella, *Quito Colonial*. Photograph by Jessie Reeder.

the catalog with a statement of responsibility that identifies the authors with Ecuador yet sketches as well the nation's divisions: "Responsible to an ideological commitment and responsible to manifest the truth before all in the historical moment to which we belong, we want to reflect, at least in its larger aspects, the social, economic, and political panorama of our country, of this corner of *Indo-América*, as we might call it, composed in the majority by *Indians*, by *cholos*; (plebian people as you say) and, like all bourgeois countries, formed as well by oppressed classes and oppressive classes."[15] As in Andrade Marín's and Tupac Amaru's works, Rodríguez and Estrella's division of the national body takes a substantially different form than did the divisions proffered by the editors of *El Ecuatoriano* or the Plaza Grande paintings. Yet those divisions remain, and they continue to be natural, inevitable, and constitutive of the actually existing republic. The structure of republican representation that Estrella and Rodríguez identify as profoundly feudal and colonial consists of power-inflected relationships among multiple sorts of others.

In their paintings and caricatures Estrella and Rodríguez envision social relations within Quito as standing in for a larger society defined by three social classes: the feudal (or oligarchic) powers, the church, and the oppressed. While that framing suggests that the artists are in some way identified with the final category, their partial distinction from it had already been established by their earlier presentation of themselves as having the task of enlightening the oppressed national body. Artists, then, served as the ideal representatives for the oppressed—its republican other: "Art, noble expression of human intelligence, ought to be brought to the popular consciousness in order to teach it its routes, correct the defects of our collective organism, and above all to make us feel a longing for justice and the reclamation of rights."[16] Such ambivalent movement between identification and representation in Rodríguez's and Estrella's images and statements points, once again, to the distinction-making structures of republican practice. Addressing injustice using the language of democratic idealism means making sense of the experience and existence of internal otherness. Republican representation highlights the extent to which others are the national majority, and it draws attention to how that majority invokes the republican responsibility of the few.

In the justifications and criticisms of existing republican order launched by Andrade Marín, Tupac Amaru, and the editors of *El Ecuatoriano*; by the Plaza Grande paintings; and by the exhibit *Quito Colonial*, we catch a glimpse of the complex rhetorical ecology by which republican Ecuador functioned. Those texts and images show a republican polity that ordered the nation by separating a majority of others from an elite minority through the uneven distribution of representation. Whether the status quo of national order was the subject of critique or celebration in those artifacts, they coincided in imagining an oligarchic republic in which a nation-made-other sacrificed its sovereignty and in calling leaders into responsibility for those sacrificial others. By entering positions of representation, the rhetor-self consistently pulled away from the nation even while remaining closely tied to it and fundamentally responsible for it. The relationship between populace and leaders here is not the classical ideal of representative democracy in which leaders are responsible *to* the people. It forms instead an oligarchic republic in which leaders are set apart from and responsible *for* their subjects. In this scheme leaders do not cease to be Ecuadorians, do not entirely abdicate identification and affiliation with the Patria, yet the nation has become something other than self. In the oligarchic republic, leaders are the elect; they are other than the nation of others.

"Making Everything Ugly"

That sense of being set apart, both other-yet-not and compatriot-yet-not, appeared not only in texts and images that sought to order and organize systems

of authority and resistance but also in artifacts that aimed to capture the degradation of the nation or picture a national ideal. In the late nineteenth and
mid-twentieth centuries, that impulse appeared most starkly in negotiations
over the purpose and possibilities of different visual genres. Of particular
interest for this discussion of republican otherness are treatments of beauty
and ugliness that used images of national spaces and populations to invoke
elite viewers' relationships with the nation as other by fixing attention on
matters of representation. Such arguments over representation and aesthetics, like the efforts to organize national space, sought to naturalize republican othering through careful framing of the polity and its indigenous others.
They mitigated the ways that elites claimed sovereignty, allowing them to
refuse identification with the other-majority while also remaining in a relationship with it. Such mechanisms give further insight into the persuasive
workings of what Allen (writing of the United States) terms a "two-pronged
citizenship of domination and acquiescence."[17] In Ecuador, as in the United
States, that "two-pronged citizenship" provided a deeply problematic yet du-
rable system for reconciling the uneven distribution of republican sovereignty. It assigned different roles to different members of the republic, giving the
sacrificial role almost entirely to the indigenous other.

In 1911 the Ecuadorian photographer José Domingo Laso put together a
picture book of Quito scenes titled *Quito a la vista*. In that book's preface,
the editors (Laso and J. Roberto Cruz) reported that they saw the volume as
"filling a gap that continues to be felt among us in terms of illustrated publications depicting the capital of the Republic." They objected to the images
of Quito circulated internationally by "foreign tourists," and they bemoaned
photographs that showed Ecuador as a "savage or conquerable country."
Such images, they argued, gave viewers "an impoverished idea of our population and our culture." In response, they proposed a visual project that was
"vindicating, a work of perfect patriotism"; it featured those national scenes
"in which the industries and splendid beauty of the Ecuadorian land offer
objects worthy of being perpetuated by art." This collection of photographs,
in other words, used its images of Quito to forward an accurate vision of
the nation, one produced from within. Of particular concern to the editors
was correcting what they believed to be the distorted national image that
had emerged thanks to foreign photographers' fascination with Ecuadorian
indigeneity. Such photography, they complained, overemphasized the "indigenous element," hiding the true beauty and progress of the country and
"mak[ing] everything ugly."[18] This was a strange critique of existing photography to come from Laso, who was himself known for producing romantic,

costumbrista photographs featuring indigenous subjects. Yet that invocation of national beauty and ugliness, its explicit link to indigeneity, and its contradictory relation with Laso's own oeuvre call further attention to the complicated role of otherness in republican practice.

Laso and Cruz's treatment of ugliness and indigeneity in photography echoes interestingly, if oddly, in another critique of art launched thirty years later by members of the academic organization the Instituto Indigenista del Ecuador (IIE, or Indigenist Institute of Ecuador). In that case the left-leaning social scientists of the IIE found fault with artistic indigenista depictions of indigenous people, arguing that those paintings distorted reality by making indigenous people and their lives appear ugly. Unlike Laso and Cruz, the members of the IIE were focused on the dignity of indigenous communities rather than the dignity of the nation. At the same time the IIE's concern for indigenous uplift was always situated in national terms—its campaign against degrading images was, fundamentally, oriented toward making the nation beautiful. There are, then, striking similarities between these two texts and the images that accompanied them. Both texts negotiate the national status of indigenous people and critique visual materials for distorting the image of the nation. They also work with slippery associations of self and other in which the status of indigenous people as representative of the nation swells and fades yet remains persistently salient.

Framing Others In and Out

In one sense Laso and Cruz's preface to *Quito a la vista* quite clearly positioned indigenous people as other in the sense of a constitutive exterior. Images of indigenous people made the nation appear ugly, so patriotic photographers would emphasize the nation's white-mestizo modernity and high culture. Patriotism and a search for national redemption inspired Laso and Cruz to exclude Indians from the frame and emphasize instead the grand buildings and parks of the capital.

For the most part the photographs included in *Quito a la vista* replicate that sense that indigenous people were fundamentally exterior to a proper vision of the nation. They privilege images of architecture: colonial-era churches, scientific institutions, grand promenades. Though most of the photographs do include human figures, those figures seem incidental. They were caught within the frame because the photos were taken during the course of daily life. Not surprisingly, given Laso and Cruz's stated goals, the humans traversing those Quiteño scenes are marked as white-mestizo and largely as affluent: women appear in full skirts and stylish hats, children wear knickers and bonnets, priests don clerical robes, men sport suits and fedoras.

Despite that general purity, however, the album seems haunted—by the indigenous people left out of the photographs but invoked by Laso and Cruz's own words, by the photos' curious framing, and by the long tradition of city scenes that preceded *Quito a la vista*'s appearance. Calling those prior images and their own careful framing to mind, Laso and Cruz effectively, if unintentionally, repopulated their photographs, asking viewers to remember what was not there. Both their words and their photographs called attention to matters of framing: if previous image makers have aimed their cameras or positioned their easels to highlight Indians, Laso must be framing his shots as well to leave the impoverished beyond the margins. But even then, it seems, it was not quite possible to frame the city's indigenous denizens out entirely.

Throughout *Quito a la vista*, not only in the language of the preface, the editors call attention to their active framing in ways that invoke indigenous presence and align indigenous others with an actually existing nation whose troubles haunt the beautiful photographs that Laso and Cruz sought to provide. The album lacks a photograph of one of Quito's most iconic spaces, the monastery of San Francisco de Quito—the first religious building built in the city after the conquest. It is not hard to guess that the church, with its large plaza given over to a popular market, simply couldn't be photographed without capturing indigenous figures in the frame. In a more active sense, the third and fourth photographs in *Quito a la vista* show two sides of the Plaza Grande in ways that similarly call attention to indigenous absence (figs. 35 and 36).

Rather than providing the iconic, straight-on view used in the four paintings described earlier and in other popular images of the plaza, these two photographs strike odd angles, partially obscuring the buildings they purport to display and drawing attention to the difficulty of capturing the Plaza Grande without indigenous figures. The third photograph offers an oblique view of the presidential palace, Carondelet, and the fourth shows the facade of the archbishop's palace. Like the Plaza Grande paintings, these photographs were clearly taken from the upper stories of adjacent buildings, but where the paintings ask the viewer to gaze straight across the square, Laso's photographs were taken at closer angles: we see Carondelet from the perspective of the archbishop's palace and the archbishop's palace from the Municipio. In the Carondelet photograph in particular, the awkwardness of framing threatens to betray the mission to which it was summoned. An electric street lamp

Fig. 35.   José Domingo Laso, *Palacio del Gobierno*, 1911. Photograph. In Laso and Cruz, *Quito a la vista*.

Fig. 36.   José Domingo Laso, *Palacio Arzobispal*, 1911. Photograph. In Laso and Cruz, *Quito a la vista*.

erupts into the foreground of the frame, highlighting Quito's modern system of lighting but also cutting through the southern third of the building. A tree in the plaza garden blacks out a portion of the center of the building. The right-hand edge of the palace is closely cropped at the edge of the photograph, while a section of an adjacent building appears beyond its edge at the left side of the photograph. The image, in other words, seems just slightly haphazard and out of control. It is not a particularly good photograph of the plaza or of the building behind it.

The awkwardness of the photograph calls attention to Laso and Cruz's explicit indication that their primary task has been about framing: showing the modern nation and excising egregious Indians. In it, we see a national ideal functioning in active contrast to another existing, widely circulated, and familiar vision of the nation. The typical views of the Plaza Grande had to be reoriented and repositioned for them to provide the cleared vision of the nation that Laso and Cruz had promised. The visible contrast between the plaza photographs in *Quito a la vista* and their more familiar predecessors brings the nation-othering sense of representation and republican oligarchy into play.

Laso and Cruz relied on the common sense that photography captures the real. By depicting national spaces cleared of Indians, they hoped to picture the real nation as other-than-indigenous. Yet the very care they took to exclude indigenous people from their images ended up calling the frame of the nation into question and invoking that other who haunts republican polity. There is a sense that excluding Indians from the photographs was no easy task: the authors emphasize the "scrupulous care that we have taken to ensure that all our photographs appear clean and free of those groups to which we have just referred."[19] Creating such clean images required that photographers "trouble themselves," engage "special care," and practice heightened awareness. They had to take their photographs from odd angles and omit certain scenes. The viewer gets the sense, then, that simply walking into the street, setting up the camera, and taking photographs would not allow the sort of photograph desired. Laso and Cruz were not alone in that urge to improve reality for the sake of an interested realism: Joaquín Pinto painted regularly from photographs, appreciating their realism, yet he argued that the work of the painter was to present their scenes "ennobled, even improved . . . according to the judicious and beautiful conception of the painter."[20] In *Quito a la vista* as in Pinto's paintings, the supposed realism of positivist representation comes into focus as artifice. Laso and Cruz are providing the nation aestheticized, not the nation as it is.

Quito a la vista makes Quito modern, beautiful, and filled with potential. Where the editors' preface notes the problem to be excluded (i.e., indigenous people), the introduction to the album triumphantly lists all Quito's historical and contemporary accomplishments, including reference to an extending network of urban electrification, a soon-to-be-completed citywide system of plumbing, and the trans-Andean railway that connected Quito to the world in 1908.[21] What's worth noting here, then, is that such emphasis on beauty and modernity, progress and potential, required an active, intentional, and explicit excision of indigenous figures. That move implies that the nation's problems are likewise blocked out of the picture and placed on the shoulders of an indigenous other that haunts the spaces of government yet can also be framed out of them to enable a new and somehow purer nation.

But since Ecuadorian viewers seeing their nation thus depicted would have been quite aware of the excluded national problems that dogged hope for modern progress, it is too simple to suggest that the excised Indians truly serve here as the nation's constitutive exterior. Instead, though they linger at the edge of the frame, their absent presence calls attention not to the edge of the nation but to the nation-not-shown, the "ugly" nation-other from which Laso and Cruz hope to distinguish themselves and their viewers. Indians, in *Quito a la vista*, thus stood in for the larger context of the nation. Laso and Cruz proposed to represent a wide-ranging national beauty by pulling the best of the nation apart from its problems. They avoided the "ugly" distortions enacted by other image makers by enacting a parallel "beautifying" distortion.

Distortions and Dignity

Thirty-five years later, in the pages of a book edited by the IIE, another discussion of distortion and national vision similarly contested the beauty and ugliness of indigenous images as representative of the nation's otherness. In 1946 the IIE edited a book titled *Cuestiones indígenas del Ecuador* (Indigenous questions of Ecuador). The collection, featuring Ecuador's most prominent social scientists, included a manifesto written by institute members, two chapters outlining scholarly approaches to the "Indian problem," ten chapters offering social scientific studies of Ecuadorian Indians, an extensive bibliography, and an album of photographs featuring indigenous subjects. The opening manifesto lays out the IIE's understanding of indigeneity, making it clear that indigenous people were simultaneously the body of the nation and an other. They were both a distinct racialized culture and a place-based, racially ambiguous class integral to the nation.

The manifesto's circuitous definition of "Indian" bears quoting at length:

> To attempt to define in advance who the Indian is, in a Continent where the majority is racially mixed, is to create a phantasm, an ambiguous and unnecessary pursuit. . . . The Indian problem overlaps entirely with the peasant proletariat, whether pure Indians or descended from an indefinable mixture, without the need to discriminate among sanguinary groups in order to lift them to a higher level of life. The indigenist question is fundamentally a question of economics and politics, not biology. Thus, if the indigenous peasant obtains a good salary, his own parcel of fertile land, and access to cultural improvement, the fact of being pure Indian or mestizo ceases to be of importance. Even now both pure Indians and mestizos appear in the hierarchies of the bureaucracy, military, Church, and university, but a massive percentage still remain at the margins, and they ought to be transformed into an efficient agricultural factor with the economic and cultural capacity necessary for their own improvement. It is the noble pride of belonging to the Indian race, historical foundation of America, that should inspire them. [Until then] the vitality of those nations with indigenous proletariat majorities remains fatally affected.[22]

For the IIE, then, indigenous heritage was problematically ambiguous. It was not possible to determine exactly who was an Indian in biological terms, yet "belonging to the Indian race" ought to be a source of pride and motivation for the "indigenous proletariat majorities." The status of that other and yet integral majority "fatally affected" the nation.

In response, leaders and scholars were tasked with transforming that national other into an "efficient agricultural factor" and providing it with "the economic and cultural capacity necessary for [its] own improvement." In this definition, then, the Indian was both central to the glory of the nation and central to its problems, both the nation's fatal flaw and its future potential. The Indian other was, troublingly, the future of the nation. The solution to that problem of the national other, according to the IIE, required establishing systems of order and administration. Economics and politics, not biology, concerned the authors. A good salary, land ownership, education, and hygiene, if extended toward the indigenous majority, would save it and, thus, the nation.

Yet republican order was not the only sort of representation that concerned the members of the IIE. Their manifesto blended discussion of political reform with a diatribe about aesthetic representation that indicted literary and artistic indigenistas for envisioning indigenous others in ways that demeaned the nation. The IIE manifesto condemned the *feísta* ("ugly-ist") paintings produced by artists such as Eduardo Kingman and Oswaldo Guayasamín, arguing that they degraded indigenous people and replaced indigenous realities with a dangerous and destructive artistic license.[23] In his chapter of *Cuestiones*, the famous social scientist Pio Jaramillo Alvarado expanded that criticism. He excoriated literary and artistic indigenismo, arguing that its visual form "took the Indian as model in order to deform him, having ignored his spirit, stereotyping it using an imported and degenerate impressionism." Jaramillo Alvarado continued with a critique grounded in aesthetic and rhetorical terms: "though the beautiful Andean landscape and the indigenous man have indeed been faithfully interpreted in the painting and sculpture of Quito, the modernist reaction has gone too far and must return to reasonable aesthetic proportions."[24] The "improved" realism practiced by Pinto and costumbrismo, in other words, represented the nation better than did the expressivist social realism of the indigenistas.

Enacting that preference for romantic realism, the editors of *Cuestiones* provided readers with a more appropriate set of representative images. The photographic album included at the back of the book, the opening manifesto asserted, "is a demonstration that the human type of the Ecuadorian Indian is of noble expression, even in those groups pummeled by the misery to which they are condemned."[25] For the IIE the album offered an alternative depiction of Ecuador's indigenous people that corrected the excesses of artistic indigenismo; it used photography to forward an argument about the beauty of indigenous communities and the nation as a whole even in the face of exploitation. Like their predecessors, however, the visual arguments composed by the IIE positioned indigenous people as the nation precisely by making that nation other than the reader and viewer. Rejecting the representation offered by their indigenista compatriots as too distancing, the IIE nevertheless returned to the distancing strategies of earlier eras.

Though the members of the IIE were fierce critics of the status quo who genuinely hoped for an end to oppression and worked consistently in favor of indigenous communities, their approaches exemplified those traditions of investigation, classification, and administration that made the nation other from its governing elites. In addition, as A. Kim Clark points out, popular uptake of the indigenistas' efforts often reinscribed rather than upended commonsense beliefs about the cultural strangeness of indigenous people.[26] The depictions of indigenous people provided in the IIE album corroborate this sense—maintaining visual values drawn not only from romantic costumbrismo but also scientific and anthropological photography. Ironically, though the institute's indigenistas criticized pictorial indigenismo for the ways its intentionally ugly style failed to capture the "genuine interpretation of the Ecuadorian Indian," their own chosen images, though sometimes beautiful, still emphasize poverty, distance from civilization, and social degradation.[27]

The "Album indigenista," published both as part of *Cuestiones* and as a separately bound album, features thirty-four photographs of Ecuadorian indigenous people. Only the subject of the final photograph is identified by name: the indigenous communist leader Dolores Cacuango. Despite *Cuestiones*'s assertion that the album would show the dignity of Ecuador's indigenous people, its photographs are inconsistent in the level of respect they pay their indigenous subjects. In some cases, such as in the photographs *Casique de los indios colorados*, *India Zámbiza*, and *Casique de Otavalo*, indigenous figures appear regal, distant, and wise (the classic image of the noble savage, perhaps) (figs. 37–39). In others, including one captioned "One cup too many!—the Indian tragedy," no word but "degraded" seems appropriate to describe the vision of indigenous life offered (fig. 40). The album honored a sense of indigenous nobility and criticized the effects of racism and failed policy. It also, however, repeatedly visualized poverty and exclusion as endemic to indigenous life in ways that called into question how representative the beauty and dignity of indigenous others might actually be.

The IIE's declared mission to use indigenista texts to "create in the conscience of citizens the urgency, the categorical imperative, to elevate the indigenous problem to the first level [of concern] in the solution of national problems" makes clear that the continued image of indigenous otherness was a necessary component for activating the collective sympathy of those responsible for the nation made of others. As representatives for the popular other, leaders were called to address the "economic misery that affects the majority of the population forming the peasant class, misery that affects the national life in all its manifestations."[28] Cultivating that responsibility in the conscience of the nation's leaders, however, required getting the picture right.

According to *Cuestiones*, the distorted, demanding Indians of artistic indigenismo got the balance wrong, using an imported aesthetic inappropriate to the particular realities of Ecuador. The heavy, rebellious, exaggerated

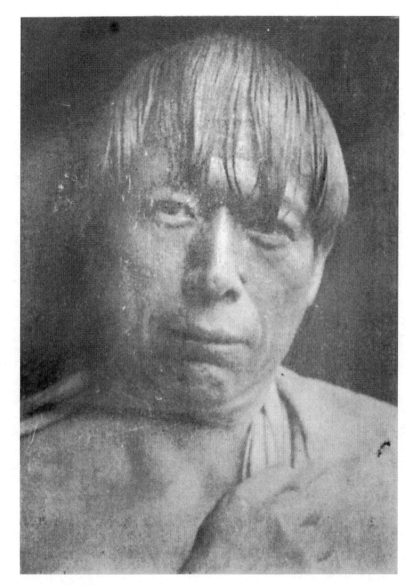

Fig. 37.   *Casique de los indios Colorados—Santo Domingo, Provincia de Pichincha,*
n.d. Reprinted in Instituto Indigenista Ecuatoriano, "Album indigenista." Photograph by Jessie Reeder.

Indians painted by Kingman and his colleagues threatened authority and
made the nation ugly. They ruptured the republican system. Such Indians
were, for the social scientists of the IIE, so entirely other that they could not
summon the necessary representation or responsibility from elite viewers.

Fig. 38.   *India Zámbiza—Prov. de Pichincha,* n.d. Reprinted in Instituto Indigenista Ecuatoriano, "Album indigenista." Photograph by Jessie Reeder.

The aestheticized realism of the album's photographs, however, whether they showed indigenous dignity or degradation, maintained a patina of beauty. That aesthetic representation, in turn, validated representative processes in the political realm by calling attention to the responsibility that the

Fig. 39.   *Casique de Otavalo—Prov. de Imbabura*, n.d. Reprinted in Instituto Indigenista Ecuatoriano, "Album indigenista." Photograph by Jessie Reeder.

elect owed to the masses. The visual order of beauty and ugliness in the album reinstated republican systems of identification and division even as the text as a whole critiqued the republic's neglect and exploitation of indigenous populations.

Fig. 40.   *Una copita de más!—La trajedia india,* n.d. Reprinted in Instituto Indigenista Ecuatoriano, "Album indigenista." Photograph by Jessie Reeder.

Representing Others

This chapter's analysis of order and beauty, representation and responsibility, suggests that contradictions of interiority and exteriority are endemic to
the creation and maintenance of republican nation-states. The relative political power, economic stability, and cultural homogeneity of a given republic
might mitigate or hide the sacrifices of representation, but they are never
absent. Negotiating interiority and exteriority and finding ways to maintain
internal others in their liminal state presents one of the fundamental rhetorical problems of republican life, both historically and in the present moment,
both in Ecuador and beyond.

The popular people in whom sovereignty resides quite easily become a
restive mass that troubles stability and modernity; a national *we* shifts fluidly
to a national *they*. Nations are made up of others. The quintessential task of
nation making, then, is to find ways of imagining those others in relation
to the self that allow for a sense of community. Scholars have frequently
interpreted that process as emphasizing proximity: in imagining the nation
we imagine a sense of "we" that allows the nation to cohere. In the examples discussed here, however, there has been another force at work. Division

coincides with identification as the primary means of making the public whole. Much as we might wish it were different, that process of distinction and othering is as fundamentally republican as the more typically recognized strategies of identification. Distancing oneself from internal compatriots allows space for practices of administration; it redresses national failings without extending responsibility, and it lays the lines of faction that transect any human conglomeration. In this sense, these pages echo the forms of border and demos formation that Etienne Balibar addresses when he writes that "border areas—zones, countries, and cities—are not marginal to the constitution of a public sphere but rather are at the center." The center of a public conglomeration rests not only at the point where power is concentrated but also at the place of the *problem*, "the sites where a people is constituted through the creation of civic consciousness and the collective resolution of the contradictions that run through it."[29]

This chapter has suggested that internal divisions between self and other play crucial roles in making republican polity work and in justifying the inequities of representation. The next chapter inverts the equation, examining moments of identification in which nonindigenous rhetors do the unexpected and position themselves as if they were indigenous. Despite the somewhat dramatic difference in strategy, however, the identifications highlighted in the next chapter share a rhetorical objective with this chapter's examples of division: both identification and division attempt to claim legitimate access to the nation and resolve otherwise troubling contradictions in the experience of national life.

5

PERFORMING STRATEGIC INDIGENEITY

In March 1886, seventy-six men in the small town of Baños, Ecuador, signed an open letter to the president of the republic.[1] Their letter took the central government to task for failing to send sufficient aid to Baños after a recent eruption of Tungurahua, the active volcano towering over the town. Writing their letter not as a direct request but as a distributable broadsheet, the men attempted to shame the president into providing support for the recovery efforts by making their complaints public.

To gain persuasive purchase the Baños letter's authors sought to amplify their neglected, provincial status; they did so by tapping into preexisting anxieties about national integration and white-mestizo responsibility. Rather than using their appeal to claim the rights and protections accompanying citizenship, the literate town notables and residents who wrote and signed the letter positioned themselves as subaltern subjects in need of protection and charity from the state. The letter begins by describing its authors as "children of the field" in relation to the power of the central government and "enlightened society." It complains, "we are an integral part of the canton, the province, [and] the nation in terms of taxes and tribute, but we are savages, barbarians, and independent when it comes to needing help and protection," concluding, "in utopian theories and with sarcastic irony you call us a *sovereign community!*"

Though they made their white-mestizo status clear in their titles and signatures, the authors articulated their local problems as if they were Indians, tapping into a well-established area of national concern. Their introductory phrases established the letter writers' marginalization by presenting it in the familiar terms of inclusion and exclusion by which indigenous communities were articulated with the nation-state. Identifying themselves with images more commonly associated with indigenous supplicants than with white-mestizo citizens, the authors adopted a stylized indigeneity to deepen the legitimacy of their appeal.

The Baños letter's claims—about barbarity, misery, and sovereignty—indexed contemporary debates about the status of indigenous people. They touched especially on the commonplace associations discussed in earlier chapters that aligned indigenous people with rusticity, labor, and tribute. Such references steeped in the ubiquitous commonplaces of indigeneity would have been familiar to the intended audience of political elites in Quito, as well as to a more local audience of literate artisans and landowners.[2] Those readers might themselves have used similar terms to discuss indigenous neighbors they considered to be natural inferiors or to engage in political debates over how best to administer the nation's indigenous population. The Baños letter's claim on the state, in other words, would almost certainly have been recognized as an appeal based on appropriated terms of indigeneity.

Because, until fairly recently, *othering* has been the primary relational strategy used by white-mestizo Ecuadorians to imagine their indigenous compatriots, performances of an indigenous self like the Baños letter stand out as incongruous yet compelling rhetorical moves. Inasmuch as they appear to break with norms of identification and division, such performances reveal areas of contention within their rhetorical ecology. The Baños letter, with its assumed indigenous voice, offers a compelling instance of one such boundary-rupturing rhetorical move: a tactic of identification and appropriation based in the embodiable potential of topoi. That sporadically engaged yet remarkably persistent aspect of the commonplace is at the heart of the rhetorical performances described here. It allows rhetors to carry topoi with them, sometimes fully inhabiting them, and thus negotiate matters of inclusion and exclusion as a thoroughly corporeal matter of public bodies. Tracing the work of embodiable topoi draws attention, in other words, to the ways that what Kenneth Burke terms the "consubstantial" nature of identification uses powerful physicality to organize and segment the community.[3]

The embodied, consubstantial aspect of topoi becomes particularly clear in the changing status of indigeneity in Ecuador between the end of the nineteenth and the middle of the twentieth century. Over that period, performances of stylized indigeneity gained rhetorical force in Ecuador as they took on corporeal terms. Indigeneity became an increasingly embodiable element in white-mestizo performances of self. Its available physicality was a source of persuasive power, aggregating features, behaviors, and histories commonly associated with indigenous bodies but making them assumable by actors from across the socioethnic spectrum whose appeals would benefit from the social circumstances indexed by an indigenous subject position.[4] This chapter traces the history of such performances, exploring how appropriated indigeneity functioned as an argument for a national self. It demonstrates how shifting needs for national legitimacy made such performances increasingly corporeal over time and animated the rhetorical force of the commonplace as embodiable. Beginning from the Baños letter's example of white-mestizos speaking as if indigenous and looking at a series of similar appeals, the chapter follows developments in such appropriations that parallel the transformation from nineteenth-century romanticism to twentieth-century social realism, from careful distance to intimate proximity.

Late nineteenth-century performances of indigeneity depended primarily on invocations of social type, inhabiting a vaguely embodied subject position predicated on assumptions about the roles and tasks that indexed indigeneity. By the mid-twentieth century, as romanticism gave way to social realism, performances of indigeneity placed more emphasis on physical conditions and inheritable traits. That later era's increasing focus on mestizaje and on incorporating indigenous people into the body of the nation gave embodiable topoi of the indigenous self more widespread rhetorical force than they had previously. Appropriating indigeneity for white-mestizo use, those topoi helped authorize white-mestizo national visions and provided distance from an actually indigenous past and present.

That use of embodied topoi of indigeneity for national persuasion in Ecuador calls attention to how appropriations of rhetorical legitimacy delimit the public body, and it emphasizes how ideals of access and inclusion can sustain republican publics predicated on exclusion and division. Tracing how contradictory performances of public construction in Ecuador transmit "social knowledge, memory, and a sense of identity through reiterated [behavior]," then, this chapter demonstrates that even profound identification can be a means of division through reiterated appropriation.[5] Close attention to the arrangement and use of bodies in the body politic makes clear how thoroughly identification and division coexist in the ecologies of rhetorical constitution.

On Embodiable Topoi

That topoi should be assumable means of self-definition ought not to be surprising in light of the arguments advanced in previous chapters. Those analyses have demonstrated that the commonplace patterns that inform identification are lively and available; such features also make them implicitly embodiable.

Aristotle's notion of *energeia*, which "makes the lifeless live" and actualiz-es "things or [makes] them appear to be engaged in activity," gives Ralph Cintrón's understanding of topoi as "social energy" a particularly physical basis. As Cintrón explains, "If the point is emotion, motion, action, and ac-tualization—and most importantly if our subject is politics—we might look to verbal and non-verbal crystallizations that have sufficient *umpf* to actualize the body politic."[6] In other words, the energy of topoi is generative in a cor-poreal sense; it not only moves but makes the public body.

Understanding the ways that topoi inhabit and motivate bodies, however, requires something more than the metaphoric language of Cintrón's analysis. The embodied use of topoi is not solely a matter of symbolic appropriation— it brings active, physical bodies to bear on matters of symbolic and material concern to the lived experience of the public. Making sense of those topoi, then, demands attention to the ways that persuasion is both material and symbolic, a matter of energy and substance. In that sense Burke's intricately incarnate notions of identification and persuasion lend useful insight into how rhetors appropriate and embody common sense for rhetorical purposes. His discussions of identification as grounded in questions of "substance" frame the physicality of rhetorical influence in ways useful for understand-ing how topoi of indigeneity have moved in Ecuadorian rhetorical ecologies. Threading those Burkean theories into the specific practices of Ecuadorian rhetors like the Baños authors further unwinds the ways that commonplaces in general are knit with physicality.

In *A Rhetoric of Motives*, Burke suggests that identification is always a ques-tion of achieving "consubstantiality." Identifying with a position, we become "'substantially one' with a person other than [ourselves] . . . at once a distinct substance and consubstantial with another."[7] In his elaborations on consub-stantiality, that shared substance of identification is frequently corollary to genetic familial relations; it is decidedly carnal. His explanatory anecdotes for identification as consubstantiality—from the rupture of birth to an afraid-of-heights father's momentary urge to drop his son over a ledge—make even more clear that Burke sees identification as not only risky but fleshy: a matter for bodies in relation. His anecdotes also demonstrate, however, the ambi-guities that prevent identification from being sheer transubstantiation. In identifying with another, we become "substantially one" rather than "wholly one" with that other, just as biological offspring both share the body of their mother and yet also remain distinct from it.

Identification, in this sense, leads us to tread an ambiguous terrain in which we are both "one" and "other"—physically aligned with the positions of another yet not quite that other. For Burke, dwelling in that ambiguity allows a public *"acting-together"* through which members of the public "have common sensations, concepts, images, ideas, attitudes."[8] The examples provided by the Ecuadorian context suggest, however, that such *"acting-together"* need not necessarily mean that "one" and "other" act together. It may, in fact, mean that one acts *on* or *in place of* that other. Consubstantial identification, in other words, is not only a matter of rhetor and audience identifying with each other. Sometimes it involves identification with a third substance to draw the audience into a new relationship with the rhetor or with one another. As the case of Ecuadorian rhetors embodying indigeneity also makes clear, the rites of identification can include a three-stage movement from identification to appropriation and then to dissociation that makes the other into self and, in the process, sets the other aside.

Burke addresses that movement from inclusion to expulsion in characteristically stark language when he explains consubstantiality in terms of the scapegoat. The scapegoat, he writes, "is profoundly consubstantial with those who, looking upon it as a chosen vessel, would ritualistically cleanse themselves by loading the burden of their own iniquities upon it."[9] Scapegoat rituals, for Burke, perform their communal effects through an initial identification (the people with the scapegoat), then a move to division (the people from scapegoat), and then a return to identification (the people against the scapegoat). As the philosopher Beth Eddy explains of Burke's use of consubstantiality and identification to understand religious feeling, "The possibility that identical symbolic acts can enact opposite social intentions—that rites of identity can play on consubstantiality's ability both to identify and to divide—provides symbol-using animals with their greatest religious asset and simultaneously their greatest liability. Sometimes we want to bring opposites together; sometimes we need to separate them and guardedly keep them apart."[10] Consubstantiality makes room for both. It allows a sort of transfusion in which the substance of self and other flows among bodies, relying on identification yet making possible appropriation and division. What neither Burke nor Eddy notes, though, is that there is a possible transference of selfhood from the rejected scapegoat to the valued community.

That transference is very much at work in Ecuadorian white-mestizo performances of indigeneity. Identifying with indigeneity by appropriating indigenous voices, those rhetors claim legitimacy for themselves and set aside other possible appeals. By embodying topoi of indigeneity, Ecuadorian rhetors index and incorporate available assumptions about indigenous people. They reproduce what Cintrón terms the "contradictory, collective passions and convictions that constitute a people" through a corporeal com-mon sense.[11] Thus, for example, invocations of social type in the Baños letter accessed the accumulated assumptions of late nineteenth-century white-mestizo Ecuadorians concerning indigenous people. They called into service the body of a rustic Indian rather than a white-mestizo landholder, and in the process they secured rhetorical agency for the landholder rather than his indigenous compatriots. Performing indigeneity activated storehouses of social energy connected to the physical features and material histories of indigenous people as understood by white-mestizos. Along the way it made the letter's appeal to government intervention and charity more compelling, even as it displaced possible indigenous appeals. Embodying indigeneity, nonindigenous people gained consubstantiality with a stylized indigenous subject and invoked the relationships of exploitation and obligation that ex-isted between the state and indigenous people.

Nineteenth- and mid-twentieth-century Ecuadorian white-mestizos typi-cally imagined indigenous people as problematic figures. The rhetorical strategy of speaking as if one were an indigenous person could hold pro-ductive appeal in dominant contexts only if it engaged both the desire for distance and the anxious obligation that white-mestizos associated with an indigenous subject. The language of consubstantiality is useful for under-standing the resulting push and pull over unequal terms. Burke suggests that consubstantiality can be "symbolically established between beings of un-equal status" without necessarily removing those status inequalities.[12] Such unequal identification, for Burke, seems to invoke a relationship in two di-rections (between rhetor and audience). But his discussion of consubstanti-ality in terms of the scapegoat also makes clear that consubstantial relations between beings of unequal status need not be mutual. Sometimes those of higher status find it convenient to displace subalterns by claiming identifica-tion with them.

That is certainly the sort of Burkean symbolic identification between be-ings of unequal status at work in embodied topoi of indigeneity in Ecuador. In such appropriative identifications, performing indigenous subjectivity helped legitimize the experiences of a national public. Positioning them-selves as indigenous, white-mestizos invoked the figure of the Indian to serve political ideologies that had little positive impact on the lives of in-digenous communities.[13] As in the Baños letter, those white-mestizos made themselves, and the nation, "substantially one" (i.e., consubstantial) with indigenous people to claim the attention of the nation. Those claims to an indigenous self also pushed a troubling indigenous other further away.

Such coexistence between identification and division in performances of indigeneity goes beyond Burke's own assessment that identification occurs always in concert with division. The sort of dissociation at work in the Ecuadorian example doesn't just allow white-mestizos to side with one group against another. Instead, appropriation is a means of changing the valence of national conversation. The ambiguous, appropriative interplay between identification and division in embodiable topoi calls for blending Burke's sense of identification as both partisan and "compensatory to division" with rhetorical theorists Chaim Perelman and Lucie Olbrechts-Tyteca's approach to dissociation in terms of conceptual redefinition. Describing the embodiable topoi of indigeneity in terms of identification and dissociation invokes both Burke's exploration of the "ways in which individuals [or groups] are at odds with one another" and Perelman and Olbrechts-Tyteca's invocation of the "desire to remove an incompatibility" between propositions and create a lasting coherence.[14]

Seeing dissociation as both the rejection of a connection and the effort to create a lasting coherence in the public body by changing the meaning of an existing position allows us to understand an otherwise contradictory fact: embodiable topoi simultaneously perform indigeneity as a symbolic body for the nation and elide the participation of indigenous people within the nation. In other words, the physical appropriation of indigeneity simultaneously underlines the place of the rhetor within the national body and reifies the marginality of the appropriated subjectivity. Rejecting the direct participation of indigenous people but also taking on that rejected indigeneity, the dissociation inherent to embodiable topoi takes different forms across different eras. At each moment, however, its force comes from a white-mestizo desire simultaneously to invoke legitimacy by incorporating a stylized indigenous subjectivity and to remain separate from the negative valence of actually being indigenous.

Such performances of stylized indigeneity depend on a slippage between what we might call "real" indigeneity and the nexus of circumstances and attributes that signal indigeneity. Or to appropriate Robert Berkhofer's terms, they call attention to the distinction between "real" indigenous people and the "Indian" as a colonial invention. The colonizer's stylized Indianness produces an indigenous subject position that facilitates colonial ends and constrains the actions of indigenous people when they appeal to the state. Scott Lyons calls such dictated terms of performance "rhetorical imperialism": they exercise "control of others by setting the terms of the debate" and "*identify* [those others] by describing them in certain ways."[15] Rhetorical imperialism is insidiously constitutive, facilitating both the identification of indigenous others and identification with the nation. It convenes the subject positions from which indigenous people must speak, and it allows white-mestizos to speak *as if* indigenous. In Ecuador, where white-mestizos could access indigenous subjectivity through their own mestizo heritage, the appropriations made possible by rhetorical imperialism were similar to, but also distinct from, those examined in U.S.-based studies of rhetorical appropriation.[16] Performances of indigeneity by white-mestizos made an indigenous self increasingly central to national legitimacy even as they redefined indigeneity in their own favor.

Of course, indigenous social actors in Ecuador also performed their own indigeneity within and against the terms of rhetorical imperialism, assuming and altering their performances in tension with those already in circulation. As previous chapters show, indigenous people appropriated the state's paternalistic language about indigenous communities and turned state strategies for development to their own ends. Given these complexes of performance and response, it is difficult to assert a firm boundary between real and performed indigeneity, not because indigeneity ceases to exist but because the signals that communicate indigeneity are quite often the stylized subjectivities of embodiable topoi, shaped by the rhetorical imperialism of dominant white-mestizos and by the resistance of indigenous peoples.

Social Types and Nineteenth-Century Embodiable Topoi

In the second half of the nineteenth century, performances of indigeneity like the Baños letter flirted with physical appropriation by engaging the commonplace energy invested in romantic social types. These white-mestizo identifications with indigeneity were inchoately corporeal, making use of the patterns built up around some of their moment's most recognizable types circulated in visual contexts: Indians as miserable laborers, pastorally romantic and culturally isolated. From scientific treatises that treated indigenous populations alongside the flora and fauna of natural history to travel narratives that bemoaned the backwardness and squalor of Ecuadorian Indians and costumbrista painting that made indigenous laborers available for view, the amodern rusticity of the generic indigenous type was cast in bodily terms of comportment and attire.[17] Through their circulation in print, political debate, classrooms, and public spaces, such images made indigenous bodies and the meanings associated with them widely available to literate white-mestizos.

Balancing notions of barbarian degradation and romanticized dignity, late nineteenth-century images of indigenous social types could then be mapped onto the terrain of the long-standing debate over the proper relationship between white-mestizos and indigenous people in the emerging nation-state.

The Baños letter exemplifies this appropriation of social type, matching its era's increasing focus on the state's responsibility for its indigenous population. The assumable form of the miserable indigenous type provides the main force of the letter's appeal. It begins with recognizable references to indigenous pastoral simplicity, comparing the residents of Baños to "children of the field." With the next lines the authors index the history of indigenous exploitation by presenting themselves as suffering the "indifference and cruel indolence" of the regional tax collectors. Then, they outline their place in the nation in words that, ironically, presage Brooke Larson's far more recent (2004) argument that white-mestizos saw indigenous people as "unalterable and suffering laborers" who provided but did not participate in the modernization of Ecuadorian society.[18] The authors of the Baños letter assert, "We are members of the social body when it comes to giving our energy and resources to sustain society, and we are insignificant pariahs when we need her help" to restore prosperity.[19] Driving home their invocation of indigenous subjectivity, the authors describe their community as "tyrannized, oppressed and devalued" and as having "lost the strength to . . . claim what belongs to [them]." They end the introductory paragraphs with the lines quoted earlier: "we are savages, barbarians, and independent when it comes to needing help and protection."

If the opening paragraphs of the letter reference indigenous social types through the terms of romanticism and exploitation, more physical aspects of those types emerge in later paragraphs that shift to complaints about unrequited labor for the sake of the nation. These paragraphs complain that the town's residents had been solely responsible for the labor to reopen roadways destroyed by volcanic detritus. Echoing those costumbrista images that recorded indigenous public works labor, the authors invoke forced conscription, noting, "since long ago it has been our regular task to work the roads and bridges [of our region]" and complaining that this work had been done by the people of Baños alone: "without salary, without help, without reimbursement, we are always employed in these [public] works" that are, they note, then used to transport the wealth of the region to the capital as taxes. As chapter 3 makes clear, the exploitative labor that the letter imagines as done by Baños' residents was more likely performed by local indigenous communities drafted through forced conscription. In this vein the letter also echoes the history of indigenous resistance to conscription as well as indigenous communities' increasingly frequent petitioning of the central state for protection against exploitation.[20] The letter, in other words, uses references to laboring social types to cue its readers to the commonplaces of indigeneity. Aligning themselves with the plight of indigenous communities, the authors fit themselves into an ongoing national conversation and gain rhetorical legitimacy in the process.

Though the juridical establishment of indígenas as "miserable persons" "unfit to exercise the rights of citizenship" ended with tribute's abolition in 1857, the condition of indigenous "misery" remained a commonplace of nineteenth-century discourse, invoked regularly in official documents and popular petitions.[21] Ecuadorian political elites regularly asserted indigenous peoples' fundamental lack of civilization, offered policies designed to control indigenous communities, and expressed paternalistic concern for indigenous uplift. This pattern of misery, exploitation, and appeal to charity positioned indigenous populations as the archetypical representations of the subjugation of the people before the paternal state. White-mestizos (and indigenous people) attempting to perform a subjectivity credible to the state could adopt such tropes of misery to appeal to the dominant notions of indigeneity in circulation.

In their use of that larger national conversation, the Baños authors appropriated the terms of physical misery and exploitative labor for their own ends. Their descriptions of the Baños community conjured powerful stereotypes about the neediness of indigenous people and the responsibility of the state to provide for them.[22] The availability of the trope of indigenous misery thus allowed the authors of the Baños letter to stand in the place of the indigenous social type through what rhetoricians John Jones and Robert Rowland term a "shared sense of victimage," encouraging an audience of white-mestizos to identify the commonplaces of the indigenous social type with the particular concerns of the authors.[23] The Baños authors made their concerns consubstantial with the concerns of indigenous people; they identified with indigeneity "even [though] their interests were not joined," because the available commonplace of indigenous misery allowed their interlocutors to see them in parallel terms.[24]

The letter projects a stylized indigenous subjectivity to make space for paternalistic intervention, responding to a rhetorical situation in which appeals to the government as paternal figure were the norm. In this context, *el indio* becomes the archetypal subject in need of charity, the depth of misery that legitimizes both the subject's claim on the state and need for a strong government. With its appeal to the state based on the unrewarded labor of the people, the letter highlights the government's corollary obligation to intervene paternalistically to relieve communal suffering. It also engages that central anxiety of many white-mestizos at the time: how to imagine a modern republic despite what they described as the persistent backwardness of indigenous communities.

Though the commonsense meanings associated with indigenous social types were widely available to late nineteenth-century Ecuadorians, the letter's explicit connection between social types and the idea of the nation links it particularly closely to the nation-making indigeneity of costumbrismo. The appeals to physicality at work in costumbrista social types provide visual insight into a wider rhetorical ecology whose patterns and energies allowed performances of stylized indigenous subjectivity to carry peculiar and powerful force.

While costumbrista artwork proliferated throughout the second half of the nineteenth century, it was never a monolithic form. The ways that costumbrista artists positioned subject and audience shifted, for example, as image makers invoked different sorts of social relations. As discussed in earlier chapters, most costumbrismo, especially that produced by foreign artists (ca. 1850–70), emphasized a distancing, European gaze. In that sense costumbrismo eschewed any sense of embodied interaction between viewer and subject. Art historian Trinidad Pérez suggests, however, that some costumbrismo, especially work by Joaquín Pinto, did promote a sense of encounter between subject and viewer.[25] That move in the genre was related in part to the growing national market for costumbrista paintings and, more particularly, to the changing social values of those domestic purchasers.[26] Paying attention to the increased sense of relationship visible in late costumbrismo sheds light on how embodying the topoi of indigeneity might have strengthened the Baños letter's demand that the central government recognize its community's needs.

That changing relationship is visible, for example, in popular costumbrista depictions of the *aguatero*, or water carrier. Quito's aguateros were among the most commonly reproduced costumbrista figures. The indigenous peons tasked with carrying potable water from public plazas to private residences were ubiquitous figures in nineteenth-century Quito. Their initial popularity likely coincided with the fascination that Quito's system of water distribution evoked among European travelers. Aguateros' common presence in the city's public spaces—filling their jars from plaza fountains—made them frequent subjects of photography, lithography, and painting (including the four Plaza Grande paintings discussed in chapter 4). Some of those images, following classic costumbrista style, place aguateros in isolation. Many, however, expand to include the fountain as well. In these pictures the indigenous aguatero bearing his burden is bent dramatically at the waist, resting a large pottery urn on the small of his back. The urn sits vertically, towering half again the height of the man. Ropes knotted around the urn and passed across the man's chest secure its precarious balance. The man's gaze is directed toward the ground in front of him and he is fully occupied by his task (fig. 41).

Fig. 41.   Ernest Charton, *Porteur d'eau*, n.d. Watercolor on paper. Collection of Modern and Republican Art, Ecuadorian Ministry of Culture, Quito, Ecuador.

Owing to the initially European market for costumbrismo and the tendency for elite Ecuadorians in that era to identify themselves culturally with Europe, these traditional aguateros emphasize the gaze of the viewer. They place the objective viewer as fundamentally exterior to the scene and its passive, exotic subject. This relationship between viewer and image does not leave much space for the sort of paternal engagement we see invoked in the Baños letter. These costumbrista Indians are exotic objects of fascination, not subordinate members of a shared national public. Their labor invokes cultural observation, not civic obligation. In these images the aguatero's passive receipt of the viewer's gaze and his status as exotic object limit the possibility for the viewer to encounter the social type as a member of a shared public.[27]

That lack of shared publicity evident in traditional aguatero images (and in a corollary politics that provided separate forms of administration for indigenous communities) is effectively explained by the absence of one of the key elements of publicity identified by publics theorists. Michael Warner, for example, notes that publics are based on a "relation among strangers." That relationship is, however, not organized around encounters with mysterious, exotic outsiders. Instead, "In the context of a public . . . strangers can be treated as already belonging to our world. More: they *must* be. We are routinely oriented to them in common life." In a similar vein, rhetorical theorists Robert Hariman and John Louis Lucaites assert that "publics by their nature require . . . embodied forms of sociality (or they will not be effective)."[28] A sense of encounter and of common (even if virtual) space are, in other words, foundational elements of publicity. That is, for these theories of the public, the inclusivity of a public extends only so far as its members can imagine themselves in relation with one another. To the extent that Ecuadorian artifacts treating indigeneity allow no possibility of encounter between viewer and subject, then, they also elide the public relationship between themselves and an indigenous other. Traditional costumbrista aguateros, then, do not invoke a sense of shared publicity, because they lack a sense of encounter and instead emphasize an objectifying distance between viewer and viewed. Such Indians were not available for identification or appropriation.

As the century progressed, however, the conditions emerged for a sense of public encounter that did include indigenous people. Those conditions, however, complicate existing understandings of the "we" created by publicity, not just for Ecuador but for theories of the public in general. Warner, Hariman and Lucaites, and other publics theorists predicate publics on the possibility of equality and access. They critique actually existing publics for excluding marginalized populations, arguing that "legitimate" publics must on principle, as Nancy Fraser puts it, allow "all who are potentially affected [to] participate as peers in deliberations concerning the organization of their common affairs."[29] For this scholarship, the "we" of a legitimate public must be common or else publicity itself is endangered. And yet the unequal, illegitimate publics of actually existing democracy remain among our only available examples of publicity. The example of public practice in Ecuador helps make sense of that gap between ideal and actually existing, between legitimate and illegitimate.

In Ecuador, changing political values at the end of the nineteenth century, particularly those advocated by Liberals, brought indigenous people increasingly into the sphere of stranger relations and embodied sociality described by Warner and Hariman and Lucaites. The shape of those relations as invented by white-mestizo elites, however, did not move from exoticism to Warner's equality-based "co-membership" or Fraser's legitimate public. The sort of publics creation at work in the embodied social encounters of nineteenth-century Ecuador instead retained inequality within co-membership. These may have been illegitimate publics, yet they functioned as publics. White-mestizos appropriating an indigenous self still imagined indigenous people as inferior compatriots; they simply placed them within the public body rather than outside it.

Much of Joaquín Pinto's costumbrista work envisions that sort of common embodied publicity. According to Pérez, Pinto's costumbrismo "moves away from stereotyping figures to the point where, without ceasing to represent social and ethnic types, he individualizes them in terms of physical features, anatomy, range of gestures, expression, volume and colour." Pinto's images, in other words, move the viewer from external observation into a sense of physical encounter. Pérez continues, "Pinto's work, moreover, reduces the distance between the image and the viewer by humanizing the figures. He abandons any claim to objectivity in the gaze and takes up a position directly facing the characters he represents."[30] Pinto's version of the rondín discussed in the introduction (fig. 1), for example, alters typical depictions by turning the watchman's body slightly and raising his gaze to meet that of the viewer. That watchman also appears to lift his lantern intentionally toward the viewer, as if to shed light on the street between them. In Pinto's *Rondín*, then, viewers approach the watchman as they might have met him in the darkened Quito street; earlier paintings of the night watchman presume no such familiar encounter.

Pinto's alterations of costumbrismo evoke an encounter between viewer and subject and envision a sense of national publicity that begins to include indigenous people as inferior compatriots. These changes foster a shared public culture through a version of what Hariman and Lucaites term the "performative embodiment of social codes."[31] The terms of shared publicity offered by Pinto's costumbrismo and by artifacts like the Baños letter, however, are hierarchical in ways that might trouble even the theories of publicity offered by scholars who critique Jürgen Habermas's image of the bourgeois public sphere. Such theories recognize that access to bourgeois publicity has often been premised on exclusions and the inability of subalterns to bracket identity or even enter the dominant spaces of public life.[32] Yet because they have as their goal an effort to understand the possibilities for productive, plural publicity, such theories still tend to imagine publics and counterpublics in terms of mutual access. One might be excluded from a particular public while participating in another, or one might work to expand access to a closed public. Inequality, however, remains anathema to any functioning public in these theories.

Fraser, for example, argues that theorists of "actually existing democracy" must "render visible the ways in which social inequality taints deliberation within publics" but also makes clear that "an adequate conception of the public sphere requires not merely the bracketing, but rather the elimination, of social inequality." Warner, for his part, emphasizes that "without a faith—justified or not—in self-organized publics, organically linked to our activity in their very existence, capable of being addressed, and capable of action, we would be nothing but the peasants of capital—which of course we might be, and some of us more than others." He continues, "This is why any distortion or blockage in access to a public can be so grave, leading the people to feel powerless and frustrated."[33] For these theorists, in other words, inequality and exclusion are foundational problems of publicity, but they reveal the failures of public spheres rather than serving as troubling features rife within the practice of publicity.

The insights made available by the Ecuadorian context by no means undermine such assertions about the destructive influence of inequality on publics. They do, however, recognize that inequality is as endemic to publics as it is anathema to their ideal. That recognition moves the role of inequality even more fully into the center of discussion over publics, suggesting that publicity can be a means of establishing Burkean consubstantiality "between beings of unequal status."[34] In this sense, as Pinto's images emphasize common publicity over an objective gaze, they also introduce and reproduce a shared but hierarchical national public. That sense of embodied encounter still "provides a community with both models for civic action and a sense of collective agency," as described by Hariman and Lucaites, but the available models are not founded on assumptions of equal status.[35] Such encounters build co-presence without the burdens of equality or concomitant guarantees of equal access to public agency. They help clarify how the body politic makes sense of and comes to accept its divisions and exclusions, building a common sense of republican sovereignty out of structural inequality.

That sense of publicity without equality is quite visible in Pinto's revision of the popular aguatero image. Though he produced sketches of traditional aguateros, he does not appear to have carried any of those sketches into a final painting.[36] In fact, Pinto's only extant painting of a water carrier is a 1904 oil painting titled *Orejas de palo* (fig. 42), which departs significantly from traditional tropes. Those differences emphasize how Pinto, perhaps because of his investment in representing the lived experience of Quito's streets and people, abandoned the distance of traditional costumbrismo and invoked instead shared physical presence and a sense of paternalistic obligation. The subject of the painting, a blind man dressed in a ragged poncho, stands upright and walks directly toward the viewer. A barrel rests crosswise on the man's upper back and is strapped in place across his chest. The ends of the barrel frame the man's head, forming the wooden ears that give the painting its name. The man holds a staff to guide his walk across the uneven cobbles of the plaza beneath him. Where the traditional image of the aguatero invokes a ubiquitous laborer available to the observing gaze of the Europeanized viewer, a figure so common as not even to appear in municipal discussions over the problem of potable water, Pinto's blind man is a specific character. As Pérez suggests, his direct approach and the demand implied in his gaze evoke an incipient interaction with the viewer. That moment of implied interaction in public transforms the role of the viewer from observation into encounter. It allows the creation of a sense of mutual publicity and shared nationality that undergirds the sense of white-mestizo paternalistic obligation so key to appeals like the one in the Baños letter.

The traditional aguatero image implies that the indigenous porter is more a mechanism of transport than a co-member of society. This view, which relegated indigenous people to a status as the means for—but not members of—the national public, however, was in competition with the one visible in *Orejas de palo* and in the Baños letter, which asked white-mestizos to relate to indigenous people through a sort of noblesse oblige oriented toward the recuperation of the degraded Indian. Based in charity, this relationship did not change the material status of indigenous people, as exploitation and rigid social hierarchies continued apace; however, the means by which that status

Fig. 42.   Joaquín Pinto, *Orejas de palo*, 1904. Oil on canvas. Collection of the Museo Alberto Mena Caamaño, Centro Cultural Metropolitano, Quito, Ecuador.

was legitimated altered. The blind man of Pinto's *Orejas de palo* is physically present for the viewer and thus makes demands on the viewer. He advances directly through the image, presenting himself as a subordinate compatriot worthy of both pity and control. The viewer's task is to engage as modern citizen with the degraded, yet recuperable, Indian.

Extrapolating from the ways that the shared physical encounter in Pinto's images convenes a viewer at once compatriot and superior makes space for understanding the appeals of the Baños letter in more depth. The letter, like Pinto's aguatero, engages an indigenous voice to invoke the obligations of its readers, particularly that of the central state for its marginalized communities. It frames that obligation, however, in terms of shared publicity without democratic equality. The physical invocation of social type and shared public space in both artifacts emphasizes an appeal to the neediness of the subject, marking an assumption that the proper relationship between white-mestizos and indigenous people was a relationship of charitable obligation. The "performative embodiment of social codes" in Pinto's paintings and in the Baños letter helped white-mestizo citizens imagine the sort of inclusive access to the national public that publics theorists suggest is a precondition for publicity without requiring inclusion to mean equality.[37] As A. Kim Clark notes of Ecuadorian national identity, "it is the [idea of] inclusiveness, the very universalizing tendencies of the idiom [of inclusiveness] through which the national community is imagined, that allows various social groups to see different populations and regions as either central or not to the national community."[38] As chapter 1 demonstrates, nineteenth-century white-mestizo elites were quite aware of the ideological *need* for an inclusive national public, but they were also invested in limiting the reach and the implications of such universal accessibility. Appropriating the terms of indigeneity to build identification but also establish distance served that contradictory need well. The shared but unequal publicity introduced in costumbrista images like Pinto's and in the Baños letter did the important work of allowing white-mestizos to imagine themselves as responsible, controlling co-members of a carefully segregated national body.

A Fascination with Indigenous Corporeality and Spirituality

If at the end of the nineteenth century invocations of indigeneity emphasized the inchoately physical terms of indigenous labor and white-mestizo paternalism, the rise of the twentieth century brought an explicit corporeality to discourse about the Indian and the nation. It brought, as well, a corollary increase in the intensity of white-mestizo identification with, appropriation of, and dissociation from indigeneity. That growth in embodied relation and exception can be traced to several trends at the national and continental levels. Mercedes Prieto notes that the emergence of sociology as an academic discipline during the first decades of the twentieth century fostered discussions in the Ecuadorian academy that positioned indigenous peoples as physically degraded, racially dissolute, and civically incapable—corporeal problems caused by years of colonization and exploitation.[39] By the second decade of the twentieth century, those academic discussions had direct impact on political discourse about indigenous citizenship, grounding its possibilities in questions of hygiene, diet, and training.

Around the same time the idea of mestizaje—emphasizing the inherent cultural-racial mixture of Latin American peoples—came more to the fore in national and continental discourse. Long a factor in discussions of the national body, in the 1920s and 1930s mestizaje became a central means of interpreting national character. The idea that all Latin Americans shared in indigenous and European heritage and that indigenous heritage was central to making the Americas distinct gained increasing commonsense force.[40] In this context the possibilities of indigeneity as embodiable topoi grew exponentially, helping make a national self that included indigeneity while excluding Indians.

As chapter 2 makes clear, the questions of indigenous spirituality and corporeality that dominated political, academic, and cultural debate starting in the second quarter of the twentieth century presumed an innate link between such corporeal spirituality and the land. They fused landscape, or the "fuerzas telúricas" (forces of the earth), with the indigenous body.[41] That same narrative, influenced by notions of mestizaje, connected those indigenous fuerzas telúricas with the character of the national body and the idea of a national "we." Such telluric connection allowed white-mestizo Ecuadorians to appropriate indigeneity and simultaneously position the mestizo as the truly autochthonous national figure.

An article in one of the first issues of *Letras del Ecuador* neatly demonstrates that fusion of land, physicality, and indigeneity to characterize a mestizo nation. The article, titled "La tristeza: Disfraz de la Raza" (Melancholy: The disquise of the Race), responded to European characterizations of the "South American race" as fundamentally melancholic.[42] Its author, Arturo Montesinos Malo, echoed common suggestions that "congenital melancholy" was a "commonplace of [Ecuadorian] physiognomy." Melancholy was, in other words, a simultaneous matter of local psychology, spirituality, and physicality. It was genetic and phenotypic.

The source and subject of that physical melancholy, however, was slippery for Montesinos. On the one hand, he invokes both José Vasconcelos's and José Martí's emphases on Latin Americans as a mestizo people. Early paragraphs contrast "nuestra raza" (our race) with the "pure white" and speak of that South American "race" in the first-person plural. At the same time,

Montesinos's main indicators of that race and its sadness suggest a more singular source. Both his text and the photograph placed in the center of the page make clear that for Montesinos and his editors, national melancholy is grounded in the nations' indigenous character. In fact, the first thing that grabs the reader's attention when turning to the article is the large portrait photograph of a rondador that illustrates it (fig. 2). The photograph fills nearly a sixth of the page, dominating the center of the article. Its caption, "in the American continent lives a melancholy race," links the indigenous rondador of the photograph firmly to the "Raza" in the title of the article. If the article's first paragraphs suggest that the titular race was mestizo, in other words, the photograph suggests with equal power that its melancholy was indigenous.

The photograph, by the German-Ecuadorian photographer Bodo Wuth, was produced in a style straddling costumbrismo and indigenismo, much like the photographs published in the album accompanying *Cuestiones indígenas del Ecuador*. Such photographs frequently illustrated articles in *Letras* and other contemporary periodicals, featuring indigenous subjects as common national characters. Wuth's photograph appeals to multiple tropes of indigeneity to establish a simultaneous melancholy and dignity for its subject. From the camera's low angle to the photograph's strong backlight and its presentation of the rondador against a studio canvas suggesting a leaden sky, the image makes its tristeza palpable. It also makes tristeza indigenous: the rondador's face appears in slight shadow, accentuating a high forehead, deep-set eyes, and long nose that easily bespoke indigeneity. His long braid and poncho only emphasize that ethnoracial location further.[43]

On the one hand, this image of the rondador invoked the sorts of distancing typical of traditional costumbrismo: the rondador seems removed from the viewer and cast as an object of observation. On the other, the intended relationship between viewer and subject in Wuth's photograph is clarified—brought closer together—by Montesinos's words. The article's title, text, and caption all encourage viewers to imagine themselves in relation to the melancholy rondador, even to see themselves as part of a melancholy race; readers, author, and illustration are all part of a national "we" that Montesinos evokes again and again. In this sense Montesinos stages an encounter between the rondador of Wuth's photograph and the readers of the article. The indigenous rondador embodies the trait that defines all of Montesinos's readers. Ecuadorian melancholy may be an indigenous melancholy, but it infuses Ecuadorian features more broadly.

Montesinos's text quickly provides an implicit explanation for the place of the indigenous rondador in the article's narrative of mestizaje. Enacting a gradual appropriation of indigeneity into national culture, Montesinos writes,

> [Our] melancholy begins high up in the desolate white peaks of the Andes. From there it descends with the icy breeze onto the bald heads of the minor mountains and, encountering the weak friendship of the grasslands, finally materializes as music. The shepherd elaborates that melancholy . . . melody that descends into the valleys and enters the sleepy villages, where it is transformed into the *yaraví* [a type of Incaic music]. When the Andean plaint enters the city it seems to civilize itself and arrives at the portals of harmony. From there emerges the *pasillo* [a criollo dancing song], the marriage of the telluric sighs with the suicidal verses of poets writing in their own blood.[44]

The gradual civilization of the Andean melody as it descends from jagged peaks through grasslands and villages and into the city follows a route similar to that asked of indigenous people themselves, under pressure to culturally assimilate to mestizo modernity. The path of that music is also a powerful performance of the Indian in the mestizo, especially since the ancient melody's final destination is the suicidal musings of the Ecuadorian poet. This phrasing, which placed the urban (read also, white-mestizo) poet as the inheritor and product of ancient indigenous melodies, nicely encapsulates the force that embodiable topoi gained in mid-twentieth-century Ecuador.

In an era marked by political upheaval, economic disaster, and war, many Ecuadorian artists and intellectuals imagined the state of their nation in terms of a melancholy inherited from the land and from indigenous predecessors. But they asserted also the possibility of national rebirth and progress that moved from indigeneity to mestizaje. Some Ecuadorian scholars of the time, noticing the resilience of the "aboriginal race," argued for the "possibility of a future indigenous spiritual renaissance."[45] Often, however, that renaissance was to occur not in indigenous communities but within mestizo bodies. Articles like Montesinos's appropriated the potential for indigenous spiritual renaissance, implying that the mixture of European and indigenous cultures made white-mestizos more fit to reinvigorate the spiritual *fuerzas telúricas* of pre-Columbian cultures. Left-leaning mid-twentieth-century authors and artists in particular moved to identify with the indigeneity active in their own bodies. Locating national melancholy inside their own collective chests, they made themselves indigenous to envision the nation's inevitable emergence from melancholy into greatness.

This vision of spiritual renaissance through mestizaje facilitated claims to national greatness grounded in physical appropriation of indigenous spirit. It emphasized the indigeneity incarnate in each Ecuadorian, housing desirable indigeneity in mestizo bodies and mestizo cultures rather than in indigenous bodies and indigenous cultures. As Marilyn Grace Miller demonstrates in *Rise and Fall of the Cosmic Race*, political use of the idea of mestizaje is at least as old as the criollo notion of American distinction.[46] However, the second quarter of the twentieth century was the heyday of mestizaje in Latin America, thanks in part to the visionary success of José Vasconcelos's argument in *Cosmic Race* that Latin America would see the emergence of a new and powerful mestizo race—the hopeful harbinger of the future.[47] Vasconcelos's ideas arrived quickly in Ecuador, brought on the wings of an artistic awakening in both Mexico and Ecuador and articulated within Ecuador as early as 1928 in the writing of Benjamín Carrión. Though many Ecuadorian politicians and intellectuals doubted that indigenous people would ever be fully integrated into national culture, they still perceived the nation in terms of the mixture of Spanish transplants and American aboriginals, even as they identified themselves as *blancos*.[48]

The pages of the arts-and-culture periodicals published in Quito during that era frequently brought together the twin ideological forces of mestizaje and indigenismo. Notions of mestizaje in mid-twentieth-century Ecuador were inflected by the continued presence of a large, culturally distinct population of indigenous people and by the visibility of indigenista approaches in the arts and social sciences. Where Miller describes mestizaje and indigenismo as two distinct tendencies (suggesting that "the rhetoric of *mestizaje* [in Ecuador] frequently interfaces or clashes with the concerns of *indigenismo*"), the discussions available in *Letras* and other periodicals make clear that indigenismo and mestizaje regularly fused, informing and shaping each other.[49] Social science indigenismo, for example, often subsumed the future of indigenous peoples to the process of cultural mestizaje. In general, the discourse of both mestizaje and indigenismo in Ecuador appropriated indigeneity for mestizos, laying claim to indigenous voice, culture, and even biology as integral to white-mestizo national culture. Montesinos's "Tristeza" is just one example among many. As one Ecuadorian intellectual, Luís Monsalve Pozo, declared in his prize-winning essay on the "Indian problem," in areas of study as divergent as "economics, politics, religion, jurisprudence, ethics, education, sociology, and biology, we find [in Ecuador] a fascination for rediscovering the Indian and a vehement desire to capture his accent and his cry."[50] This combined fascination and appropriative urge appeared also in the Law of Artistic Patrimony, approved by the 1945 Constitutional Assembly. In one article it strikes down Catholic-inspired regulations prohibiting traditional indigenous festivals; in the next it requires the ministry of education to "find ways to maintain traditions and record the national folklore, incorporating it into modern Ecuadorian culture."[51] Indigenous cultural activity provided the nation with a living folkloric past and simultaneously needed to be brought into a mestizo present. In that same vein contemporary photographs, artwork, and illustrations repeatedly positioned contemporary mestizos as the inheritors of a stylized indigenous subjectivity, presenting indigenista images as "art expressive of [Ecuadorian] life" or "the age of majority for the national pictorial arts."[52]

This appropriation of indigeneity by white-mestizos and its attendant suggestion that mestizos had inherited autochthonous culture was especially powerful in Ecuador thanks to the overarching influence of the land-indigeneity topos. Images of landscape that so fully integrated indigenous figures into the land that they appeared as yet another starkly lined mountain or craggy cascade suggested that the white-mestizo nation, which had inherited the land, had also inherited its indigeneity. Another article by Monsalve Pozo, in the November 1940 issue of the periodical *Mar Pacífico*, took this linkage of land and culture to a whole new level, suggesting the extent that mestizaje had become a commonplace for understanding the physical, carnal absorption of indigeneity into the body of the white-mestizo nation. That article argues that not only Ecuador's people but also its geography are best understood in the terms of mestizaje. Though the references are mostly oblique, Monsalve posits a sort of geographic intercourse where the fertile, tropical coast and the humid, verdant Amazonian rainforest play the feminized Indian to the masculine, European dominance of the volcanic Andes. Through their "copulation and struggle" they produce the nation.[53] The nation, mestizo even in its territory, inherits carnal indigeneity from the land.

The suggestion that indigeneity was most properly incarnate in mestizo bodies was not unique to Monsalve Pozo; rather, that physical language that placed the emphasis of mestizaje on a Euro-American absorption of an indigenous body appeared repeatedly in Ecuadorian texts.[54] The physical references of this narrative spoke to a generalized sense that positioned mestizos as the culmination of a long process that absorbed the best of many cultures. Embodying cultural place and national space often resulted, then, in intensely physical descriptions of mestizo indigeneity. The carnal aspect of mestizaje was never far beneath the surface, and it provided the impetus for a national public moving from backwardness into greatness. Autochthonous cultural identity was absorbed, breathed, physiological. And its future was mestizo.

All these tropes of mestizaje and indigenismo shared an unspoken assumption that indigeneity as a mark of cultural distinction provided an essential prologue to the nation but could not be a permanent feature of the national present. And mestizaje and indigenismo served, despite many of their disseminators' good intentions toward their indigenous compatriots, to build an inclusive ethnic "we" through the exclusion of contemporary indigenous people. Mid-twentieth-century performances of indigeneity excluded contemporary indigenous people from the body of the nation as a largely unintended consequence of the fact that mestizaje and indigenismo's partisans needed to embody their own indigeneity (or rather, their *partial* indigeneity) to advance their projects of social uplift and undergird their claims to history and geography for the sake of the national public.

From one perspective these mid-twentieth-century performances of indigeneity as an embodiable topos exemplify identification as consubstantiality at its most explicit. White-mestizos identified themselves with the legitimacy and potential of the nation, giving the national public a historical legacy that could be found in their own blood and breath.[55] From a different perspective, however, accepting the legitimacy of these performances required indigeneity to achieve a commonsense meaning that ceased to include contemporary indigenous populations. Thus, the consubstantial identification with indigeneity prompted through its use as an embodiable topos required a basic dissociation: it demanded that the audience shift the legitimate claim to indigenous heritage from indigenous people to mestizos, incorporating the nation as indigenous through mestizo bodies while marginalizing the possibility of modern indigenous citizenship. The body of the national public could then be profoundly indigenous in nature without significantly altering the political and cultural hegemony of white-mestizos.

Extending Embodiable Topoi

Articulating the emergence of indigeneity as an embodiable topos from the late nineteenth into the mid-twentieth century provides important context for artifacts like the Baños letter, Pinto's costumbrismo, Montesinos's "Tristeza" article, and other reflections on mestizaje. The peculiar, contradictory, legitimizing force of embodiable topoi allowed white-mestizos to negotiate and benefit from the problematic place of indigenous people within the nation.

Claiming and redirecting the social energies stored within indigenous bodies, white-mestizos were able to position their own appeals in prominent terms of the discussion over the legitimate identity of the nation and the nature of the national public.

Such use of strategic appropriation to summon the attention of the nation-state suggests that identification and division play coterminous, not just compensatory, roles in the making of national publics. Attending to embodiable topoi reminds us that rhetorical appropriation happens not only when rhetors usurp arguments, styles, or themes but also when they adopt statuses, statures, and personas. Corporeal appropriation, including its contradictory absorption and rejection of the appropriated body, claims and reorients rhetorical legitimacy in contexts of public inequality. Such legitimacy comes, in other words, from rhetors inhabiting particular bodies and territories at the expense of others. It may require a sort of rhetorical colonialism, marginalizing previous inhabitants. As this analysis indicates, however, such marginalization is not always characterized by straightforward erasure in favor of an ideal. In contexts where interests are in conflict or histories are fraught (as they usually are), claiming legitimate consubstantiality with the national body may require the sort of tricky play between identification and dissociation, between appropriation and denial, visible in stylized performances of indigeneity.

The ways that performances of indigeneity served as embodiable topoi and made national legitimacy a physical, material matter in the Ecuadorian context show how identification, appropriation, and dissociation are enmeshed with one another. Being of one substance with indigeneity reimagined it in service of the national self. Such performances of an indigenous self take the actualizing force of topoi to another level, incarnating it. They also point simultaneously toward the strength and the porousness of national identification. As the discourse of carnal mestizaje makes particularly clear, identifications *bleed* and *breathe*. They are lived yet partial. They make individuals "substantially one" with one another in ways that appropriate and separate. Consubstantiality "allows identity to transform and . . . facilitates the catharsis those changes in identity necessitate."[56] Topoi, primary means of carrying consubstantiality forward, negotiate the permeability of national identification. That recognition of nationalisms in terms of shared but contested substance leads now into the conclusion of this study—a reflection on how commonplace solidity and fluidity illuminate the implications of national identification.

CONCLUSION

¿DE QUIÉN ES LA PATRIA?

"To whom does the Fatherland belong?" It's a question that has been answered in many different ways over the course of Ecuador's republican history. "The people" has almost always been the official answer. As the foregoing chapters have made clear, however, who constitutes the people and what roles those people play in the nation-state have been roundly contested both within and beyond the centers of national power. In practice Ecuador has belonged mostly to the affluent, the light-skinned, the Westernized. Even so, social movements, political groups, and individual Ecuadorians continue to respond to the implicit questions of national belonging with new (or, rather, renewed) answers that repeatedly reenvision the "whom" of the Patria.

Answer One: "La Patria Ya Es de Todos"

During the months leading up to the late September 2008 vote on their new Constitution, Ecuadorians were once again flooded with explicit discussions of national constitution. Quito's newspapers printed daily updates on the progress of the Constitutional Assembly. Passengers on interprovincial buses flipped through printed copies of the proposed charter. Both the *no* and the *sí* campaigns held rallies that filled the streets with marchers and left graffiti on walls and bridges. Posters urging support for the new Constitution appeared on every flat surface, and radio and television stations were blanketed with advertisements sponsored by the office of the president.

In its efforts in favor of the new Constitution, the administration of President Rafael Correa adopted a simple, populist slogan: "*¡La Patria ya es de todos!*" (The fatherland is already everyone's!). One advertisement from that campaign shown frequently on Quito's television stations during the summer of 2008 gives a particularly clear dramatization of who and what the

Patria and its "everyone" might be. That advertisement weaves patriotic motifs of flag waving into panoramic views of Ecuadorian territory and tableaus of Ecuadorians at work and play.[1] After the opening scene, in which two children run across the screen with an enormous Ecuadorian flag, the ad moves quickly to three introductory sketches meant to represent the country's three regions. In the first, a young indigenous woman dressed in the brightly colored skirt and shirt typically worn by Kichwa women from Cayambe tends a herd of cattle. She picks a dandelion from the mountain field at her feet and, turning toward the camera, blows its seeds into the wind. In the second scene the camera pans across a bubbling Amazonian stream surrounded by thick jungle and zooms in on a long-haired indigenous man raising a handful of water to his lips. The man wears a loincloth and a bead necklace; the colors of the Ecuadorian flag splash like ceremonial paint across his chest. In the third scene an Afro-Ecuadorian boy runs through the surf of an ocean beach, a kite flying in the wind behind him. Returning to the Highlands, the closing image of the advertisement's first half tracks a soaring condor across the sky. Yellow and red bands stream from the condor's wings to form the tricolor Ecuadorian flag against the blue sky and then fade to a sunset view of the Andean range wrapped in clouds. Following that transition, the remainder of the advertisement opens with yet another flag raising and a marked transition to faster, more driving music. The rest of the ad features Ecuadorians whose Western-style clothing, light skin, and social location mark them as mestizos. In that second half the focus of the advertisement shifts from establishing identity and place to promoting images of economic activity and production.

Answer Two: "Queremos una Patria para los Ecuatorianos"

In March 2012 thousands of protestors walked from Ecuador's Amazonía to highland Quito to dramatize their claim to speak for the nation and demand a "Fatherland for Ecuadorians." This March of Plurinational Resistance for Water, Life, and the Dignity of the People, organized by grassroots and national indigenous groups, called attention to the ways that large-scale mining interests, particularly transnational corporations, threatened the nation and the rights of its peoples. The marchers voiced their objection to massive natural resource exploitation in terms that had been authorized by the Constitution approved three and a half years earlier: they raised concern for the natural world, spoke in defense of the vulnerable, sought protection for popular sovereignty, and demanded respect for national diversity. Their march, a river of people organized around indigeneity but speaking for national diversity, aimed to embody the plural nation that had been invoked by the 2008 Constitution.

The Marcha Plurinacional was far from the first of such marches. It followed in the footsteps of other indigenous protests over the past three decades that have carried demands from Ecuador's rural periphery to its urban center. Through these marches and strikes and through the decades of organizing and centuries of resistance discussed in this book, indigenous communities in Ecuador have asserted themselves as national forces to be reckoned with. The Marcha Plurinacional brought those histories to bear on current concerns, supplementing established strategies with new rhetorical resources.

The Marcha began with a rally on March 8 in Zamora Chinchipe Province in the southern tip of Ecuador. From there it wound upward through the inter-Andean basins of the Highlands, attracting new participants and cheering crowds. Along the way it also faced counterprotests and raised the ire of the national government. Rallying the marchers as they gathered to begin their journey, one leader, Polibio Morocho, declared, "We will go forward supporting collective struggle, the claims of the *pueblos* against this neoliberal politics, this neoliberal statalism, this neoliberal government. . . . Long live the march! Long live the *pueblo!*" Later, Humberto Cholango, the president of CONAIE, Ecuador's most powerful national indigenous organization, urged the crowd, "We will climb the paths of freedom, the paths of profound change that we Ecuadorians want, to construct a new country, to construct the plurinational state, to construct the good life for our elders, for women, and for our children."[2] He concluded, "We want to say, . . . we indigenous people are not terrorists, we are *defenders* of the country, we are *defenders* of dignity, we are *defenders* of sovereignty."[3]

On March 22 the marchers arrived in Quito and tried to deliver a list of demands to the powers of the central government—the National Assembly, the Constitutional Court, and the president—but were blocked. Still, the Marcha gained national and international attention and once again brought the concerns of some marginalized indigenous communities into the center of national attention. In their claims to the state, the marchers used the available language and symbols of national constitution. Their arguments—in their "Mandate" carried to Quito; in speeches along the way; in posters, flags, and ritual performances—seized on the same populist themes activated by the campaign for the new Constitution and authorized by the approval of the

Constitution itself.[4] They hinged the future of the nation on, among other things, respect for cultural rights, limits on resource extraction, protection for dignified labor and popular economies, and greater autonomy for nations and *pueblos* within the nation-state.[5] Most of all, as Cholango's declaration that "we want a Fatherland for Ecuadorians" made clear, they claimed a national voice for themselves—acting as the true national "we" charged with defending the nation.

"NOSOTRAS Y NOSOTROS, el Pueblo Soberano del Ecuador"

These two similar yet competing answers to the question "to whom does the Patria belong?" stand on either side of Ecuador's most recent formal constitutive act, the Constitution of 2008. Their rhetorical substance responds to and calls into being national constitutions as surely as did the working groups of the Constitutional Assembly who composed the hefty text of the new Constitution in the name of "We [women and men] the sovereign people of Ecuador."[6] The anecdotes, in other words, draw attention once again to the complex rhetoricity of constitutive visions and the resilient ways that indigeneity infuses such visions in Ecuador. Despite their different political orientations—the "*¡La Patria ya es de todos!*" advertisement having been produced by the office of the president and the Marcha Plurinacional organized in opposition to the president's policies but in defense of his Constitution—the arguments advanced in these anecdotes share crucial elements, goals, and contexts. The fact that these constitutive artifacts converse with each other is not, however, merely an artifact of their political moment. The events also draw deeply from the enduring, resilient common sense that, as this study has shown, has shaped national vision over the long haul. In the Constitution, in protest marches and political speeches, in advertising campaigns and websites, the lingering questions of Ecuadorian national vision continue to circulate and return to the familiar places of indigeneity. In these new arguments about national identity being made on the ground of old assumptions, the resilience and constitutive force of topoi are driving factors. They make the nation renewed recognizable to itself.

These contemporary returns to the familiar places of indigeneity offer as well an opportunity to consider more closely the implications and uses of national identity—a factor implicit in the analyses of foregoing chapters. The campaign for the Constitution and the Marcha Plurinacional themselves give us convenient terms for assessing those stakes: they use a claim to national selfhood to access the force and effect of sovereignty. *Constitutive Visions* has examined how powerful identifications like national identities come into being and sustain themselves. Chapters 4 and 5 began, however, to raise another, parallel question about the rhetorical use of national identity, and the anecdotes discussed here bring that question further into focus. As these anecdotes suggest, making the shift from identifications to their implications helps us understand the forceful connections between the question "¿quién es de la Patria?" ("who belongs to the Patria?," i.e., the claim of national identity) and the question "¿de quién es la Patria?" ("to whom does the Patria belong?," i.e., the claim of sovereignty).

It has become commonplace, in late twentieth- and early twenty-first-century scholarship, to speak of ourselves as living in a newly transnational moment characterized by unique challenges to nation-state sovereignty. Today, the argument goes, the hermetic sovereignty of the Westphalian nation-state is under threat, dispersed or displaced by interdependence. In response, those arguments continue, we need new understandings of sovereignty, political organization, and rhetorical practice to address those changes. Without denying that there are new elements to our current transnational, interdependent moment, the constitutive scenes explored here and throughout *Constitutive Visions* make clear that dispersion, displacement, and interdependence have always been central to the making of nations and the enacting of nation-state power.

Since sovereignty has always been contested and national identity has always been key to such contestation, it is not entirely necessary to move into the twenty-first century to illuminate the connections between them. Contemporary Ecuadorian constitutional scenes, however, bring the generative presence of old patterns in present negotiations over sovereignty and identity evocatively to light. Examining them, then, draws attention to the long history of interdependence that scholars today too often identify as a threat to or a new condition of sovereignty. What these contemporary Ecuadorian examples and their antecedents make clear is that those claims that imagine sovereignty's permeability as new and as diminishing the force of national identity are attempting to read too narrow a slice of global history.

The Ecuadorian example, then, draws attention to the larger factors at work in a point made recently by political theorists Wouter Werner and Jaap De Wilde, who argue that sovereignty has always been a matter of interdependence and power contingency. Historically speaking, "threats to the state's autonomy and ability to rule have reinforced the claims to sovereignty rather than weakened them. The most passionate defenses of the idea of state sovereignty can be found in times when the freedom and independence of states is believed to be at stake."[7] What Werner and De Wilde describe and the example of Ecuador makes quite clear is that sovereignty has never been and could never be hermetic, but challenges to sovereignty make its penetrability palpable. Looking to contexts where such challenges have been perennial draws attention to the ways that the power of citizens in a republic to influence their government and the power of individual political entities to govern their own fate are always contested and negotiated over time. They never exist in a stable state.

The wide-ranging treatment of Ecuadorian constitutive visions provided up to this point, particularly its attention to how national identities have emerged through contestation, illustrates that identification and sovereignty are usefully seen in concert. Saying that Ecuador *ya es de todos* (is already everyone's) or that the marchers are *defensores de soberanía* (defenders of sovereignty) is an assertion of national identity—it places a plural people at the center of what it means to be Ecuador. Those appeals are, in the same breath, assertions of sovereignty. They use a claim to national identification to intervene in the contested terrain of national power—the terrain where popular sovereignty meets national sovereignty. In that sense the advertisement and the march emphasize a notion of sovereignty "as an argument, as a claim to authority" rather than as an objective or legal state.[8] The commonplaces of indigeneity that provide places of return for national identifications also, in other words, serve efforts to link the republican rights of the people to the autonomy and power of the nation-state.

Constitutive Visions has shown that the powerful identifications of national identity do a great deal of varied constitutive work. Among their essential tasks is the provision of the grounds on which the arguments of sovereignty play out. Both popular sovereignty (the claim of the people to have a say in their government) and national sovereignty (the claim of the state to authority and independence) draw from the active social energy made available by national identification to do their internal and external organizing work.

Tracking that rhetoric-based connection between identification and sovereignty shows another of the analytical benefits of attending to national constitution. To illuminate that benefit, the remainder of this conclusion first sketches how commonplaces of indigeneity continue to give force to the arguments at work in twenty-first-century debates over Ecuadorian constitution. Then, it examines how those tactics of identification serve as strategies of sovereignty. Considering how claims of belonging and identification underlie claims of belonging and sovereignty, these closing words highlight the porous, negotiated, and interstitial nature of republican belonging in both senses. It suggests as well how important the piecemeal yet powerful affiliations that make national identity are, and have always been, to the rhetorical practice of sovereignty.

Familiar Topoi, New Constitution

Both of the campaigns discussed here—the movement for the new Constitution and the Marcha Plurinacional—do their rhetorical work by asserting what it means to be Ecuadorian. They identify themselves with the nation and leverage that identification to speak to and as the republic. The images at play in the "Patria" advertisement and the Marcha should not surprise anyone who has been thus far convinced of the constitutive resilience of commonplaces nor of the central role played by topoi of indigeneity in Ecuadorian national visions. In the brief video and the month-long trek, rhetors imagining the nation engage many of the same topoi of national identity that proliferated across the nineteenth and twentieth centuries, though they alter those topoi to fit the conditions of the twenty-first century. Indigenous bodies tether the nation to the land; indigenous marchers carry the voice of *la naturaleza* into the city. An indigenous girl tends the national flock; indigenous workers position themselves as the productive national soul. Indigenous people are the prologue for a modern nation or the center of a plurinational one. Nation, territory, labor, other, self—the specific contexts are different, but the patterns remain hauntingly familiar.

That reliance on resilient patterns of indigeneity appears, paradoxically yet familiarly, in response to a document whose stated purpose is to enact profound change in the old national patterns. The 2008 Constitution, after all, was intended to make new Ecuador's "project of life in common," replacing a long history of exclusive politics with "a Constitution that is liberatory, that is founded in tolerance, and that is founded in equity."[9] Both opposition groups and President Correa's supporters imagined the preparation of a new Constitution as an opportunity to break with the past. Before the 2007 vote to authorize the Constitutional Assembly that would draft the document, the indigenous organization Ecuarunari encouraged its supporters to support the process but also pressure the government to comply with its promises. Calling for "true democracy," the editors of Ecuarunari's *Rikcharishun* newsletter warned against a return to "the false democracy

that we have lived up to this point [that] has permitted only the few to enrich themselves and the great majority of the people to be impoverished . . .
supported and legalized by the nineteen Constitutions elaborated over 177
years of republican history." Speaking a month later at the inauguration of
the Constitutional Assembly, President Correa similarly declared that the
new Constitution, "unlike the previous, ought to provide us with a true democracy, a new territorial order and adequate autonomy, the rescue of the
state, and the construction of an economic and social system built on justice
and solidarity."[10]

Though it shares some features with the previous Constitution (in effect
since 1998), the completed new Constitution, approved by Ecuadorian voters
on September 28, 2008, does indeed attempt to reimagine what it means to
be the Ecuadorian republic, making it more profoundly inclusive and more
profoundly of its people. Built in the spirit of Rafael Correa's "citizens' revolution" and in uneasy partnership with Ecuador's traditionally strong social
movements, the 2008 Constitution announces broad new rights—for individuals, collectives, and the natural world—and commits to a revolutionary
inclusion of the peoples' voices. Not only does it declare opposition to neoliberal economic structures and promote the right to the "good life" for its
citizens rich and poor, it also doubles down on the multiculturalism of its
twenty-year-old predecessor by declaring Ecuador a "plurinational state" and
imagining a country "forged by women and men of distinct peoples."[11] It
recognizes indigenous cultures and rights in ways that extend well beyond
those of any previous charter. Thanks in part to pressure from indigenous
activists, the Constitution outlines communal rights and the autonomy of
indigenous nations alongside more traditionally Western considerations of
individual rights and state sovereignty. From its opening phrases the 2008
Constitution imagines a new national era in terms of a diverse public with
roots in social struggle.

Perhaps because of that rooting in past history, the 2008 Constitution,
like the "Patria" advertisement meant to support it and the Marcha Plurinacional meant to reclaim it, also draws deeply from the familiar energies of
Ecuadorian national constitution. It invokes the dreams of Simón Bolívar
and Eloy Alfaro—imagining the new Ecuador in continuity with the heroes
of independence and the Liberal revolution. It also activates the well-worn
topoi of indigeneity; in fact, it makes them more prominent in the definition
of national identity than has any previous Constitution. It claims indigeneity as integral to identification with the nation-state as a whole. The uneasy
interplay between recognizing national diversity and claiming national

indigeneity that grounds the new Constitution is particularly visible in its preamble, worth quoting in its entirety:

WE, the sovereign people of Ecuador
RECOGNIZING our millennial roots, forged by women and men of distinct peoples,
CELEBRATING the natural world, the Pacha Mama, of which we are part and which is vital to our existence,
INVOKING the name of God and recognizing our diverse forms of religiosity and spirituality,
APPEALING to the wisdom of all the cultures that enrich us as a society,
AS DESCENDANTS of the social struggles for liberation in the face of all forms of domination and colonialism,
And with a profound commitment to the present and the future,
Decide to construct
A new form of citizenly life together, in diversity and harmony with the natural world, in order to achieve the good life, the *sumak kawsay*;
A society that respects, in all its dimensions, the dignity of persons and collectives;
A democratic country, committed to Latin American integration—the dream of Bolívar and Alfaro—to peace and solidarity with all the peoples of the earth; and,
In exercise of our sovereignty . . . we present this:
CONSTITUTION OF THE REPUBLIC OF ECUADOR

This preamble is a record of pluralism claimed and accepted. References to the republic's founding diversity appear in each of the five descriptive clauses following "We, the sovereign people of Ecuador," and that diversity is explicitly invoked in three of them. The "sovereign people of Ecuador" includes "women and men of distinct peoples"; it recognizes plural forms of worship; and it draws on the wisdom of multiple cultures. Further, that people emerges out of generations of social struggle, fights that prominently include indigenous peoples' efforts against white-mestizo exploitation. The preamble similarly evokes indigeneity to assert a strong national tie to the natural world: it uses the Kichwa term "Pacha Mama" to speak of national responsibility to Mother Earth. The sovereign people creating the new Constitution, in other words, is a people constituted from cultural complexity but drawn together by a common indigeneity. In this Constitution, then, diversity has roots in pre-Columbian soil, and the spirit that holds the contemporary nation-state together grows substantially from indigenous experience.

Like the scene-setting language of the preamble's first half, the formative act outlined in the section after "Decide to construct" also convenes a profoundly plural republic with a particularly indigenous spirit. The new society to be constructed is founded on "diversity and harmony," and it acknowledges that "the dignity of persons and collectives" has multiple dimensions. Its "new form of citizenly life together" promotes not only "el buen vivir" ("the good life" in Spanish) but also "el sumak kawsay" (the same in Kichwa). The plural state—what the Constitution's first article terms "a constitutional state of rights and justice: social, democratic, sovereign, independent, unitary, intercultural, plurinational, and secular"—is a plurality enacted through indigeneity. The structures of the new Constitution are built around an indigenous history and a future good life invoked in explicitly Kichwa terms.

That sense of a national self rooted in indigeneity bleeds outward from the Constitution into the documents and events surrounding it. In the "Patria" advertisement produced before the Constitution's approval and in the Marcha Plurinacional that used the Constitution to call the state to account, the sense of a nation founded in its indigeneity takes form and gains force. For the "Patria" advertisement, like hundreds of earlier artifacts produced by Ecuadorian elites, images of indigenous people grant legitimacy and ground regional identity. They give the spirit of the nation an indigenous body, tying the pristine beauty of nature and the rustic beauty of traditional culture to an implicit argument about national coherence and pride. Yet the advertisement's implicit transition from heritage to modernity makes clear a continued ambivalence in national identifications. The indigenous self fades from the scene as the ad moves into its second half and shifts from a celebration of history, culture, and land to an energetic paean to national productivity. That second half features more urban scenes, a faster rhythm, and modern technology. As in so many constitutions of Ecuadorian national identity, the ad uses indigenous people to set the scene, stand in for regional identities, and represent tradition, nature, and heritage. Their place in connection to the modern nation remains in question.

The arguments advanced by the marchers, for their part, put indigenous people at the very center of the nation, claiming to be its definitive people and its natural protectors. Cholango, in his opening statement, challenged state efforts to paint indigenous protestors as both marginal and threatening to the nation by positioning their actions instead as forms of national salvation. Reversing the Correa administration's depiction of indigenous activists in the Amazon as terrorists who threaten national stability, Cholango declared instead, "we are *defenders* of the country, we are *defenders* of dignity, we are *defenders* of sovereignty." Indigenous action to protect natural resources, block transnational corporations, and support the interests of local communities was, in other words, the constitutional action of true Ecuadorians. It secures the good life, guarantees the plurinational state, and makes possible a new country. Underscoring that claim, the line of marchers winding along the Highlands highways carried first a long Ecuadorian flag and then, immediately behind it, the rainbow flag of the indigenous movements. *We* indigenous people, the marchers announced in word and image, are the body of the nation. We make the nation strong.

The Constitution, the "Patria" advertisement, and the Marcha Plurinacional all engage indigenous topoi of land and landscape to enact their claims to national self-hood. In the advertisement, landscape identifies Ecuador's three regions and establishes a contemporary sense of national sublime. Indigenous people are clearly identified with two of those regional landscapes (Amazonía and Highlands) and with the natural world as a whole. It is telling, perhaps, that indigenous people appear in the introduction alongside Ecuador's national bird (the condor) and the mountain peaks whose outline grace the national seal—all common elements of the natural world. In the Constitution, indigeneity is tied to the land through the invocation of the Pacha Mama. It is a primary key to the republic's past—source of its "millennial roots" and cultural wisdom.

That invocation of the Pacha Mama also authorizes the Constitution's move to grant rights to nature—a feature that became useful for the arguments made by the Marcha Plurinacional. For the Marcha, land was both scene and context. Literal movement across Ecuadorian territory enacted the marchers' claims to represent the nation. In addition, the marchers made use of the Constitution's delegation of rights to the natural world and its assertion that "any person, community, people, or nationality is authorized to compel the public authority to comply with the rights of nature."[12] Invoking that constitutional commitment to the natural world alongside other, older elements of land-indigeneity topoi allowed the marchers to position themselves as quintessentially and naturally environmentalist—the ideal representatives of the natural world.

If the elaboration of a national self grounded in territory takes priority across the indigenous commonplaces of these examples, their competing yet intermeshed rhetorics of national identification also point toward overlapping sovereignty concerns: the claim to be Ecuador's true sovereign people and the claim of the people to be truly sovereign in the nation-state. It is no mistake that constitutions and Constitutions are at issue here. They are, after all, the essential scenes and acts of both republican national identity and republican sovereignty. Constitutions and constitutions establish the patterns by which identification with the nation leads to authority claims. In that sense the advertisement corroborates popular sovereignty as the source of the new Constitution ("¡La Patria ya es de todos!"); the march reclaims sovereignty through popular struggle ("somos defensores de soberanía"); and the 2008 Constitution serves as a resource that links the sovereignty of the people to the sovereignty of the nation ("NOSOTRAS Y NOSOTROS, el pueblo soberano del Ecuador").

Belonging and Sovereignty

Though sovereignty has often been defined at the intersection of authority and independence (e.g., "the authority of a culturally diverse people or association of peoples to govern themselves by their own laws and ways free from external subordination"), the practices of sovereignty made visible in the examples of this study are more about the process of creating and contesting authority and independence than they are about preexisting claims.[13] They make clear that sovereignty is always intersectional. Even more, far from being a fixed state of control that preceded a relatively recent emergence of transnational interdependence, sovereignty has always negotiated material conditions and been built by the intersection of clashing interests and competing stories.

In this sense rhetoricians and others interested in the arguments of sovereignty ought to look beyond the *status* of sovereignty into its profound rhetoricity. To do so, we might take a supplementary approach to the treatment of sovereignty and rhetoric most familiar to rhetoricians to date. Scott Lyons defines "rhetorical sovereignty" as "the inherent right and ability of *peoples* to determine their own communicative needs and desires in this pursuit, to decide for themselves the goals, modes, styles, and languages of public discourse." That definition of rhetorical sovereignty imagines sovereignty primarily as an inherent status—a natural right to language and influence that is owned by all. At the same time, Lyons's discussion of the conditions under which such sovereignty might be achieved makes clear the rhetoricity that preexists the claim to status. He writes, "Sovereignty, of course, has long been a contested term in Native discourse, and its shifting meanings over time attest to an ongoing struggle between Americans and the hundreds of Indian nations that occupy this land. . . . Sovereignty is the guiding story in our pursuit of self-determination, the general strategy by which we aim to best recover our losses from the ravages of colonization: our lands, our languages, our cultures, our self-respect."[14] In light of the history elaborated in this study, Lyons's assertion of sovereignty as a guiding story or general strategy makes particular sense. We gain new understanding of the nature and force of sovereignty, then, if we recognize that *status* as sovereign is relational, constitutive, and founded in contestation. Sovereignty is not a natural or a legal state that nation-states and peoples hold except when challenged. Instead, sovereignty is a matter of and for argument—the challenge itself is central to the lived practice of sovereignty.[15] Framing sovereignty in general, not just questions of linguistic sovereignty, in rhetorical terms—as what Werner and De Wilde name "a *claimed* status, with discursive functions"— offers a useful orientation for understanding what national identifications have to do with the power of the people and the rights of the state.[16] Both the history of achieving sovereignty and the experience of wielding it are rhetorical—they are characterized by claims to consubstantial identification with the sovereign body and by the activation of the social energy such identification provides. National identity and republican sovereignty, then, both rest on the well-worn places and inventive resources of the commonplace. Identification grounds stories of sovereignty, which are, in turn, told so that they might enact sovereignty. Those stories become familiar and generative because of the inventive force of topoi.

In their tie to past patterns and their efforts to establish political voice by claiming and contesting national legitimacy, the constitutional artifacts discussed earlier make that principle particularly clear. The "Patria" advertisement, the 2008 Constitution, and the Marcha Plurinacional call sovereignty into being, contest it, and, most of all, show its profoundly processual nature. They point to the ways that claims to popular sovereignty and to national sovereignty interanimate each other through the terms of national identification.

The "Patria" advertisement and the Marcha Plurinacional focus primarily on questions of popular sovereignty: defining and invoking the power of the people vis-à-vis the state. The "todos" of the advertisement invokes a nation made up of young and old; Amazonía, Highland, and Coast; modern and rustic; urban and rural. The marchers argue that they are the true people and use their slow progress across national territory to highlight their right to speak to power. But the Marcha and the advertisement are also about national sovereignty—about the power and authority of the nation-state.

The marchers both demand that the state live up to its promise of independence from transnational corporations and remind the central government that even national sovereignty in Ecuador is constitutionally plural. The advertisement, premised on the claim that "la Patria ya es de todos," suggests that the will of people is always already included in the action of the nation-state. Both artifacts, then, enact a classically republican sort of negotiation, attempting to draw acceptable connections between the power of the people and the power of the nation. That negotiation, however, is always fraught—not only for the people who, as Danielle Allen notes, are profoundly disempowered sovereigns but also for national sovereignty.[7] The ability of the republican nation-state to assert its authority is contingent on the intervention and acquiescence of the people who have defined (and been defined by) it. That was true when provincial indigenous communities called the Ecuadorian state into being during the nineteenth century and remains true as marchers subsume the authority of the central government to their own claim to national prominence.[8]

Final Words

The shape of sovereignty, then, depends largely on the same constitutive relations that drive national identification. Those relations, in turn, send us back to the language of constitutive rhetoric, particularly to Kenneth Burke's assertion that constitutions make claims to the "is" to bring the "ought" into being. In their definition of sovereignty, Werner and De Wilde also invoke the relationship between "is" and "ought," but they define it in terms of claims and responsibility. For them, the declaration of sovereignty (the *is*) precipitates certain obligations (*oughts*) on the part of the sovereign state and its interlocutors. "A claim to sovereignty," they write, "attempts to establish a relation as an institutional fact (the 'fact' of being the supreme or ultimate authority and the 'fact' of being an independent authority) and [as an outcome of that claim establishes] a set of rights and responsibilities." In this sense, the is-ought of sovereignty claims implies a fairly linear equation: if the people and other political entities accept the state's claim to be sovereign, then the claim triggers certain recognized powers, rights, and obligations. The Ecuadorian context makes clear, however, that a more Burkean version of the constitutive is-ought is also at work in sovereignty claims. In that case, the declaration of an *is*—of sovereignty—attempts to bring into being what *ought* to be: authority, popular rule, and so on. National constitutions declare the people and the state to be sovereign so that they might become sovereign. In this sense, then, sovereignty truly is "a speech act to (re-)establish the claimant's position as an absolute authority, and to legitimize its exercise of power."[19]

The claim made by the "*¡La Patria ya es de todos!*" slogan shows this is-ought aspect of sovereignty particularly clearly. Its definition of the Patria appears to announce an absolute national inclusion imagined not simply as a hortatory ought but as an actually existing condition. It declares that everyone belongs to the nation-state and the nation-state belongs to everyone. This, it asserts, is already the state of things and it is natural, a given. A bit of familiarity with Ecuadorian usage, however, clarifies that the claim to universal sovereignty is a Constitutional wish: an *ought* that hopes to bring into being an *is*. In Spanish, "ya," though translated into English as "already," can also be used to indicate intention. Such usage is particularly common in Ecuador. There, a parent summoned from work by a child's call will respond, without moving, *Ya vengo*—"I'm already coming." The slogan's claim that the country already belongs to everyone, in other words, is best understood in context as a hopeful expectation for the future, a declaration that aims to be performative; *ya* allows the phrase to enact its goal through its own statement. The Patria and the Constitution, this slogan asserts, are ours in common because we declare them to be so. That declaration of absolute inclusion attempts to establish a "motivational fixity" that, to appropriate Burke's thoughts on the vision of equality in the U.S. Constitution, makes its definitive claim to inclusion in the hopes that all may be included.[20]

The constitutional wishes for sovereignty at work in the Constitution itself and in the Marcha Plurinacional are perhaps less stark than those visible in the language-based ambiguity of "*¡La Patria ya es de todos!*" They are no less present, however. As the opening words of chapter 1 suggest, the grand claims of the new Constitution have been contested and incomplete from the very first days of their authority. The Marcha itself shows that the *is* of a plurinational state, the good life, and respect for the rights of nature are, in practice, *oughts* that require struggle to actualize. The marchers, for their part, declare themselves to be the nation, yet the national stories they engage and the route they travel from margin to periphery ought to remind us of just how thoroughly their claim to place indigenous voices at the center of the nation is and has been contested.

The journey from the 1861 Constitution's invocation of a popular sovereignty grounded in the whole people but enacted by the few to the 2008 Constitution's explicit celebration of a plurinational, intercultural, actively

sovereign people has followed a long path of contested identity and identification. Indigenous communities, labor organizers, artists, politicians, authors,
and academics have spent one hundred and fifty years drawing on, altering,
and disputing Ecuadorian constitutions, using the topoi of national identity to push from the anemic popular commitments of the mid-nineteenth
century to the robustly democratic declarations of the early twenty-first. The
prevalence of topoi of indigeneity in recent constitutive visions speaks, then,
not only to the influential roles played today by indigenous political actors
and social movements but also to the resilience and coherence those commonplaces provide. The familiar ways those topoi show up in contemporary constitutions ground the new republic announced in the 2008 Charter
in the long history that precedes and surrounds it. The 2008 Constitution
does its generative work on the terrain of previous constitutive acts, scenes,
agents, and attitudes. It returns, then, not only to Bolívar and Alfaro but also
to Rafael Brito and Carlos Larrea G., to the Baños authors and José Domingo
Laso, to the indígenas of Nayón and of Zámbiza, to the National Journalists Union and Dolores Cacuango, to Joaquín Pinto and Eduardo Kingman.
Building a new national coherence in the face of change, the Constitution
returns once again to familiar commonplaces.

The resilient topoi that feed such national visions make clear, in other
words, that the progressive expansion of sovereignty is not, precisely, a
steady march of progress that leaves the past behind with each step toward
the present.[21] A narrative of teleological development cannot effectively capture the processes of national constitution, in part because it imagines the
key elements under discussion—republics, nations, identifications, and
sovereignties—as outcomes rather than negotiations. This, after all, is the
lesson of the histories of permanence and change examined in the foregoing chapters: powerful identifications such as nationalisms come into being, are sustained, and then do constitutive work—including the work of
sovereignty—through the encounter of familiarity and novelty and the inventive action of the commonplace. Those inventive returns made possible
by resilient topoi use claims about national identity to convene and contest
sovereignty. If national identity emerges in the messy confluence of identification and dissociation, self and other, the experience of sovereignty that
grows from the nation is also a complicated, constructed, constitutive affair.

As the 2008 Constitution, the "Patria" video, the Marcha Plurinacional,
and the preceding chapters demonstrate, resilient topoi both trouble and
sustain the *ought* of rhetorical constitutions. Because building new visions
so often depends on the recognition of earlier patterns and draws from the

shared sources of social energy that allow a public to be convened, those new visions rarely represent a true break with the past. They are built in negotiation with the constitutive visions of their predecessors. Paying attention to the resilience of topoi and their re-creation over time helps demonstrate how strategies of inclusion and exclusion coexist in constitutions of national identity, how the hortatory wish of democracy and nation sustains practices of exclusion, and how national publics wield sovereignty in the face of limitations and contestation. Rhetorical scholarship that takes the durability of commonplaces seriously will not necessarily undo the patterns on which those topoi are based. It will, however, serve a refractory purpose. Splitting resilient commonplaces into spectra of common sense, rhetorical studies like the one offered here bring before our eyes the complexes of identification and dissociation that together compose and sustain our constitutive visions.

NOTES

Preface

1. Albornoz, "Alphabet in the Andes" (hereafter cited in text).
2. For more on this point, see C. Olson, "Places to Stand."
3. Mao, "Doing Comparative Rhetoric," 66.
4. Such resources come from across disciplinary boundaries: from the early work of cultural anthropologists like Clifford Geertz and James Clifford to the critical interventions of indigenous scholars Linda Tuhiwai Smith and Devon A. Mihesuah, from rhetorical ethnographers considering the ethics of their fieldwork to rhetorical historians plumbing the politics of historiographic research. Clifford and Marcus, *Writing Culture*; Geertz, *Interpretation of Cultures*; Mihesuah, *American Indians*; L. Smith, *Decolonizing Methodologies*; Cintrón, *Angels' Town*; Cushman, *Struggle and the Tools*; Mortensen and Kirsch, *Ethics and Representation*; Murphy et al., "Politics of Historiography"; Brooks, "Reviewing and Redescribing"; Atwill et al., "Octalog II"; Agnew et al., "Rhetorical Historiography"; Agnew et al., "Octalog III"; Gale, "Historical Studies"; Glenn, "Truth, Lies, and Method"; Jarratt, "Rhetoric and Feminism."
5. See, for example, Gries, "Practicing Methods"; Mao, "Chinese Rhetorical Tradition"; Mao, "Doing Comparative Rhetoric"; and Romano, "Historical Catalina Hernández."
6. Mao, "Doing Comparative Rhetoric," 66.
7. For more information on these literacy projects, see Rodas, *Crónica de un sueño*. For more contextual insight on the political organizing surrounding the literacy projects, see Becker, *Indians and Leftists*.
8. This book uses the term "white-mestizo" to reference the light-skinned minority that has maintained economic, cultural, and political hegemony in Ecuador since independence. My goal here is not to establish specific racialized traits but to examine the circulation of ideas about related subject positions. White-mestizo, then, designates an elite but contested subject position that values the Euro-American in part through its simultaneous appropriation and denigration of an indigenous, Afro-Ecuadorian, or mestizo other.
9. A. Clark, "Ecuadorian Indians," 54.
10. I'm indebted, in this definition of rhetoric, to Jack Selzer, Ralph Cintrón, and Kenneth Burke, among others. Selzer, "Rhetorical Analysis"; Cintrón, *Angels' Town*; Burke, *Rhetoric*.
11. Mao, "Doing Comparative Rhetoric," 66.
12. See, for example, A. Clark, "Indians"; A. Clark, "Race"; K. Clark, "Formación del estado"; and Kingman Garcés, *Ciudad y los otros*.
13. Graff, *Literacy Myth*.
14. Hawhee and Olson, "Pan-Historiography."
15. Ibid.
16. I received a Foreign Language and Area Studies grant from the Department of Education to study Quichua and my tenure line was funded by a grant from the Mellon Foundation.

Introduction

1. The Spanish word *rondador* refers specifically to the pan flute played by the men in these images. *Rondín* is the more accurate term for the nineteenth-century pan flute player shown in the garb of a night watchman (*rondín* refers to his making the "rounds" of the city but invokes the rondador as well). Titles for later images of men playing rondadors often label the instrument and the player together. I use *rondador* here to suggest the ways that the figure, the flute, and the music blend, together indexing national identity.

2. In this sense my study of national identity through national visions resonates with Mauricio Tenorio Trillo's discussion of national images in Peru: "Countless studies have shown that nationalism requires the constant influence, transformation, destruction, and reinvention of local traditions and identities. But the consideration of national images cannot contribute essentials to those who search for identities. National images help to ask questions related to identity, but not to affirm real or negate fake identities. In dealing with national images one does not ask, for instance, who were the genuine Peruvians and how they really thought and felt; rather, one aims to find out what part of some people's historiographically visible existence they believed to signify Peruvianness. All in all, the destinies of the various identities within a nation are constantly changing, challenging, and utilizing the nation according the specific circumstances." Where Tenorio Trillo sees identity as only true or false, however, I approach both identity and vision in terms of "find[ing] out what part of some people's historiographically visible existence they believed to signify [Ecuadorianness]." "Essaying," 65–66.

3. Such debate over the nation-state's relevance and survival takes many forms but appears most often in the work of scholars focused on the social, political, and economic effects of globalization. See, for example, Bahri, "Response"; Buell, "Nationalist Post-nationalism"; Fraser, "Transnationalizing"; Hardt and Negri, *Empire*; Hardt and Negri, *Multitude*; Hesford and Schell, "Introduction"; and Ugarteche, "Transnationalizing." This study is more in line with the work of scholars who position the porous sovereignty and identifications currently "new" to U.S. and European nation-states in a longer history of contested national spheres in a colonial and neocolonial context. See, for example, Hutchings, "Whose History?"; Quijano, "Coloniality of Power"; and Randeria, "De-politicization of Democracy."

4. Cervone, "Retorno de Atahualpa"; Kingman Garcés, *Ciudad y los otros*; Muratorio, "Images of Indians."

5. C. Miller, "Aristotelian *Topos*," 142; Cintrón, "Democracy," 100.

6. Aristotle, *Topics*, bk. 1, pt. 1, p. 1.

7. See not only Cintrón, "Democracy," and C. Miller, "Aristotelian *Topos*," but also LaWare, "Circling the Missiles"; Perelman and Olbrechts-Tyteca, *New Rhetoric*; and Romano, "Historical Catalina Hernández."

8. McKeon, "Creativity," 199; Leff, "Topics of Argumentative Invention," 23, 24.

9. Connecting more recent treatments of topoi to ancient writing on the subject, whether Greek or Roman, can be difficult. Contemporary scholars have been primarily fascinated with ideological topoi (what Crowley and Hawhee term "commonplaces") and less concerned with structural topoi (which Crowley and Hawhee call "common topics"). Ancient rhetorical theories often emphasize the opposite, focusing on structural topics (comparison, degree, etc.) and relegating conceptual topoi to a brief treatment of "special topics" (e.g., in Aristotle's *On Rhetoric*) or omitting them altogether. Contemporary students, then, can hardly be blamed for wondering if the current scholarly focus developed ex nihilo. Closer analysis shows that the contemporary topos does have ancient roots in its broader concern with finding ways to "reason from opinions that are generally accepted." Leff notes that "rhetoricians must draw their starting points from

accepted beliefs and values relative to the audience and the subject of discourse. When these beliefs and values are considered at a high level of generality, they become 'commonplaces' or 'common topics' for argumentation." All topical theories, in other words, rest on the idea that arguments can be built from social patterns. Crowley and Hawhee, *Ancient Rhetorics*; Aristotle, *On Rhetoric*; Leff, "Topics of Argumentative Invention," 23.

10. Cintrón, "Democracy," 100–101.

11. Cintrón's definition makes room for the visual, noting how signs and symbols provide meaning, but his brief nod to the visual is less theoretically rich than his treatments of linguistic topoi such as "democracy."

12. C. Miller, "Aristotelian *Topos*," 142; McKeon, "Creativity," 199; Cintrón, "Democracy," 101.

13. Kennedy Troya, "Territorio y el paisaje," 7.

14. Mirzoeff, *Right to Look*, 2.

15. C. Miller, "Aristotelian *Topos*."

16. Finnegan, "Recognizing Lincoln," 33.

17. Finnegan, "Visual Studies," 235.

18. C. Miller, "Aristotelian *Topos*," 134.

19. McKeon, "Creativity," 201, 202.

20. C. Miller, "Aristotelian *Topos*," 134, 143, 142.

21. Ibid., 141 (emphasis in the original).

22. McKeon, "Creativity," 199.

23. I am not the first scholar of Ecuadorian contexts to take this agglutinative approach to national-identity formation. Ernesto Capello, in *City at the Center*, uses a very similar method to examine the multiple moments and modes through which Quiteños positioned their city as central.

24. Haeckel, quoted in McIntosh, *Background of Ecology*, 8.

25. Krebs's definition appears, sometimes without citation, in many ecology textbooks. It is described as the current standard in Begon, Harper, and Townsend, *Ecology*, xi.

26. Edbauer, "Unframing Models," 8, 9 (emphasis in the original).

27. Begon, Harper, and Townsend, *Ecology*, xi, 3, xi.

28. Edbauer, "Unframing Models," 20.

29. Consigny, "Rhetoric and Its Situations," 181.

30. For a more detailed take on this pre-Columbian history, see Ayala Mora, *Época aborigen I*; Ayala Mora, *Época aborigen II*; and Salomon, *Native Lords of Quito*.

31. For more on the Republic of Spaniards and the Republic of Indians, see Coronel Feijóo, *Valle sangriento*; Jácome, "Economía y sociedad"; Miño Grijalva, "Economía"; Pólit Montes de Oca, "Conquista del Perú"; Salomon, "Crisis y transformación"; and Terán Najas, "Sinopsis histórica." For more on the Quito School, see Kennedy, *Arte*; Kennedy Troya, "Miguel de Santiago"; Navarro, *Artes plásticas*; Vargas, *Historia*; and Vargas, *Arte ecuatoriano*.

32. Guerrero's studies of tribute and later forms of ethnic administration offer a useful overview of indigenous-state relations in the late colonial and early republican periods. "Dominated Populations"; *Administración de poblaciones*.

33. For an overview, see Ayala Mora, *Independencia*.

34. For more detailed analyses of tribute's role in the early republic, see Guerrero, "Dominated Populations," and Sattar, "*Indígena o Ciudadano.*"

35. Both "criollo" and "white-mestizo" refer to the light-skinned, European-identified Ecuadorians who dominated Ecuadorian culture in the nineteenth and twentieth centuries. I use "white-mestizo" to reference Ecuador's dominant ethnopolitical class throughout the periods of this study. "Criollo" refers more specifically to the urban, landholding Highlands aristocracy of the nineteenth century. For discussions of the broader challenges of nation making in Latin America, including some specific treatment of Ecuador,

see Castro-Klarén and Chasteen, *Beyond Imagined Communities*, and Larson, *Trials of Nation Making*.

36. Ecuador's "Progressive Era" should not be confused with the period of the same name in the United States. Where U.S. Progressives advocated social reforms and sponsored projects of uplift, education, and moral improvement, Ecuadorian Progressives hailed from a Coastal elite whose affluence was built on agricultural export income (especially cacao) and dominance of the country's financial institutions. Their period in power represents an alliance between those Coastal elites and the large landholders who dominated the central highlands, and it favored the interests of those two groups.

37. Kingman Garcés, *Ciudad y los otros*, 86. All translations of Spanish-language scholarship and primary sources are the author's, unless otherwise noted.

38. Cañizares-Esguerra, "Postcolonialism"; Kennedy Troya, "Artistas y científicos"; Poole, *Vision, Race, and Modernity*.

39. Kennedy Troya and Ortiz Crespo, "Continuismo colonial."

40. Carbo, *Ecuador en Chicago*; Fitzell, "Teorizando la diferencia"; Muratorio, "Images of Indians."

41. Mera, *Cantares*; Mera, *Catecismo explicado*; Mera, *Cumandá*.

42. For studies of Pinto's work, see *Joaquín Pinto*; Ortiz Crespo, *Joaquín Pinto*; Gallegos de Donoso, Vargas, and Villalba, *Pintores ecuatorianos*.

43. For a general biography of Martínez, see Jurado Noboa, *Luís A. Martínez*. For more on Martínez's mountaineering, see Banco Central del Ecuador, *Paisajes del Ecuador*, and Martínez, *Andinismo*. For more on his interventions in Ecuadorian agriculture, see Martínez, *Agricultura del interior*, and Martínez, *Agricultura ecuatoriana*.

44. A. Clark, *Redemptive Work*.

45. President Páez dissolved the 1937 Constitutional Assembly before it could produce a final document and reconvened an assembly more fully under his control in 1938. That Constitution was never completed because Páez was overthrown; the radical 1945 Constitution was fully approved before being annulled the next year by President Velasco Ibarra, who then oversaw the passage of a more moderate document in 1946.

46. The Aryan fascism of Hitler's Germany evoked fairly unanimous revulsion in Ecuador. The Spanish Civil War and Franco's Catholic fascism, however, divided the nation along accustomed liberal and conservative lines.

47. Plaza Lasso, *Problems of Democracy*, 20, 27, 31. Like most white-mestizos of his day, Plaza Lasso did not see indigenous people as his equals. He does appear to have been genuinely interested in indigenous education, though, writing, "If the *indígena* is to be transformed into a free human being, a complete citizen of this country and if his country is to transform itself into a true democracy, incorporating them to political and civic activities, the only effective route of action is to give the Indian a practical and clear [*sensible*] education" (quoted in de la Torre and Salgado, *Galo Plaza*, 37).

48. See K. Clark, "Medida de la diferencia," and Prieto, *Liberalismo y temor*.

49. See, for example, Garcés, "Condiciones de vida," and Jaramillo Alvarado, "Indio."

50. Greet notes that the artists called indigenistas had ambiguous relationships with that term and its derogatory origins. Greet quotes Oswaldo Guayasamín, for example, as declaring in 1974, "I have never been an Indigenist painter. Indigenism is a pictorial trend that is equivalent to painting Indian ponchos, sashes, and hats, sometimes beautiful, other times dirty and ugly, leaving human character behind or using it as a pretext for the decorative." *Beyond National Identity*, 1.

51. Greet offers a compelling argument that Ecuadorian indigenismo ought not be seen as a merely internal, national trend but as a "constantly evolving means for Latin American artists from countries with large Native American populations to negotiate a distinct, yet modern, identity in an increasingly international cultural sphere" (ibid., 2).

52. For more on the movement of artists within and beyond the Americas, see ibid., as well as C. Olson, "Raíces Americanas."

53. Farrell, "Sizing Things Up," 1.

Chapter 1

1. Hedgecoe, "Hyper-Political Wave."

2. Conaghan, "Ecuador," 58.

3. For more on the possible causes of Ecuador's frequent reconstitution, see Gargarella, "Towards a Typology"; Lucero, "Crisis and Contention"; and Walsh, "(Re)articulation."

4. Burke, *Grammar*; Burke, "Questions and Answers," 334. For more on symbolic action, see also Burke, *Rhetoric*. For discussion of symbolic action and nonsymbolic motion, see Burke, "(Nonsymbolic) Motion," and Hawhee, *Moving Bodies*.

5. Burke, *Language*, 3; Burke, *Rhetoric*, 42.

6. Burke, *Grammar*, 358.

7. See C. Olson, "Places to Stand," for more on how a U.S.-centric focus has affected the development of constitutive rhetoric.

8. In this study, the words "Constitution" or "Constitutions" written with a capital "C" refer to political Constitutions. When "constitution" appears in lower case, it references the broader meaning treated here: constitutions as the conglomeration of political documents, visual culture, civic debates, citizenly experiences, and narratives that carry national topoi and authorize consistent identifications even in the midst of change.

9. Burke, "Questions and Answers," 334.

10. Charland, "Constitutive Rhetoric." There is an established and growing body of scholarship in constitutive rhetoric. Almost none of it references Burke's *Grammar of Motives* chapter, "The Dialectic of Constitutions," 323–401. For work relying on Maurice Charland instead, see Bacon, "Acting as Freemen"; Drzewiecka, "Reinventing and Contesting Identities"; C. Smith, "Discipline"; Stein, "'1984' Macintosh Ad"; Sweet and McCue-Enser, "Constituting 'the People'"; and Tate, "Ideological Effects." For scholarship referencing other Burkean ideas, see Morus, "SANU Memorandum"; Thieme, "Constitutive Rhetoric"; and Zagacki, "Constitutive Rhetoric." A few scholars use "constitutive rhetoric" in ways parallel to Charland but do not cite his work; see Asen, "Reflections," and Leff and Utley, "Instrumental and Constitutive Rhetoric."

11. Charland, "Constitutive Rhetoric," 134.

12. D. Anderson, *Identity's Strategy*, 37; G. Clark, *Rhetorical Landscapes*, 4.

13. Burke, "Questions and Answers," 334.

14. Burke, *Grammar*, 341.

15. For discussions of attitude and the hexed pentad, see Burke, "Questions and Answers," and Burke, *Grammar*, 443.

16. Burke, "Questions and Answers," 334 (emphasis in the original).

17. Ibid., 333.

18. Ibid., 334.

19. Burke, *Grammar*, 387. Burke used both "beneath" and "behind" to refer to the same general idea of a Constitution-supporting constitution.

20. Maiguashca, "Electoral Reforms," 104.

21. Guerrero, "Dominated Populations," 273.

22. Borja y Borja, *Constituciones del Ecuador*, 64.

23. The Constitutions of 1861 and 1878 describe the republic as composed of "all Ecuadorians united under the same pact of political association." The Constitution of 1945 invokes the Ecuadorian nation as "constituted in an independent, sovereign, democratic, and unitary state under a regime of liberty, justice, equality and work, with the goal of promoting individual and communal well-being and supporting human solidarity."

24. Guerrero, "Dominated Populations"; Sattar, "Indígena o Ciudadano."

25. Mora, quoted in Maiguashca, "Electoral Reforms," 105.

26. This specific list appears in the Constitutions of 1861 and 1869. Later Constitutions intersperse rights and responsibilities throughout the document.

27. The Constitutions of 1929 and 1945 replace *nación* with *pueblo*, signaling heightened populism and emphasizing that the people as a whole carried sovereignty. The Constitution of 1946 notes only that "National Sovereignty is exercised through the organs of Public Power that this Constitution establishes."

28. Burke, *Grammar*, 323, 358.

29. Actas de la asamblea, 1861; Mora Lopez, *Ecuador en la Constituyente*, 1–6.

30. Burke, *Grammar*, 373.

31. Moñino, quoted in Viqueira Albán, *Propriety and Permissiveness*, 38.

32. In this era one occasionally sees "citizen" used as a more general term applied to petitioners, regardless of their actual citizenship status. My treatment of citizenship here addresses the Constitutional meaning, not that more colloquial use, largely because "Indian" and "citizen" were often mutually exclusive terms for referencing petitioners.

33. Feehan, "Burke's Dualistic Theory," 42.

34. If this were a study of the U.S. Constitution, I would suggest the same for that context. The invocation of "We the people," after all, invokes a far larger nation than the founders were willing to admit into active participation. The assertion that Constitutions create consistency from the stuff of contingency is not limited to Ecuador and ought to inflect broader understandings of rhetorical constitution.

35. Burke, *Grammar*, 323.

36. Maiguashca, "Electoral Reforms," 92, 93; de la Torre and Salgado, *Galo Plaza*, 20.

37. Guerrero, "Dominated Populations," 273. The history of Afro-Ecuadorian political oppression is beyond the scope of this project, but it should be noted that Afro-Ecuadorians have also been regularly excluded from participation and have been less visible than indigenous people, thanks, in part, to the narratives examined here.

38. Guerrero, "Imagen ventrilocua," 214.

39. Burke, *Grammar*, 373, 357.

40. Ibid., 368, 367.

41. Guerrero, "Dominated Populations," 294.

42. Hajicek, "Canvas as Nation."

43. B. Anderson, *Imagined Communities*; Castro-Klarén, "Nation in Ruins"; Hobsbawm, *Nations and Nationalism*.

44. Kennedy Troya, "Artistas y científicos," 230.

45. Catlin, "Traveller-Reporter Artists"; Pérez, "Exoticism," 100.

46. Muratorio, "Images of Indians," 115, 114.

47. Burke, *Grammar*, 362, 365.

48. Pérez, "Exoticism," 110.

49. Chapter 5 discusses much of Joaquín Pinto's work as an exception to this general claim about costumbrismo.

50. Hariman and Lucaites, *No Caption Needed*, 12, 13.

51. Prieto, *Liberalismo y temor*, 39.

52. *Mestizaje* refers to the processes of racial mixture that, according to some, defines Latin American identity. In 1925 the Mexican philosopher José Vasconcelos published an influential treatise claiming that the mestizo was humankind's racial future and, therefore, that Latin America represented the next stage of human development. It is unclear whether the Ecuadorian intellectuals influenced by Vasconcelos conceived of mestizaje in primarily biological or cultural terms. For more, see A. Clark, "Race," and Prieto, *Liberalismo y temor*. Even where the carnal sense of mestizaje was suppressed, however, assumptions about cultural mixture played key roles in Ecuadorian intellectual, political, and artistic circles.

53. Ecuador and Peru maintained border hostilities throughout the first half of the twentieth century, preventing much cultural exchange.

54. Prieto, *Liberalismo y temor.*

55. Carrión, "Premio Aguilera," 7.

56. Burke, *Grammar*, 365.

57. Ibid., 368.

58. Charland, "Constitutive Rhetoric," 133.

59. Adelman, "Introduction," 1, 12.

60. D. Anderson, *Identity's Strategy*, 42.

Chapter 2

1. Carrión, *Cartas al Ecuador*, 44.

2. Mera, *Cantares*, 29.

3. B. Anderson, *Imagined Communities*; Castro-Klarén and Chasteen, *Beyond Imagined Communities*; Hobsbawm, *Nations and Nationalism.*

4. Bolívar, "Delirium."

5. Juan León Mera's reference to "ponchos and sandals" points immediately to indigenous people. His invocation of the *molle hijo* has a similar resonance, as the fruit of the *molle hijo* tree was traditionally used to make a version of *chicha*, a mildly intoxicating beverage consumed in Andean indigenous communities. *Cantares*, 26, 29.

6. The elite tendency to equate rural (indigenous) identity with amodernity, illiteracy, and lack of citizenship should not be surprising to U.S. scholars of composition and rhetoric. Peter Mortensen, in "Figuring Illiteracy," notes that in the early twentieth-century United States, "illiteracy was held to be endemic to rural life, and its persistence there at the turn of the century was thought to be hampering the agricultural modernization needed to support the rising demands of city dwellers." Also similar to my concern for the lasting force of such commonplaces of rusticity, Mortensen notes that this "insistence on situating the unlettered in rustic bodies" has consequences even today (144).

7. Burke, *Rhetoric*, 22 (emphasis in the original).

8. Kennedy Troya, "Territorio y el paisaje," 7, 12.

9. Powell, "Writing the Geography," 74.

10. Guerrero, *Imágenes del Ecuador.*

11. *Acta de la pública.*

12. Villavicencio, *Geografía de la república.*

13. See, for example, Cevallos, *Geografía de la república*; Mera, *Cantares*; and Wolf, *Geografía y geología.*

14. Grijalva Calero, *Plástica y literatura*, 21.

15. G. Clark, *Rhetorical Landscapes*, 8.

16. Ibid., 18, 26.

17. The Shyris, also known as the Quitus, occupied the central highlands region of what became Ecuador prior to the arrival of the Incas.

18. Villavicencio, *Geografía de la república*, 8.

19. Mera, *Cantares*, 99, 104.

20. Kennedy Troya, "Territorio y el paisaje," 11.

21. Leonhardt Abram, "Andes en el corazón," 41.

22. It may not be a coincidence that 1906 was the year that the final push began on the railway link between Quito and Guayaquil that would be completed in 1908.

23. Pinto, quoted in *Joaquín Pinto*, 1.

24. Kennedy Troya, "Paisajes patrios," 83.

25. Grijalva Calero, *Plástica y literatura*, 21.

26. Vargas, *Historia*, 87–88.

27. Villavicencio, *Geografía de la república*, vii.

28. Mera, *Cantares*, 34.

29. Villavicencio, *Geografía de la república*, vii.

30. Martínez, *Agricultura ecuatoriana*, 5.

31. Kennedy Troya, "Paisajes patrios," 106.

32. For example, according to A. Kim Clark, indigenous communities at the turn of the century used Liberal political language to interrupt exploitation and bring the system of public works labor to a standstill. Their petitions, Clark argues, helped bring the state into being. "Indians"; "Formación del estado."

33. In this period, canton Quito included not only the relatively small urban area of the city of Quito but also a large outlying area that, from its farthest points, was more than a day's walk from the capital itself.

34. The initial request has disappeared, leaving only the responses of the parochial authorities.

35. Thirty-five years later the new Liberal government would describe itself as committed to these same goals but introduce them as if they were new objectives that would allow the nation to emerge from the stagnation of the Conservative Era. While Liberals had different plans for pursuing these goals, the objectives themselves actually changed little. For more on the late nineteenth-century version of these goals, see Kingman Garcés, *Ciudad y los otros*. For discussion of their enactment in the Liberal Era, see A. Clark, *Redemptive Work*, 43.

36. Kennedy Troya, "Paisajes patrios."

37. Roberto Donoso, juzgado político of Cangagua, writing to the jefe político of Quito, March 25, 1862, in Oficios y solicitudes, 1862, 118–19.

38. List of indígenas possessing fallow land, March 1862; report from the parish of Tumbaco to the jefe político of Quito, March 15, 1862; petition from the "Gobernador de Indígenas" of Quinche, January [26?], 1862, all in ibid., 164–65, 112–13, 652.

39. Letter from Rafael Brito, 1862, in ibid., 668 (emphasis mine).

40. Petition from Rafael Lopez Conde of Tumbaco, October 20, 1862, in ibid., 467–70.

41. Letter from Manuel Quesadan of Lloa, March 12, 1871; response by Maxiano Ramírez, juez civil of Lloa, to the petition of Manuel Quesadan, March 15, 1871, both in Oficios y solicitudes, 1871, 301, 302.

42. Formal petition in favor of the indígena Mariano Barajo, parish of Tocachi; formal petition in favor of the indígena A— Guamon, parish of Tocachi; formal petition in favor of the indígena Joaquín Laso, parish of Tocachi, July 8, 1870, all in Oficios y solicitudes, 1870, 804, 478, 481.

43. Velasco, *Historia antigua*. This dispute was finally settled nearly a century later through the groundbreaking work of the anthropologist Frank Salomon, published as a dissertation in 1978 and a book in 1986. Through a mixed-method ethnohistory entirely new at the time, Salomon demonstrated that not only were there organized communities in the Quito area prior to the Incan conquest but those communities and their traditions had survived surprisingly intact into the present day of his research. Salomon, *Native Lords of Quito*.

44. For a full report on Jijón y Caamaño's lifelong research, see Jijón y Caamaño, *Ecuador interandino y occidental*.

45. Prieto, *Liberalismo y temor*, 80.

46. A. Clark, "Racial Ideologies," 381.

47. Carrión, *Cartas al Ecuador*, 82.

48. See, for example, Mistral, *Escritos políticos*, and Vasconcelos, *Cosmic Race*. For more on this pan-Latin American rhetorical ecology, see C. Olson, "Raíces Americanas."

49. Carrión, *Cartas al Ecuador*, 13, 15.

50. Ibid., 81.

51. Carrión's invocation of the Maya is unusual. The Incas, Cara (Shyris), and Quitus are far more common points of reference, given their clear occupation of (what became) Ecuadorian territory. His reference suggests a desire to forge parallels between Ecuador and revolutionary Mexico (ibid.).

52. Carrión found evidence of that second vocation in both the fine arts traditions drawn from Europe and the artisan traditions fostered in indigenous communities.

53. A. Clark, "Racial Ideologies," 390.

54. *Revista del Mar Pacífico*, "Personalidad," 16.

55. *Previsión Social*, "Hogar indígena," 7, 8.

56. Garcés, "Industría," 93.

57. *El Día*, "Higienización."

58. A. Clark, "Race," 201 (emphasis in the original).

59. Prieto, *Liberalismo y temor*, 93.

60. Ibid., 123–64, 140. In *City at the Center* Capello offers an evocative study of the ways indigenous communities in Quito appropriated this emphasis on private property to defend their claims to prime real estate at the edge of the city.

61. A. Clark, "Racial Ideologies," 382; Prieto, *Liberalismo y temor*, 91.

62. Fernández, "Nucanchic alpa," 1.

63. A. Clark, "Racial Ideologies," 390.

64. Becker, *Indians and Leftists*.

65. A. Kim Clark points out that the FEI did particularly well in Cayambe, where the indigenous organizer Dolores Cacuango was actively promoting indigenous literacy through informal schools with indigenous instructors. See "Racial Ideologies" for more.

66. Fernández, "Nucanchic alpa," 1.

67. Ministerio de Gobierno, *Informe del Ministro*, 6, quoted in A. Clark, "Racial Ideologies," 383.

68. Ibid., 378.

69. *Nucanchic Allpa*, available in pdf from the archive maintained by Dr. Marc Becker at http://www.yachana.org/.

70. Asamblea general de campesinos, "Asamblea."

71. Quoted in A. Clark, "Racial Ideologies," 379 (translation mine).

72. "Manifiesto."

73. González y Contreras, "Aclaraciones," 12.

74. I encountered the article in question as a clipping in the collection of the Casa de la Cultura Ecuatoriana. The clipping is dated 1945 but includes no other publication data. While the article's references to place make clear that it was originally published in Mexico, it was fairly common for periodicals in Ecuador to reprint foreign articles that discussed local artists.

75. Icaza, "Nace en el Ecuador," 1.

76. Velasco Ibarra, quoted in *Letras del Ecuador*, "Señor presidente," 1.

77. Just eighteen months later Velasco Ibarra would write privately to Conservative leader Jacinto Jijón y Caamaño to complain that he believed the Casa de la Cultura to be a den of leftist intrigue and sedition.

Chapter 3

1. A. Clark, *Redemptive Work*.

2. See, for example, Garcés, "Condiciones de vida"; Martínez, *Agricultura ecuatoriana*; and Federico Páez, "Mensaje del Señor encargado del Mando Supremo de la república," in Actas de la asamblea, 1937.

3. Hariman and Lucaites, *No Caption Needed*, 13.

4. See *Joaquín Pinto*; Gallegos de Donoso, "Juan León Mera"; and Pérez, "Exoticism."

5. The remaining tableaus depict the traditional figures of the year's many religious festivals, often masked and in costume. Traditionally, many of those festival roles, especially those done in whiteface masks, would have been played by indigenous people or *cholos/as* (acculturated indigenous people).

6. Discussions from the municipal council in the years leading up to the inauguration of electric lighting suggest that maintaining a system of consistent lighting for the city was a source of great concern. In that era Quito's streets were illuminated by lanterns lit with tapers or gas and hung from the walls of homes lining the streets. Council meeting minutes suggest that there were several aborted attempts to modernize the lighting (to move away from hand-lit tapers) and regular complaints about the quality and style of the lighting. Pinto himself, in 1891, petitioned the municipal council to exempt him from having to maintain the lighting around his home due to the age and inadequate height of the walls.

7. Kingman Garcés, *Ciudad y los otros*, 41.

8. See, for example, Actas del cabildo, 1888, 129–31; and Actas del cabildo, 1891, 63.

9. Even in the small scale of the topographic map at the front of this book, it is possible to see the steep ridges that separate inter-Andean valleys from one another.

10. Letter from Elias Laso, January 1862, in Oficios y solicitudes, 1862, 2:8–10.

11. Carbo, *Ecuador en Chicago*, xii.

12. Mora Lopez, *Ecuador en la Constituyente*, 38. Thanks to Judith Caballero for translation help. Ministry of Public Instruction, quoted in A. Clark, *Redemptive Work*, 49.

13. Kingman Garcés, *Ciudad y los otros*.

14. A. Kim Clark's chapter "The Contradictions of Redemption: The Uneven Development of Alausí" in *Redemptive Work*, for example, describes how indigenous laborers were forcibly recruited for hygiene-improvement projects in the white-mestizo communities of Chimborazo during an outbreak of bubonic plague. When indigenous laborers carried the infection home to their communities, however, there was no parallel local or national government investment in those communities, and the fatality rates there were higher than in the more urban areas. For more on the neocolonial basis for nation building, see ibid; Kingman Garcés, Goetschel, and Mantilla, "Obras públicas"; and Larson, *Trials of Nation Making*.

15. I am in debt to A. Kim Clark for this insight. She examines such indigenous resistance in far more depth and detail in "Indians, the State, and Law," her study of labor conscription in the parish of Alausí in Chimborazo Province.

16. Letter from the tenencia parroquial of Cangahua, August 13, 1870, in Oficios y solicitudes, 1870, 499; letter from the teniente político of Chimbacalle, July 12, 1897, in Oficios y solicitudes, 1895–1899, 269.

17. Letter from José Antonio Gallardo, tenencia parroquial of Alangasí, August 28, 1870, in Oficios y solicitudes, 1870, 569; letter from Rafael Andrade to Manuel E. Ordones, teniente parroquial of Santo Domingo de los Colorados, January 13, 1895, in Oficios y solicitudes, 1895–1899, 102.

18. Cosmo Terán, tenencia política of Cumbayá, March 19, 1894, in Oficios y solicitudes, 1891–1894, 564.

19. Letter from Teodomiro Ávila, teniente político of Sangolquí, September 4, 1893, in ibid., 361; letter from the tenencia política of Conocoto, August 3, 1896; and tenencia política de Zámbiza, August 23, 1897, both in Oficios y solicitudes, 1895–1899, 202, 291.

20. A. Clark, *Redemptive Work*, 86.

21. A. Clark, "Indians."

22. Letter from Carlos Larrea G., July 29, 1897, in Oficios y solicitudes, 1895–1899, 273.

23. Letter from the indígenas of Nayón and Zámbiza, August 3, 1897, in ibid., 281.

24. A. Clark, "Ecuadorian Indians," 56.

25. Becker, *Indians and Leftists*, 5.

26. Kingman Garcés, Goetschel, and Mantilla, "Obras públicas," 365.

27. Gallegos de Donoso, "Juan León Mera," 10.

28. LaWare, "Encountering Visions," 230.

29. A. Clark, "Ecuadorian Indians," 57.

30. Becker, *Indians and Leftists*, 28, 12, 38.

31. Comité de Huelga, "Huelga."

32. Fernández, "Indios se alzan."

33. Fernández, "Indios 'comunistas.'"

34. See, for example, Garcés, "Condiciones de vida," 26.

35. K. Clark, "Medida de la diferencia," 115.

36. *Los Andes*, "Nacionalidad por trabajo," 4.

37. For a more detailed analysis of similar connections among work, education, and citizenship in the United States, see Wan, "Producing Good Citizens."

38. Prieto, *Liberalismo y temor*, 91.

39. A. Clark, "Racial Ideologies," 383.

40. Rodas, *Crónica de un sueño*, 39–45.

41. A. Clark, "Ecuadorian Indians," 57, 58.

42. Beck and Mijeski, "*Indígena* Self-Identity," 121.

43. E. Kingman, "Nacionalismo," 5.

44. Vasconcelos, *Cosmic Race*.

45. Only one rural scene in *Hombres* breaks the communal pattern. Tellingly, that print, *En los surcos*, shows an indigenous man using an ox-driven plow to till a field. Given that indigenous collective action was linked to tradition for Kingman, the introduction of modern agricultural tools quite reasonably interrupts that communal theme.

46. E. Kingman, "Nacionalismo," 5.

47. For more recent, detailed studies of Kingman's work and his political and intellectual affiliations, see Greet, *Beyond National Identity*; and Moreno Aguilar, *Kingman*.

48. Pacheco Pérez, introd. to *Gente del Ecuador*, 1.

49. N. Kingman, quoted in Oña, "Arte de Kingman," 61.

50. This neglect continues. Today the mural is little known and difficult to see. What was the Ministry of Agriculture is now an office building for the armed forces that allows limited access, and portions of the mural are buried behind a bank of Plexiglas cubicles.

51. N. Kingman, "Boceto," 172.

52. Lasso, "Eduardo Kingman," 17; Vacas Gómez, "Eduardo Kingman," 2; Terán, "Materialismo dialéctico," 18.

53. E. Kingman, *Ayuda artística*, 4; Terán, "Materialismo dialéctico," 17.

54. This material implies another way that Burke's definition of rhetoric in terms of "identification" rather than "persuasion" can help make space for a wider array of symbolic practices to be understood as rhetorical. Here, for example, I am less interested in the ability of indigenista artwork to persuade a particular audience to join indigenous struggles than I am in how these images oriented viewers toward a new vision of the nation. By attempting to alter the terms of identification by which viewers would recognize compatriots and imagine their own place in the nation, the indigenistas were reorganizing the rhetorical milieu in which they lived. Their images engaged the commonplaces of indigenous labor and national identity to affect national common sense.

55. A. Clark, "Ecuadorian Indians," 57.

56. See, for example, Becker, *Indians and Leftists*; A. Clark and Becker, *Highland Indians*; and Pallares, *Peasant Struggles*.

57. *Revista del Mar Pacífico*, "Personalidad," 16.

58. De la Torre, "Usos políticos," 237.

Chapter 4

1. Ministerio de Previsión Social, *Día del indio*, 5.

2. A. Clark, "Indians"; de la Torre, "Usos políticos"; Guerrero, "Dominated Populations"; Sattar, "Indígena o Ciudadano"; Williams, "Administering the Otavalan Indian."

3. See Fitzell, "Teorizando la diferencia," and Muratorio, *Imágenes e imagineros*.

4. For visual-culture scholars, see Grijalva Calero, *Plástica y literatura*; Muratorio, "Images of Indians"; Pérez, "Exoticism"; and Pequeño Bueno, *Imágenes en disputa*. For scholars examining modernization projects, see Kingman Garcés, *Ciudad y los otros*, and Prieto, *Liberalismo y temor*.

5. Cintrón, "Democracy"; Fraser, "Rethinking"; Paley, "Toward an Anthropology."

6. Davis, *Inessential Solidarity*; Isocrates, "Nicocles," 6; Burke, *Rhetoric*, 22; Derrida, *Of Grammatology*, 313.

7. Davis, *Inessential Solidarity*, 56, 62.

8. This distinction between the "other" of ontology and the other of social life, incidentally, is likely the source of Davis's frustration with Burke, who claims simultaneously that identification-through-consubstantiality is our originary state and that "identification is compensatory to [essential] division." Burke, always attentive to the ambiguities of substance, sees a difference between individual origins and communal experience. Burke, *Rhetoric*, 22; Davis, *Inessential Solidarity*, 22–26.

9. *El Ecuatoriano*, "Oligarquía," 389, 390 (emphasis in the original).

10. Cintrón, "Democracy," 113, 106.

11. Allen, *Talking to Strangers*, 41.

12. Andrade Marín, "Indio," 145, 146; Tupac Amaru, "Carta de Tupac Amaru," 3. Though this columnist invokes the name of the last member of the Inca family who led a short-lived rebellion against the Spanish colonizers in the late sixteenth century, *El Día*'s Tupac Amaru wrote only occasionally about indigenous issues.

13. Andrade Marín, "Indio," 146; Tupac Amaru, "Carta de Tupac Amaru," 3.

14. Rodríguez and Estrella, *Quito colonial*.

15. Ibid., 5 (emphasis in the original).

16. Ibid., 7, 6.

17. Allen, *Talking to Strangers*, 41.

18. Laso and Cruz, *Quito a la vista*, 1.

19. Ibid.

20. Pinto, quoted in *Joaquín Pinto*, 1.

21. Laso and Cruz, *Quito a la vista*, 4.

22. Instituto Indigenista Ecuatoriano, *Cuestiones indígenas*, i–ii.

23. Note this word is F-E-I-S-T-A, from *feo* or "ugly," not F-I-E-S-T-A, meaning "party."

24. Jaramillo Alvarado, "Indio," 35–36.

25. Instituto Indigenista Ecuatoriano, *Cuestiones indígenas*, iii.

26. K. Clark, "Medida de la diferencia," 115.

27. Instituto Indigenista Ecuatoriano, *Cuestiones indígenas*, iii.

28. Ibid., iv.

29. Balibar, "World Borders," 72.

Chapter 5

1. Open letter to the president of the Republic of Ecuador, March 4, 1886, in Hojas volantes, 395–98. Signatories to the letter include the parish's chief executive, several civil judges, and the schoolmaster.

2. I have not been able to determine the actual circulation of this broadsheet, so I can make claims only about its imagined audience, not its actual readership.

3. Burke, *Rhetoric*, 21.

4. My emphasis on the portability of topoi expands on recent scholarship about circulation in rhetoric and publics theory. See, for example, Edbauer, "Unframing Models"; Finnegan and Kang, "Sighting the Public"; L. Olson, "Pictorial Representations"; and Warner, "Publics and Counterpublics."

5. Taylor, *Archive and the Repertoire*, 2.

6. Cintrón, "Democracy," 101.

7. Burke, *Rhetoric*, 21.

8. Ibid.

9. Burke, *Grammar*, 406.

10. Eddy, *Rites of Identity*, 73–74.

11. Cintrón, "Democracy," 101.

12. Burke, *Rhetoric*, 46.

13. Guerrero documents patterns of nineteenth-century white-mestizo elites speaking for indigenous people in political contexts. The speaking *as if* of the embodiable topos is an extension of that more widely practiced paternalism. Guerrero, "Dominated Populations"; Guerrero, "Construction."

14. Burke, *Rhetoric*, 22; Perelman and Olbrechts-Tyteca, *New Rhetoric*, 413.

15. Berkhofer, *White Man's Indian*, 3; Lyons, "Rhetorical Sovereignty," 452.

16. For studies of how nonindigenous rhetors appropriate and commodify indigeneity in the U.S. context, see Black, "Mascotting"; Ono and Buescher, "Deciphering Pocahontas"; and Rogers, "Deciphering Kokopelli." Lester Olson's "Pictorial Representations" and *Emblems of American Community* examine instances in which the appropriated image of the Indian stands in for the American body politic, though in *Emblems* Olson notes that the alien nature of the Indian remains prominent.

17. For an analysis, see Castro-Klarén, "Nation in Ruins"; Poole, *Vision, Race, and Modernity*; and Pratt, *Imperial Eyes*. For examples, see González Suárez, *Aborígenes*; and Humboldt, *Aspects of Nature*.

18. Larson, *Trials of Nation Making*, 120.

19. Such complaints would have invoked indigeneity for contemporary readers. The legacy of indigenous tribute meant that tax paying was closely connected to indigeneity in Ecuadorian common sense, and white-mestizo resistance to taxation was regularly phrased in terms of white-mestizos rejecting being treated like Indians. For more, see Guerrero, "Dominated Populations."

20. President Gabriel García Moreno used the "miserable Indian" as a defining trope in his midcentury modernization project, and the Liberal Party emphasized indigenous misery in their efforts to end debt peonage. See, for example, A. Clark, "Indians." Clark demonstrates indigenous communities' regular appropriation of similar language to invoke the state in their defense. Prieto, *Liberalismo y temor*; Williams, "Administering the Otavalan Indian," 38.

21. Guerrero, "Dominated Populations," 291.

22. A. Clark, "Indians."

23. Jones and Rowland, "Reagan at Moscow State," 92.

24. Burke, *Rhetoric*, 20.

25. Pérez, "Exoticism," 111. While it is difficult to determine how Pinto's actual artwork circulated, his prominent positions in arts academies and connections with major artists and scientists suggest his influence. The fact that Pinto is often identified as one of Ecuador's first artists to envision the nation also points toward the role he played in shaping the idea of the body politic.

26. The cascades that ran down the volcano Pichincha were diverted into fountains and cisterns throughout Quito. But without a citywide system of plumbing, the only way for water to travel from the cisterns into private homes was on the backs of these specialized porters.

27. Kang, "Coming to Terms"; Yeh, "We're Mexican Too"; Bell, "Transnational Public Sphere."

28. Warner, "Publics and Counterpublics," 56; Hariman and Lucaites, *No Caption Needed*, 45.

29. Fraser, "Transnationalizing," 20.

30. Pérez, "Exoticism," 111.

31. Hariman and Lucaites, *No Caption Needed*, 33.

32. Fraser, "Rethinking."

33. Ibid., 77; Warner, "Publics and Counterpublics," 52–53.

34. Burke, *Rhetoric*, 46.

35. Hariman and Lucaites, *No Caption Needed*, 34. It is also possible that the paintings connected to these sketches were lost. Pinto sold many of his works, and many were not preserved.

36. Hariman and Lucaites, *No Caption Needed*, 34.

37. Ibid., 33.

38. A. Clark, *Redemptive Work*, 8.

39. Prieto, *Liberalismo y temor*, 32, 81.

40. See, for example, Carrión, *Creadores*; Carrión, *Mapa de América*; and Vasconcelos, *Cosmic Race*. For scholarly discussion of mestizaje in Ecuador specifically, see Beck and Mijeski, "*Indígena* Self-Identity"; A. Clark, "Race"; Espinosa Apolo, *Mestizaje*; and Roitman, *Race, Ethnicity, and Power*. For analyses of mestizaje as a phenomenon in other parts of twentieth-century Latin America, see Gould, *Die in This Way*; Klor de Alva, "Mestizaje"; M. Miller, *Rise and Fall*; and Saldaña-Portillo, *Revolutionary Imagination*.

41. Prieto, *Liberalismo y temor*, 165.

42. Montesinos goes on to argue that the commonplace of "melancholy" has become a mask that Ecuadorians hide behind to justify their struggles.

43. Though the rondador performs a stylized indigeneity, we cannot know if the photographer's model would have identified himself *as* indigenous. Some indigenista photographs apparently present "real" indigenous people, but there were photographs taken in the same period that present "real" white-mestizos posing as pastoral Indians for studio portraits.

44. Montesinos Malo, "Tristeza," 9.

45. Prieto, *Liberalismo y temor*, 32.

46. M. Miller, *Rise and Fall*, 2.

47. Vasconcelos, *Cosmic Race*, 9.

48. A. Clark, "Race"; Prieto, *Liberalismo y temor*.

49. M. Miller, *Rise and Fall*, 119.

50. Monsalve Pozo, "Indio," 3.

51. *Letras del Ecuador*, "Ley de patrimonio artístico," 18.

52. Icaza, "Nace en el Ecuador"; Diez-Canseco, "Discurso."

53. Monsalve Pozo, "Ecuador," 15.

54. See, for example, *Revista del Mar Pacífico*, "Afirmación y horizonte," and Diez-Canseco, "Discurso."

55. See Taylor's *Archive and the Repertoire* for a discussion of performance as a means of maintaining histories in the face of colonial erasure.

56. Burke, *Rhetoric*, 21; Eddy, *Rites of Identity*, 73.

Conclusion

1. One version of the ad is available on YouTube; see "La Patria," *Mensaje del Gobierno.*

2. CONAIE is the Confederación de Nacionalidades Indígenas del Ecuador (Confederation of Indigenous Nationalities of Ecuador).

3. A video of Morocho's and Cholango's speeches is available on the website of Ecuarunari (Ecuadorian Federation of Kichwa), "Marcha por la vida."

4. The political rivalry between Rafael Correa's "twenty-first-century socialism" and Ecuador's plurinational, antineoliberal social movements may seem odd to U.S. readers unfamiliar with Ecuador's recent political history. Suffice it to say that the conflict revolves around Correa's often demagogic political style, his administration's overfierce response to criticism, and his suspicion of traditional social movements on the one hand and the formal indigenous movement's own entrenched political commitments and search for greater influence on the other. Both sides of the conflict offer largely left-wing solutions to Ecuador's economic and social problems. They object to the excessive influence of transnational corporations, actively seek social reforms in favor of Ecuador's lower classes, and pursue new levels of environmental protection. They differ to varying extents on how to pursue those goals, and their differences are especially stark on the question of how (or whether) to exploit the country's substantial subsoil natural resources.

5. For a description of the mandate, see Charupi, "Marcha Plurinacional al Arbolito." For a full copy, see Ecuarunari, "Mandato."

6. The "pocket version" available from the National Assembly weighs in at an impressive 218 pages.

7. Werner and De Wilde, "Endurance of Sovereignty," 284.

8. Kalmo and Skinner, "Introduction," 7.

9. *El Comercio,* "Acosta define."

10. Ecuarunari, "Nuestra propuesta," 4; Correa, "Intervención," 4.

11. Asamblea Constituyente, *Constitución de la república,* 16, 15.

12. Ibid., 52.

13. Tully, *Strange Multiplicity,* 195. Tully's relatively recent definition of sovereignty attempts to account for the reality of interdependence in the contemporary world, yet retain a sense of the context in which states are able to exercise some sense of independence.

14. Lyons, "Rhetorical Sovereignty," 449–50.

15. Kalmo and Skinner, "Introduction."

16. Werner and De Wilde, "Endurance of Sovereignty," 287.

17. Allen, *Talking to Strangers,* 41. Speaking of the experience of individual citizens and communities, Allen explains that "democratic citizenship requires rituals to manage the psychological tension that arises from being a nearly powerless sovereign" (ibid.).

18. See A. Clark, "Indians."

19. Werner and De Wilde, "Endurance of Sovereignty," 292, 287.

20. Burke, *Grammar,* 357, 73.

21. Adelman, "Introduction," 2.

BIBLIOGRAPHY

ARCHIVAL SOURCES

Archivo de la Función Legislativa. Quito, Ecuador

Actas de la asamblea nacional constituyente de 1861.
Actas de la asamblea nacional constituyente de 1906.
Actas de la asamblea nacional constituyente de 1937.

Archivo Metropolitano de la Historia de Quito. Quito, Ecuador

Actas del cabildo, 1888.
Actas del cabildo, 1891.
Oficios y solicitudes al jefe político como presidente del consejo, 1871. Vol. 1.
Oficios y solicitudes dirigidos al jefe político, 1862. Vol. 2.
Oficios y solicitudes dirigidos al jefe político, 1891–94.
Oficios y solicitudes dirigidos al jefe político, 1895–99.
Oficios y solicitudes dirigidos al jefe político como presidente del consejo, 1870.
Oficios y solicitudes dirigidos al presidente del consejo, 1862.

Biblioteca Aurelio Espinosa Pólit. Cotocollao, Quito, Ecuador

Hojas volantes. 4 vols.

E-Archivo Ecuatoriano

Asamblea General de Campesinos. "La asamblea general de campesinos de los cantones Yaguachi y Milagro, a los obreros y campesinos en general." 1928. E-Archivo Ecuatoriano. http://www.yachana.org/earchivo/.
Comité de Huelga. "Huelga de los sindicatos 'Tierra Libre' y 'El Inca': Los crímenes de los latifundistas, autoridades, y servidumbre." March 18, 1931. In Hojas volantes, 1931–40, vol. 2. Original copy held by the Biblioteca Aurelio Espinosa Pólit. Cotocollao, Quito, Ecuador. Reference: D. Polit Partid (985 1931–40). E-Archivo Ecuatoriano. http://www.yachana.org/earchivo/.
"Manifiesto que el comité ejecutivo de la Federación Indígena dirige al pueblo ecuatoriano." February 1945. E-Archivo Ecuatoriano. http://www.yachana.org/earchivo/.
Nucanchic Allpa. March 17, 1936; May 28, 1940; November 5, 1944; October 5, 1946. E-Archivo Ecuatoriano. http://www.yachana.org/earchivo/.

Fundación Posada de las Artes Kingman

Kingman, Eduardo. "La ayuda artística." 1949.
———. "Nacionalismo en arte." 1951.

PUBLISHED TEXTS

Acta de la pública y solemne instalación de la escuela democrática de Miguel de Santiago, celebrada el 31 de enero de 1852. Quito: Imprenta del Gobierno, 1852.

Adelman, Jeremy. "Introduction: The Problem of Persistence in Latin American History." In *Colonial Legacies: The Problem of Persistence in Latin American History*, edited by Jeremy Adelman, 1–14. New York: Routledge, 1999.

Agnew, Lois, Laurie Gries, Zosha Stuckey, Vicki Tolar Burton, Jay Dolmage, Jessica Enoch, Ronald L. Jackson II, et al. "Octalog III: The Politics of Historiography in 2010." *Rhetoric Review* 30, no. 2 (2011): 109–34. http://dx.doi.org/10.1080/073501 98.2011.551497.

Agnew, Lois, James J. Murphy, Cheryl Glenn, Nan Johnson, Jan Swearingen, Richard Leo Enos, Jasper Neel, et al. "Rhetorical Historiography and the Octalogs." *Rhetoric Review* 30, no. 3 (2011): 237–57. http://dx.doi.org/10.1080/07350198 .2011.581935.

Albornoz, Miguel. "Alphabet in the Andes." *Ecuador*, September–October 1949.

Allen, Danielle S. *Talking to Strangers: Anxieties of Citizenship After Brown v. Board of Education*. Chicago: University of Chicago Press, 2004.

Amaru, Tupac. "Una carta de Tupac Amaru al Dr. Pablo A. Suárez." *El Día*, February 4, 1935.

Anderson, Benedict. *Imagined Communities: Reflections on the Origin and Spread of Nationalism*. 3rd ed. London: Verso, 2006.

Anderson, Dana. *Identity's Strategy: Rhetorical Selves in Conversion*. Columbia: University of South Carolina Press, 2007.

Los Andes. "Nacionalidad por trabajo." April 1939.

Andrade Marín, Carlos. "El indio y el seguro social campesino." In Instituto Indigenista Ecuatoriano, *Cuestiones indígenas del Ecuador*, 145–65.

Aristotle. *On Rhetoric: A Theory of Civic Discourse*. 2nd ed. Translated by George A. Kennedy. New York: Oxford University Press, 2007.

———. Topics. Alex Catalogue. eBook Collection (EBSCOhost). Accessed April 19, 2013. http://library.wisc.edu.

Asamblea Constituyente. *Constitución de la república del Ecuador*. 2008. http://www .asambleanacional.gov.ec/documentos/constitucion_de_bolsillo.pdf.

Asen, Robert. "Reflections on the Role of Rhetoric in Public Policy." *Rhetoric and Public Affairs* 13, no. 1 (2010): 121–43. http://dx.doi.org/10.1353/rap.0.0142.

Atwill, Janet, Linda Ferreira-Buckley, Cheryl Glenn, Janice Lauer, Roxanne Mountford, Jasper Neel, Edward Schiappa, et al. "Octalog II: The (Continuing) Politics of Historiography." *Rhetoric Review* 16, no. 1 (1997): 22–44. http://dx.doi .org/10.1080/07350199709389078.

Ayala Mora, Enrique, ed. *Época aborigen I*. Vol. 1 of *Nueva historia del Ecuador*. Quito: Corporación Editora Nacional, 1988.

———, ed. *Época aborigen II*. Vol. 2 of *Nueva historia del Ecuador*. Quito: Corporación Editora Nacional, 1988.

———, ed. *Época colonial I*. Vol. 3 of *Nueva historia del Ecuador*. Quito: Corporación Editora Nacional; Editorial Grijalbo Ecuatoriana, 1988.

———, ed. *Época colonial II*. Vol. 4 of *Nueva historia del Ecuador*. Quito: Corporación Editora Nacional; Editorial Grijalbo Ecuatoriana, 1989.

———, ed. *Época republicana II*. Vol. 8 of *Nueva historia del Ecuador*. Quito: Corporación Editora Nacional, 1996.

———, ed. *Independencia y periodo colombiano*. Vol. 6 of *Nueva historia del Ecuador*. Quito: Corporación Editora Nacional, 1989.

Bacon, Jacqueline. "'Acting as Freemen': Rhetoric, Race, and Reform in the Debate over Colonization in *Freedom's Journal*, 1827–1828." *Quarterly Journal of Speech* 93, no. 1 (2007): 58–83. http://dx.doi.org/10.1080/00335630701326860.

Bahri, Deepika. "Response: A World of Difference." *College English* 70, no. 5 (2008): 522–28.

Balibar, Etienne. "World Borders, Political Borders." Translated by Erin M. Williams. *PMLA* 117, no. 1 (2002): 71–78. http://dx.doi.org/10.1632/003081202X63519.

Banco Central del Ecuador. *Paisajes del Ecuador*. Quito: Banco Central del Ecuador, 1984.

Beck, Scott H., and Kenneth J. Mijeski. "*Indígena* Self-Identity in Ecuador and the Rejection of *Mestizaje*." *Latin American Research Review* 35, no. 1 (2000): 119–37.

Becker, Marc. *Indians and Leftists in the Making of Ecuador's Modern Indigenous Movements*. Durham: Duke University Press, 2008.

Begon, Michael, John L. Harper, and Colin R. Townsend. *Ecology: Individuals, Populations, and Communities*. Oxford: Blackwell Science, 1996. http://dx.doi.org/10.1002/9781444313765

Bell, Vikki. "The Potential of an 'Unfolding Constellation': Imagining Fraser's Transnational Public Sphere." *Theory, Culture, and Society* 24, no. 4 (2007): 1–86. http://dx.doi.org/10.1177/0263276407083018.

Berkhofer, Robert F., Jr. *The White Man's Indian: Images of the American Indian from Columbus to the Present*. New York: Knopf, 1978.

Black, Jason Edward. "The 'Mascotting' of Native America: Construction, Commodity, and Assimilation." *American Indian Quarterly* 26, no. 4 (2002): 605–22.

Bolívar, Simón. "My Delirium on Chimborazo." Translated by Frederick H. Fornoff. In *El Libertador: Writings of Simón Bolívar*, edited by David Bushnell, 135–36. Oxford: Oxford University Press, 2003.

Borja y Borja, Ramiro. *Las constituciones del Ecuador*. Madrid: Ediciones Cultura Hispánica, 1951.

Brooks, Kevin. "Reviewing and Redescribing 'The Politics of Historiography': Octalog 1988." *Rhetoric Review* 16, no. 1 (1997): 6–21. http://dx.doi.org/10.1080/07350199709389077.

Buell, Frederick. "Nationalist Postnationalism: Globalist Discourses in Contemporary American Culture." *American Quarterly* 50, no. 3 (1998): 548–91. http://dx.doi.org/10.1353/aq.1998.0030.

Burke, Kenneth. *A Grammar of Motives*. Berkeley: University of California Press, 1969.

———. *Language as Symbolic Action: Essays on Life, Literature, and Method*. Berkeley: University of California Press, 1966.

———. "(Nonsymbolic) Motion/(Symbolic) Action." *Critical Inquiry* 4, no. 4 (1978): 809–38. http://dx.doi.org/10.1086/447966.

———. "Questions and Answers About the Pentad." *College Composition and Communication* 29, no. 4 (1978): 330–35. http://dx.doi.org/10.2307/357013.

———. *A Rhetoric of Motives*. 1st ed. New York: Prentice-Hall, 1950.

Cañizares-Esguerra, Jorge. "Postcolonialism *Avant la Lettre*? Travelers and Clerics in Eighteenth-Century Colonial Spanish America." In Thurner and Guerrero, *After Spanish Rule*, 89–110.

Capello, Ernesto. *City at the Center of the World: Space, History, and Modernity in Quito.* Pittsburgh: University of Pittsburgh Press, 2011.

Carbo, L. F., ed. *El Ecuador en Chicago, por el "Diario de Avisos" de Guayaquil, Ecuador: América del Sur.* New York: Chasmar, 1894.

Carrión, Benjamín. *Cartas al Ecuador.* Quito: Editorial Gutenberg, 1943.

———. *Los creadores de la nueva América.* Madrid: Sociedad General Española de Librería, 1928.

———. *Mapa de América.* Madrid: Sociedad General Española de Librería, 1930.

———. "El premio Aguilera, desierto." *El Día,* August 19, 1935.

Castro-Klarén, Sara. "The Nation in Ruins: Archaeology and the Rise of the Nation." In Castro-Klarén and Chasteen, *Beyond Imagined Communities,* 161–95.

Castro-Klarén, Sara, and John Charles Chasteen, eds. *Beyond Imagined Communities: Reading and Writing the Nation in Nineteenth-Century Latin America.* Washington, D.C.: Woodrow Wilson Center Press, 2003.

Catlin, Stanton L. "Traveller-Reporter Artists and the Empirical Tradition in Post-independence Latin American Art." In *Art in Latin America: The Modern Era, 1820–1980,* edited by Dawn Ades, 41–61. New Haven: Yale University Press, 1989.

Cervone, Emma. "El retorno de Atahualpa: Etnicidad y movimiento indígena en Ecuador." Paper presented at the Latin American Studies Association conference, Guadalajara, Mexico, 1997. http://lasa.international.pitt.edu/ LASA97/Cervone.pdf.

Cevallos, Pedro Fermín. *Geografía de la república del Ecuador.* Lima: Imprenta del Estado, 1888. First published 1870.

Charland, Maurice. "Constitutive Rhetoric: The Case of the *Peuple Québécois.*" *Quarterly Journal of Speech* 73, no. 2 (1987): 133–50. http://dx.doi.org/10.1080/ 00335638709383799.

Charupi, Seberino. "Así llego la Marcha Plurinacional al Arbolito." CONACNIE (Consejo Nacional de Coordinación de Nacionalidades Indígenas). March 26, 2012. http://www.conaie.org/component/content/article/3-notis3/506-asi-llego-la-marcha-plurinacional-al-arbolito (page discontinued).

Cintrón, Ralph. *Angels' Town: Chero Ways, Gang Life, and the Rhetorics of the Everyday.* Boston: Beacon Press, 1997.

———. "Democracy and Its Limitations." In *The Public Work of Rhetoric: Citizen-Scholars and Civic Engagement,* edited by John M. Ackerman and David J. Coogan, 98–116. Columbia: University of South Carolina Press, 2010.

Clark, A. Kim. "Ecuadorian Indians, the Nation, and Class in Historical Perspective: Rethinking a 'New Social Movement.'" *Anthropologica* 47, no. 1 (2005): 53–65. http://dx.doi.org/10.2307/25606217.

———. "Indians, the State, and Law: Public Works and the Struggle to Control Labor in Liberal Ecuador." *Journal of Historical Sociology* 7, no. 1 (1994): 49–72. http://dx.doi.org/10.1111/j.1467-6443.1994.tb00062.x.

———. "Race, 'Culture,' and Mestizaje: The Statistical Construction of the Ecuadorian Nation, 1930–1950." *Journal of Historical Sociology* 11, no. 2 (1998): 185–211.

———. "Racial Ideologies and the Quest for National Development: Debating the Agrarian Problem in Ecuador (1930–1950)." *Journal of Latin American Studies* 30, no. 2 (1998): 373–93. http://dx.doi.org/10.1017/S0022216X98005082.

———. *The Redemptive Work: Railway and Nation in Ecuador, 1895–1930.* Wilmington: Scholarly Resources, 1998.

Clark, A. Kim, and Marc Becker, eds. *Highland Indians and the State in Modern Ecuador.* Pittsburgh: University of Pittsburgh Press, 2007.

Clark, Gregory. *Rhetorical Landscapes in America: Variations on a Theme from Kenneth Burke*. Columbia: University of South Carolina Press, 2004.

Clark, Kim. "La formación del estado ecuatoriano en el campo y la ciudad, 1895–1925." *Procesos: Revista Ecuatoriana de Historia* 19 (2003): 117–30.

———. "La medida de la diferencia: Las imágenes indigenistas de los indios serranos en el Ecuador (1920–1940)." In *Ecuador racista: Imágenes e identidades*, edited by Emma Cervone and Fredy Rivera, 111–26. Quito: FLACSO Sede Ecuador, 1999.

Clifford, James, and George Marcus, eds. *Writing Culture: The Poetics and Politics of Ethnography*. Berkeley: University of California Press, 1986.

El Comercio. "Acosta define aspectos de nueva constitución." December 13, 2007. http://www.elcomercio.com/noticias/Acosta-define-aspectos-nueva-constitucion_0_151784971.html.

Conaghan, Catherine M. "Ecuador: Correa's Plebiscitary Presidency." *Journal of Democracy* 19, no. 2 (2008): 46–60. http://dx.doi.org/10.1353/jod.2008.0026.

Consigny, Scott. "Rhetoric and Its Situations." *Philosophy and Rhetoric* 7, no. 4 (1974): 175–86.

Coronel Feijóo, Rosario. *El valle sangriento: De los indígenas de la Coca y el Algodón a la hacienda Cañera Jesuita; 1580–1700*. Quito: FLACSO Sede Ecuador; Abya-Yala, 1991.

Correa, Rafael. "Intervención del presidente de la república, Rafael Correa, en la ceremonia de inauguración de la Asamblea Nacional Constituyente." Speech in Montecristi, Ecuador, 2007. http://presidencia.informatica.gob.ec/discursos/11-30-07DiscursoInauguracionAsambleaNacionalConstituyente.pdf.

Crowley, Sharon, and Debra Hawhee. *Ancient Rhetorics for Contemporary Students*. 4th ed. New York: Pearson; Longman, 2008.

Cushman, Ellen. *The Struggle and the Tools: Oral and Literate Strategies in an Inner City Community*. Albany: SUNY Press, 1998.

Davis, Diane. *Inessential Solidarity: Rhetoric and Foreigner Relations*. Pittsburgh: University of Pittsburgh Press, 2010.

De la Torre, Carlos. "Los usos políticos de las categorías de pueblo y democracía." *Ecuador Debate*, August 1997.

De la Torre, Carlos, and Mirena Salgado, eds. *Galo Plaza y su época*. Quito: FLACSO; Fundación Galo Plaza Lasso, 2008.

Derrida, Jacques. *Of Grammatology*. Translated by Gayatri Chakravorty Spivak. Baltimore: Johns Hopkins University Press, 1997.

El Día. "La higienización rural." February 14, 1935.

Diez-Canseco, Alfredo Pareja. "Discurso con que Alfredo Pareja Diez-Canseco, admirable novelista Guayaquileño, de tránsito en esta Capital, declaró inaugurada en la Galería de Arte 'CASPICARA' la exposición pictórica de los artistas europeos Hans y Elsa Michaelson." *Revista del Mar Pacífico*, February 1941.

Diezcanseco, Alfredo Pareja. *Historia del Ecuador*. Vol. 4. Quito: Editorial Casa de la Cultura Ecuatoriana, 1954.

Drzewiecka, Jolanta A. "Reinventing and Contesting Identities in Constitutive Discourses: Between Diaspora and Its Others." *Communication Quarterly* 50, no. 1 (2002): 1–23. http://dx.doi.org/10.1080/01463370209385643.

Ecuarunari. "Mandato de la Marcha Plurinacional." *Crónicas del Despojo*. March 22, 2012. http://cronicasdeldespojo.blogspot.com/2012/03/mandato-de-la-marcha-plurinacional.html.

———. "Marcha por la vida." http://ecuarunari.org/portal/. Also available on YouTube as "El Pangui-Zamora Chinchipe." 3:47. March 8, 2012. http://www.youtube.com/watch?v=GZFmderot8w&feature=player_embedded.

———. "Nuestra propuesta a la Asamblea Constituyente." *Rikcharishun*, August 2007.

El Ecuatoriano. "Oligarquía." December 5, 1891.

Edbauer, Jenny. "Unframing Models of Public Distribution: From Rhetorical Situation to Rhetorical Ecologies." *Rhetoric Society Quarterly* 35, no. 4 (2005): 5–24. http://dx.doi.org/10.1080/02773940509391320.

Eddy, Beth. *The Rites of Identity: The Religious Naturalism and Cultural Criticism of Kenneth Burke and Ralph Ellison.* Princeton: Princeton University Press, 2003.

Espinosa Apolo, Manuel. *Mestizaje, choloficación y blanqueamiento en Quito: Primera mitad del siglo XX.* Quito: Universidad Andina Simón Bolívar; Abya-Yala; Corporación Editora Nacional, 2003.

Farrell, Thomas. "Sizing Things Up: Colloquial Reflection as Practical Wisdom." *Argumentation* 12, no. 1 (1998): 1–14. http://dx.doi.org/10.1023/A:1007747321075.

Feehan, Michael. "Kenneth Burke's Dualistic Theory of Constitutions." *Pre/Text* 12, no. 1–2 (1991): 39–60.

Fernández, Juan. "Los indios 'comunistas.'" *El Día,* June 27, 1935.

———. "Los indios se alzan." *El Día,* March 1, 1935.

———. "Nucanchic alpa." *El Día,* Febuary 27, 1935.

Finnegan, Cara A. "Recognizing Lincoln: Image Vernaculars and Nineteenth-Century Visual Culture." *Rhetoric and Public Affairs* 8, no. 1 (2005): 31–57. http://dx.doi.org/10.1353/rap.2005.0037.

———. "Visual Studies and Visual Rhetoric." *Quarterly Journal of Speech* 90, no. 2 (2004): 234–56. http://dx.doi.org/10.1080/0033563042000227454.

Finnegan, Cara A., and Jiyeon Kang. "'Sighting' the Public: Iconoclasm and Public Sphere Theory." *Quarterly Journal of Speech* 90, no. 4 (2004): 377–402. http://dx.doi.org/10.1080/0033563042000302153.

Fitzell, Jill. "Teorizando la diferencia en los Andes del Ecuador: Viajeros europeos, la ciencia del exotismo, y las imágenes de los indios." In Muratorio, *Imágenes e imagineros,* 25–73.

Fraser, Nancy. "Rethinking the Public Sphere: A Contribution to the Critique of Actually Existing Democracy." *Social Text* 25–26 (1990): 56–80. http://dx.doi.org/10.2307/466240.

———. "Transnationalizing the Public Sphere: On the Legitimacy and Efficacy of Public Opinion in a Post-Westphalian World." *Theory, Culture, and Society* 24, no. 4 (2007): 7–30. http://dx.doi.org/10.1177/0263276407080090.

Gale, Xin Liu. "Historical Studies and Postmodernism: Rereading Aspasia of Miletus." *College English* 62, no. 3 (2000): 361–86. http://dx.doi.org/10.2307/378936.

Gallegos de Donoso, Magdalena. "Juan León Mera y Joaquín Pinto, testigos de su tiempo." In Mera, *Cantares del pueblo ecuatoriano,* 9–18.

Gallegos de Donoso, Magdalena, José María Vargas, and Jorge Villalba, eds. *Pintores ecuatorianos: Joaquín Pinto.* Quito: Editora Andina, 1984.

Garcés, Victor Gabriel. "Condiciones de vida de las poblaciones indígenas en los países americanos." *Previsión Social* 17 (1946): 11–46.

———. "La industría del Indio." In Instituto Indigenista Ecuatoriano, *Cuestiones indígenas del Ecuador,* 87–95.

Gargarella, Roberto. "Towards a Typology of Latin American Constitutionalism, 1810–60." *Latin American Research Review* 39, no. 2 (2004): 141–53. http://dx.doi.org/10.1353/lar.2004.0030.

Geertz, Clifford. *The Interpretation of Cultures.* New York: Basic Books, 1974.

Glenn, Cheryl. "Truth, Lies, and Method: Revisiting Feminist Historiography." *College English* 62, no. 3 (2000): 387–89. http://dx.doi.org/10.2307/378937.

González Suárez, Federico. *Los aborígenes de Imbabura y del Carchi: Investigaciones arqueológicas sobre los antiguos pobladores de las provincias del Carchi y de Imbabura en la república del Ecuador.* Quito: Tipografía y Encuadernación Salesiana, 1910.

González y Contreras, Gilberto. "Aclaraciones a la novela social americana." *Letras del Ecuador,* November 1945.

Gould, Jeffrey L. *To Die in This Way: Nicaraguan Indians and the Myth of Mestizaje, 1880–1965.* Durham: Duke University Press, 2003. First published 1998.

Graff, Harvey J. *The Literacy Myth: Cultural Integration and Social Structure in the Nineteenth Century.* New Brunswick: Transaction, 1991.

Greet, Michelle. *Beyond National Identity: Pictorial Indigenism as a Modernist Strategy in Andean Art, 1920–1960.* University Park: Pennsylvania State University Press, 2009.

Gries, Laurie. "Practicing Methods in Ancient Cultural Rhetorics: Uncovering Rhetorical Action in Moche Burial Rituals." In *Rhetorics of the Americas: 3114 BCE to 2012 CE,* edited by Damián Baca and Victor Villanueva, 89–116. New York: Palgrave Macmillan, 2010.

Grijalva Calero, Ximena, ed. *Plástica y literatura: Un diálogo en torno al indígena.* Quito: Banco Central del Ecuador, 2006.

Guerrero, Andrés. *Administración de poblaciones, ventriloquía y transescritura: Análisis históricos; estudios teóricos.* Lima: IEP; Quito: FLACSO-Ecuador, 2010.

———. "The Administration of Dominated Populations Under a Regime of Customary Citizenship: The Case of Postcolonial Ecuador." In Thurner and Guerrero, *After Spanish Rule,* 272–309.

———. "The Construction of a Ventriloquist's Image: Liberal Discourse and the 'Miserable Indian Race' in Late Nineteenth-Century Ecuador." *Journal of Latin American Studies* 29, no. 3 (1997): 555–90. http://dx.doi.org/10.1017/S0022216X97004781.

———. "Una imagen ventrilocua: El discurso liberal de la 'desgraciada raza indígena' a fines del siglo XIX." In Muratorio, *Imágenes e imagineros,* 197–252.

Guerrero, Juan Agustín. *Imágenes del Ecuador del siglo XIX.* Edited by Wilson Hallo. Quito: Fundación Hallo para las Investigaciones y las Artes, 1981. First published 1852 as *Libro de Pinturas.*

Guevara, Darío C. "Como mejorar la cultura del obrero ecuatoriano?" *Previsión Social* 10 (1942): 24–48.

Hajicek, Diane Elizabeth. "Canvas as Nation: The Crisis in Ecuadorian Art Criticism, 1980–Present." Master's thesis, University of Texas at Austin, 1996.

Hardt, Michael, and Antonio Negri. *Empire.* Cambridge: Harvard University Press, 2000.

———. *Multitude: War and Democracy in the Age of Empire.* New York: Penguin Press, 2004.

Hariman, Robert, and John Louis Lucaites. *No Caption Needed: Iconic Photographs, Public Culture, and Liberal Democracy.* Chicago: University of Chicago Press, 2007.

Hassaurek, Friedrich. *Four Years Among Spanish-Americans.* New York: Hurd and Houghton, 1867.

Hawhee, Debra. *Moving Bodies: Kenneth Burke at the Edges of Language.* Columbia: University of South Carolina Press, 2009.

Hawhee, Debra, and Christa J. Olson. "Pan-Historiography: The Challenges of Writing History Across Time and Space." In *Theorizing Histories of Rhetoric,* edited by Michelle Ballif, 90–105. Carbondale: Southern Illinois University Press, 2013.

Hedgecoe, Guy. "Ecuador's Hyper-Political Wave." *Open Democracy.* September 30, 2008. http://www.opendemocracy.net/article/ecuador-s-fresh-wave.

Hesford, Wendy S., and Eileen E. Schell. "Introduction: Configurations of Transnationality; Locating Feminist Rhetorics." *College English* 70, no. 5 (2008): 461–70.

Hobsbawm, Eric J. *Nations and Nationalism Since 1780: Programme, Myth, Reality.* Cambridge: Cambridge University Press, 1990.

Humboldt, Alexander von. *Aspects of Nature in Different Lands and Different Climates, with Scientific Elucidations.* Translated by Elizabeth Juliana Leeves Sabine. Philadelphia: Lea and Blanchard, 1850.

Hutchings, Kimberly. "Whose History? Whose Justice?" *Theory, Culture, and Society* 24, no. 4 (2007): 59–63. http://dx.doi.org/10.1177/0263276407080094.

Icaza, Jorge. "Nace en el Ecuador un arte expresión de la vida." *Letras del Ecuador,* June 1945.

Instituto Indigenista Ecuatoriano, ed. "Album indigenista." In Instituto Indigenista Ecuatoriano, *Cuestiones indígenas del Ecuador.*

———, ed. *Cuestiones indígenas del Ecuador.* Vol. 1. Quito: Editorial Casa de la Cultura Ecuatoriana, 1946.

Isocrates. "Nicocles, or the Cyprians." In *The Orations of Isocrates,* translated and edited by J. H. Freese, 1:35–49. London: Bell and Sons, 1894.

Jácome, Nicanor. "Economía y sociedad en siglo XVI." In Ayala Mora, *Nueva historia del Ecuador,* 3:123–60.

Jaramillo Alvarado, Pio. "El Indio, problema continental." In Instituto Indigenista Ecuatoriano, *Cuestiones indígenas del Ecuador,* 1–37.

Jarratt, Susan C. "Rhetoric and Feminism: Together Again." *College English* 62, no. 3 (2000): 390–93. http://dx.doi.org/10.2307/378938.

Jijón y Caamaño, Jacinto. *El Ecuador interandino y occidental antes de la conquista Castellana.* Vols. 1–4. Quito: Editorial Ecuatoriana, 1941.

Joaquín Pinto: Exposición antológica. Quito: Museo del Banco Central del Ecuador, 1984.

Jones, John M., and Robert C. Rowland. "Reagan at Moscow State University: Consubstantiality Underlying Conflict." *Rhetoric and Public Affairs* 10, no. 1 (2007): 77–106. http://dx.doi.org/10.1353/rap.2007.0024.

Jurado Noboa, Fernando. *Luís A. Martínez: Espada, pluma, y espátula.* Quito: Banco Central del Ecuador, 2010.

Kalmo, Hent, and Quentin Skinner. "Introduction: A Concept in Fragments." In *Sovereignty in Fragments: The Past, Present, and Future of a Contested Concept,* edited by Hent Kalmo and Quentin Skinner, 1–25. Cambridge: Cambridge University Press, 2010. http://dx.doi.org/10.1017/CBO9780511675928.001.

Kang, Jiyeon. "Coming to Terms with 'Unreasonable' Global Power: The 2002 South Korean Candlelight Vigils." *Communication and Critical/Cultural Studies* 6, no. 2 (2009): 171–92. http://dx.doi.org/10.1080/14791420902833155.

Kennedy, Alexandra, ed. *Arte de la real audiencia de Quito, siglos XVII–XIX. Patronos, corporaciones, y comunidades.* Hondarribia, Spain: Editorial Nerea, 2002.

Kennedy Troya, Alexandra. "Artistas y científicos: Naturaleza independiente en el siglo XIX en Ecuador (Rafael Troya y Joaquín Pinto)." *Estudios de Arte y Estético* 37 (1994): 223–41.

———, ed. *Escenarios para una patria.* Quito: Museo de la Ciudad, Fundación Municipal Museos, 2008.

———. "Miguel de Santiago (c. 1633–1706): The Creation and Recreation of the Quito School." In *Exploring New World Imagery: Spanish Colonial Papers from the 2002 Mayer Center Symposium,* edited by Donna Pierce, 129–55. Denver: Denver Art Museum, 2005.

———. "Paisajes patrios: Arte y la literatura ecuatorianos de los siglos XIX y XX." In Kennedy Troya, *Escenarios para una patria,* 82–107.

———. "El territorio y el paisaje: Una declaración de principios." In Kennedy Troya, *Escenarios para una patria*, 6–24.

Kennedy Troya, Alexandra, and Alfonso Ortiz Crespo. "Continuismo colonial y cosmopolitismo en la arquitectura y el arte decimonónico ecuatoriano." In Ayala Mora, *Nueva historia del Ecuador*, 8:119–39.

Kingman, Eduardo. *Hombres del Ecuador*. Quito: Editorial Atahuallpa, 1937.

Kingman, Nicolás. "Boceto de una vida." In *Eduardo Kingman*, edited by Lenin Oña, 167–74. Quito: Dinediciones, 1994.

Kingman Garcés, Eduardo. *La ciudad y los otros: Quito, 1860–1940; Higienismo, ornato, y policía*. Quito: FLACSO, 2006.

Kingman Garcés, Eduardo, Ana María Goetschel, and Cecilia Mantilla. "Obras públicas y fuerza de trabajo indígena (el caso de la província de Pichincha)." In *Las ciudades en la historia*, edited by Eduardo Kingman Garcés, 357–83. Quito: CIUDAD, 1989.

Klor de Alva, J. Jorge. "*Mestizaje* from New Spain to Aztlán: On the Control and Classification of Collective Identities." In *New World Orders: Casta Painting and Colonial Latin America*, edited by Ilona Katzew, 58–71. New York: Americas Society Art Gallery, 1996.

Larson, Brooke. *Trials of Nation Making: Liberalism, Race, and Ethnicity in the Andes, 1810–1910*. Cambridge: Cambridge University Press, 2004. http://dx.doi.org/10.1017/CBO9780511616396.

Laso, José Domingo, and J. Roberto Cruz. *Quito a la vista*. Quito: Talleres Gráficos de J. D. Laso, 1911.

Lasso, Ignacio. "Eduardo Kingman, pintor del drama obrero." In *Pintores ecuatorianos: E. Kingman*, edited by Margarita Laso, 15–19. Quito: Editora Andina, 1983.

LaWare, Margaret R. "Circling the Missiles and Staining Them Red: Feminist Rhetorical Invention and Strategies of Resistance at the Women's Peace Camp at Greenham Common." *NWSA Journal* 16, no. 3 (2004): 18–41. http://dx.doi.org/10.2979/NWS.2004.16.3.18.

———. "Encountering Visions of Aztlán." *Argumentation and Advocacy* 34, no. 3 (1998): 140–53.

Leff, Michael. "The Topics of Argumentative Invention in Latin Rhetorical Theory from Cicero to Boethius." *Rhetorica* 1, no. 1 (1983): 23–44. http://dx.doi.org/10.1525/rh.1983.1.1.23.

Leff, Michael, and Ebony A. Utley. "Instrumental and Constitutive Rhetoric in Martin Luther King Jr.'s 'Letter from Birmingham Jail.'" *Rhetoric and Public Affairs* 7, no. 1 (2004): 37–51. http://dx.doi.org/10.1353/rap.2004.0026.

Leonhardt Abram, Matthias. "Los Andes en el corazón: Intérpretes del paisaje." In Kennedy Troya, *Escenarios para una patria*, 26–51.

Letras del Ecuador. "Ley de patrimonio artístico." May 1946.

———. "El señor presidente de la república en la inauguración del Primer Salón Nacional de Bellas Artes." June 1945.

Lisboa, Miguel María. *Relação de uma viagem a Venezuela, Nova Granada e Equador*. Brussels: LaCroix, Verboeckhoven, 1866.

Lucero, José Antonio. "Crisis and Contention in Ecuador." *Journal of Democracy* 12, no. 2 (2001): 59–73. http://dx.doi.org/10.1353/jod.2001.0032.

———. "Representing 'Real Indians': The Challenges of Indigenous Authenticity and Strategic Constructivism in Ecuador and Bolivia." *Latin American Research Review* 41, no. 2 (2006): 31–56. http://dx.doi.org/10.1353/lar.2006.0026.

Lyons, Scott Richard. "Rhetorical Sovereignty: What Do American Indians Want from Writing?" *College Composition and Communication* 51, no. 3 (2000): 447–68. http://dx.doi.org/10.2307/358744.

Maiguashca, Juan. "The Electoral Reforms of 1861 in Ecuador and the Rise of a New Political Order." In *Elections Before Democracy: The History of Elections in Europe and Latin America*, edited by Eduardo Posada-Carbó, 87–115. New York: St. Martin's Press, 1996.

Mao, LuMing. "Doing Comparative Rhetoric Responsibly." *Rhetoric Society Quarterly* 41, no. 1 (2011): 64–69. http://dx.doi.org/10.1080/02773945.2010.533149.

———. "Studying the Chinese Rhetorical Tradition in the Present: Re-presenting the Native's Point of View." *College English* 69, no. 3 (2007): 216–37.

Martínez, Luís A. *La agricultura del interior: Causas de su atraso y modos de impulsarla*. Quito: Imprenta La Novedad, 1897.

———. *La agricultura ecuatoriana: Entrega 1a*. Ambato, Ecuador: Imprenta y Litografía de Salvador R. Porras, 1903.

———. *Andinismo, arte, y literatura*. Quito: Abya-Yala; Grupo Excursionista "Nuevos Horizontes," 1994.

McIntosh, Robert P. *The Background of Ecology: Concept and Theory*. New York: Cambridge University Press, 1985. http://dx.doi.org/10.1017/CBO9780511608537.

McKeon, Richard. "Creativity and the Commonplace." *Philosophy and Rhetoric* 6, no. 4 (1973): 199–210.

Mera, Juan León, ed. *Cantares del pueblo ecuatoriano*. Quito: Museo del Banco Central del Ecuador, 1983. First published 1892.

———. *Catecismo de geografía de la república del Ecuador: Texto de enseñanza para las escuelas ecuatorianas, adoptado por el Supremo Gobierno en 1874*. 2nd ed. Guayaquil: Imprenta de la Nación, 1884. First published 1874.

———. *Catecismo explicado de la constitución de la república del Ecuador*. Quito: Imprenta del Clero, 1894.

———. *Cumandá; o, Un drama entre salvajes*. Sevilla: Alfar, 1989. First published 1879.

Mihesuah, Devon A. *So You Want to Write About American Indians? A Guide for Writers, Students, and Scholars*. Lincoln: University of Nebraska Press, 2005.

Miller, Carolyn R. "The Aristotelian *Topos*: Hunting for Novelty." In *Rereading Aristotle's "Rhetoric,"* edited by Alan G. Gross and Arthur E. Walzer, 130–46. Carbondale: Southern Illinois University Press, 2000.

Miller, Marilyn Grace. *Rise and Fall of the Cosmic Race: The Cult of "Mestizaje" in Latin America*. Austin: University of Texas Press, 2004.

Ministerio de Gobierno y Previsión Social. *Informe del Ministro de Gobierno y Previsión Social, M. A. Albornoz, a la Nación*. Quito, 1931.

Ministerio de Previsión Social. *El día del indio*. Quito: Talleres Gráficos de Educación, 1943.

Miño Grijalva, Manuel. "La economía de la real audiencia de Quito, siglo XVII." In Ayala Mora, *Nueva historia del Ecuador*, 4:47–103.

Mirzoeff, Nicholas. *The Right to Look: A Counterhistory of Visuality*. Durham: Duke University Press, 2011.

Mistral, Gabriela. *Gabriela Mistral: Escritos políticos*. Translated and edited by Jaime Quezada. Mexico City: Fondo de Cultura Económica, 1994.

Monsalve Pozo, Luís. "Ecuador: Naturaleza mestiza." *Revista del Mar Pacífico*, November 1940.

———. "El Indio: Cuestiones de su vida y de su pasión." *Revista del Mar Pacífico*, June 1943.

Montesinos Malo, Arturo. "La tristeza: Disfraz de la Raza." *Letras del Ecuador*, November 1945.

Mora Lopez, José. *El Ecuador en la Constituyente de 1896*. Ecuador: Portoviejo, 1896.

Moreno Aguilar, Andrea. *Eduardo Kingman Riofrío (1913–1997)*. Quito: Banco Central del Ecuador, 2010.

Mortensen, Peter. "Figuring Illiteracy: Rustic Bodies and Unlettered Minds in Rural America." In *Rhetorical Bodies*, edited by Jack Selzer and Sharon Crowley, 143–70. Madison: University of Wisconsin Press, 1999.

Mortensen, Peter, and Gesa E. Kirsch, eds. *Ethics and Representation in Qualitative Studies of Literacy*. Urbana: NCTE, 1996.

Morus, Christina. "The SANU Memorandum: Intellectual Authority and the Constitution of an Exclusive Serbian 'People.'" *Communication and Critical/ Cultural Studies* 4, no. 2 (2007): 142–65. http://dx.doi.org/10.1080/ 14791420701296513.

Muratorio, Blanca, ed. *Imágenes e imagineros: Representaciones de los indígenas ecuatorianos, siglos XIX y XX*. Quito: FLACSO, 1994.

———. "Images of Indians in the Construction of Ecuadorian Identity at the End of the Nineteenth Century." In *Latin American Popular Culture: An Introduction*, edited by William H. Beezley and Linda A. Curcio-Nagy, 105–22. Wilmington, Del.: SR Books, 2000.

Murphy, James J., James Berlin, Robert J. Connors, Sharon Crowley, Richard Leo Enos, Victor J. Vitanza, Susan C. Jarratt, et al. "The Politics of Historiography." *Rhetoric Review* 7, no. 1 (1988): 5–49. http://dx.doi.org/10.1080/07350198809388839.

Navarro, José Gabriel. *Artes plásticas ecuatorianas*. México: Fondo de Cultura Económica, 1945.

Olson, Christa J. "Places to Stand: The Practices and Politics of Writing Histories." *Advances in the History of Rhetoric* 15, no. 1 (2012): 77–100. http://dx.doi.org/ 10.1080/15362426.2012.657056.

———. "'Raíces Americanas': Indigenist Art, América, and Arguments for Ecuadorian Nationalism." *Rhetoric Society Quarterly* 42, no. 3 (2012): 233–50.

Olson, Lester C. *Emblems of American Community in the Revolutionary Era: A Study in Rhetorical Iconology*. Washington: Smithsonian Institution Press, 1991.

———. "Pictorial Representations of British America Resisting Rape: Rhetorical Re-circulation of a Print Series Portraying the Boston Port Bill of 1774." *Rhetoric and Public Affairs* 12, no. 1 (2009): 1–35.

Oña, Lenin. "El arte de Kingman." In *Eduardo Kingman*, edited by Lenin Oña, 21–91. Quito: Dinediciones, 1994.

Ono, Kent A., and Derek T. Buescher. "Deciphering Pocahontas: Unpackaging the Commodification of a Native American Woman." *Critical Studies in Media Communication* 18, no. 1 (2001): 23–43. http://dx.doi.org/10.1080/ 15295030109367122.

Ortiz Crespo, Alfonso, ed. *Joaquín Pinto: Crónica romántica de la nación*. Quito: FONSAL; Centro Cultural Metropolitano, 2011.

Osculati, Gaetano. *Esploraziones delle regioni equatoriali lungo il Napo ed il fiume delle Amazzoni: Frammento di un viaggio fatto nelle due Americhe negli ani 1846–47–48*. Milan: Fratelli Centenari, 1854.

Pacheco Pérez, Raúl. Introduction to *Gente del Ecuador: Kingman–Tejada–Galecio; Xilografías, 1930–1950*. Quito: Centro Cultural Benjamín Carrión, 1998.

Paley, Julia. "Toward an Anthropology of Democracy." *Annual Review of Anthropology* 31, no. 1 (2002): 469–96. http://dx.doi.org/10.1146/annurev .anthro.31.040402.085453.

Pallares, Amalia. *From Peasant Struggles to Indian Resistance: The Ecuadorian Andes in the Late Twentieth Century*. Norman: University of Oklahoma Press, 2002.

"La Patria Ya Es de Todos." *Mensaje del Gobierno del Ecuador*. 0:58. November 5, 2008. http://www.youtube.com/watch?v=wpe83a5nINo.

Pequeño Bueno, Andrea. *Imágenes en disputa: Representaciones de mujeres indígenas ecuatorianas*. Quito: FLACSO; Abya-Yala, 2007.

Perelman, Chaim, and Lucie Olbrechts-Tyteca. *The New Rhetoric: A Treatise on Argumentation.* Translated by John Wilkinson and Purcell Weaver. Notre Dame: University of Notre Dame Press, 1969.

Pérez, Trinidad. "Exoticism, Alterity, and the Ecuadorian Elite: The Work of Camilo Egas." In *Images of Power: Iconography, Culture, and the State in Latin America,* edited by Jens Andermann and William Rowe, 99–126. New York: Berghahn Books, 2005.

Pinto, Joaquín. "Album de personajes populares." Hand-bound book with a series of original watercolors, 1900–1901. Private collection.

Plaza Lasso, Galo. *Problems of Democracy in Latin America.* Chapel Hill: University of North Carolina Press, 1955.

Pólit Montes de Oca, Vicente. "Conquista del Perú, Quito y descubrimiento del río de las Amazonas." In Ayala Mora, *Nueva historia del Ecuador,* 3:67–90.

Poole, Deborah. *Vision, Race, and Modernity: A Visual Economy of the Andean Image World.* Princeton: Princeton University Press, 1997.

Powell, Katrina. "Writing the Geography of the Blue Ridge Mountains: How Displacement Recorded the Land." *Biography* 25, no. 1 (2002): 73–94. http://dx.doi.org/10.1353/bio.2002.0010.

Pratt, Mary Louise. *Imperial Eyes: Travel Writing and Transculturation.* London: Routledge, 1992.

Previsión Social. "El hogar indígena de Conocoto." January–June 1946.

Prieto, Mercedes. *Liberalismo y temor: Imaginando los sujetos indígenas en el Ecuador postcolonial, 1895–1950.* Quito: Abya-Yala, 2004.

Quijano, Anibal. "Coloniality of Power, Eurocentrism, and Latin America." *Nepantla: Views from South* 1, no. 3 (2000): 533–80.

Randeria, Shalini. "De-politicization of Democracy and Judicialization of Politics." *Theory, Culture, and Society* 24, no. 4 (2007): 38–44. http://dx.doi.org/10.1177/0263276407080398.

Revista del Mar Pacífico. "Afirmación y horizonte." November 1940.

———. "La personalidad de Egas." February 1941.

Rodas, Raquel. *Crónica de un sueño: Las escuelas indígenas de Dolores Cacuango, una experiencia de educación bilingüe en Cayambe.* Quito: Proyecto de Educación Bilingüe Intercultural, 1989.

Rodríguez, Carlos, and Humberto Estrella. *Quito colonial: Exposición de arte.* An exhibition catalog. Quito: Litografía e Imprenta Romero, 1940.

Rogers, Richard A. "Deciphering Kokopelli: Masculinity in Commodified Appropriations of Native American Imagery." *Communication and Critical/Cultural Studies* 4, no. 3 (2007): 233–55.

Roitman, Karem. *Race, Ethnicity, and Power in Ecuador: The Manipulation of Mestizaje.* Boulder: First Forum Press, 2009.

Romano, Susan. "The Historical Catalina Hernández: Inhabiting the Topoi of Feminist Historiography." *Rhetoric Society Quarterly* 37, no. 4 (2007): 453–80. http://dx.doi.org/10.1080/02773940601116021.

Saldaña-Portillo, Maria Josefina. *The Revolutionary Imagination in the Americas and the Age of Development.* Durham: Duke University Press, 2003.

Salomon, Frank. "Crisis y transformación de la sociedad aborigen invadida (1528–1573)." In Ayala Mora, *Nueva historia del Ecuador,* 3:91–122.

———. *Native Lords of Quito in the Age of the Incas.* Cambridge: Cambridge University Press, 1986.

Sattar, Aleezé. "¿Indígena o Ciudadano? Republican Laws and Highland Indian Communities in Ecuador, 1820–1857." In Clark and Becker, *Highland Indians,* 22–36.

Selzer, Jack. "Rhetorical Analysis: Understanding How Texts Persuade Readers." In *What Writing Does and How It Does It: An Introduction to Analyzing Texts and Textual Practices*, edited by Charles Bazerman and Paul Prior, 279–307. Mahwah: Erlbaum, 2004.

Smith, Cynthia Duquette. "Discipline—It's a 'Good Thing': Rhetorical Constitution and Martha Stewart Living Omnimedia." *Women's Studies in Communication* 23, no. 3 (2000): 337–66.

Smith, Linda Tuhiwai. *Decolonizing Methodologies*. London: Zed Books, 1999.

Stein, Sarah R. "The '1984' Macintosh Ad: Cinematic Icons and Constitutive Rhetoric in the Launch of a New Machine." *Quarterly Journal of Speech* 88, no. 2 (2002): 169–92. http://dx.doi.org/10.1080/00335630209384369.

Sweet, Derek, and Margret McCue-Enser. "Constituting 'the People' as Rhetorical Interruption: Barack Obama and the Unfinished Hopes of an Imperfect People." *Communication Studies* 61, no. 5 (2010): 602–22. http://dx.doi.org/10.1080/10510974.2010.514679.

Tate, Helen. "The Ideological Effects of a Failed Constitutive Rhetoric: The Co-option of the Rhetoric of White Lesbian Feminism." *Women's Studies in Communication* 28, no. 1 (2005): 1–31. http://dx.doi.org/10.1080/07491409.2005.10162482.

Taylor, Diana. *The Archive and the Repertoire: Performing Cultural Memory in the Americas*. Durham: Duke University Press, 2003.

Tenorio Trillo, Mauricio. "Essaying the History of National Images." In Thurner and Guerrero, *After Spanish Rule*, 58–86.

Terán, Enrique. "El materialismo dialéctico en el arte ecuatoriano." In Rodríguez and Estrella, *Quito colonial*, 15–18.

Terán Najas, Rosemarie. "Sinopsis histórica del siglo XVIII." In Ayala Mora, *Nueva historia del Ecuador*, 4:261–309.

Thieme, Katja. "Constitutive Rhetoric as an Aspect of Audience Design: The Public Texts of Canadian Suffragists." *Written Communication* 27, no. 1 (2010): 36–56. http://dx.doi.org/10.1177/0741088309353505.

Thurner, Mark, and Andrés Guerrero, eds. *After Spanish Rule: Postcolonial Predicaments of the Americas*. Durham: Duke University Press, 2003.

Tully, James. *Strange Multiplicity: Constitutionalism in an Age of Diversity*. Cambridge: Cambridge University Press, 1995. http://dx.doi.org/10.1017/CBO9781139170888.

Ugarteche, Oscar. "Transnationalizing the Public Sphere. A Critique of Fraser." *Theory, Culture, and Society* 24, no. 4 (2007): 65–69. http://dx.doi.org/10.1177/0263276407080095.

Vacas G., Humberto. "Eduardo Kingman: Pintor de soledades." *Letras del Ecuador*, April 1945.

Vargas, Fray José María. *El arte ecuatoriano*. Quito: Biblioteca Ecuatoriana Minima, 1960.
———. *Historia de arte ecuatoriano*. Quito: Editorial Santo Domingo, 1964.

Vasconcelos, José. *The Cosmic Race: A Bilingual Edition*. Translated by Didier T. Jaén. Baltimore: Johns Hopkins University Press, 1997.

Velasco, Juan de. *Historia antigua*. Edited by Alfredo Pareja Diezcanseco. Vol. 2 of *Historia del Reino de Quito en la América Meridional*. Caracas: Biblioteca Ayacucho, 1981. First published 1789.

Villavicencio, Manuel. *Geografía de la república del Ecuador*. New York: Craighead, 1858.

Viqueira Albán, Juan Pedro. *Propriety and Permissiveness in Bourbon Mexico*. Translated by Sonya Lipsett-Rivera and Sergio Rivera Ayala. Wilmington, Del.: SR Books, 1999.

Walsh, Catherine E. "The (Re)articulation of Political Subjectivities and Colonial Difference in Ecuador: Reflections on Capitalism and the Geopolitics of Knowledge." *Nepantla: Views from South* 3, no. 1 (2002): 61–97.

Wan, Amy J. "Producing Good Citizens: Literacy and Citizenship Training in Anxious Times." PhD diss., University of Illinois at Urbana–Champaign, 2007.

Warner, Michael. "Publics and Counterpublics." *Public Culture* 14, no. 1 (2002): 49–90. http://dx.doi.org/10.1215/08992363-14-1-49.

Werner, Wouter G., and Jaap H. De Wilde. "The Endurance of Sovereignty." *European Journal of International Relations* 7, no. 3 (2001): 283–313. http://dx.doi.org/10.1177/1354066101007003001.

Williams, Derek. "Administering the Otavalan Indian and Centralizing Governance in Ecuador, 1851–1975." In Clark and Becker, *Highland Indians*, 37–55.

Wolf, Theodor. *Geografía y geología del Ecuador*. Leipzig: Tipografía de Brockhaus, 1892.

Yeh, Rihan. "'We're Mexican Too': Publicity and Status at the International Line." *Public Culture* 21, no. 3 (2009): 465–93. http://dx.doi.org/10.1215/08992363-2009-004.

Zagacki, Kenneth S. "Constitutive Rhetoric Reconsidered: Constitutive Paradoxes in G. W. Bush's Iraq War Speeches." *Western Journal of Communication* 71, no. 4 (2007): 272–93. http://dx.doi.org/10.1080/10570310701653786.

INDEX

Page numbers in *italics* indicate figures.

RHETORICAND**DEMOCRATIC**DELIBERATION

EDITED BY CHERYL GLENN AND J. MICHAEL HOGAN

THE PENNSYLVANIA STATE UNIVERSITY

Books in the series: